International Political Economy Series

Series Editor: **Timothy M. Shaw**, Visiting Professor, University of Massachusetts Boston, USA, and Emeritus Professor, University of London, UK

The global political economy is in flux as a series of cumulative crises impacts its organization and governance. The IPE series has tracked its development in both analysis and structure over the last three decades. It has always had a concentration on the Global South. Now the South increasingly challenges the North as the centre of development, also reflected in a growing number of submissions and publications on indebted Eurozone economies in Southern Europe.

An indispensable resource for scholars and researchers, the series examines a variety of capitalisms and connections by focusing on emerging economies, companies and sectors, debates and policies. It informs diverse policy communities as the established trans-Atlantic North declines and 'the rest', especially the BRICS, rise.

Titles include:

Jeffrey Dayton-Johnson
LATIN AMERICA'S EMERGING MIDDLE CLASSES
Economic Perspectives

Andrei Belyi and Kim Talus
STATES AND MARKETS IN HYDROCARBON SECTORS

Dries Lesage and Thijs Van de Graaf
RISING POWERS AND MULTILATERAL INSTITUTIONS

Leslie Elliott Armijo and Saori N. Katada (*editors*)
THE FINANCIAL STATECRAFT OF EMERGING POWERS
Shield and Sword in Asia and Latin America

Md Mizanur Rahman, Tan Tai Yong and Ahsan Ullah (*editors*)
MIGRANT REMITTANCES IN SOUTH ASIA
Social, Economic and Political Implications

Bartholomew Paudyn
CREDIT RATINGS AND SOVEREIGN DEBT
The Political Economy of Creditworthiness through Risk and Uncertainty

Lourdes Casanova and Julian Kassum
THE POLITICAL ECONOMY OF AN EMERGING GLOBAL POWER
In Search of the Brazil Dream

Toni Haastrup and Yong-Soo Eun (*editors*)
REGIONALISING GLOBAL CRISES
The Financial Crisis and New Frontiers in Regional Governance

Kobena T. Hanson, Cristina D'Alessandro and Francis Owusu (*editors*)
MANAGING AFRICA'S NATURAL RESOURCES
Capacities for Development

Daniel Daianu, Carlo D'Adda, Giorgio Basevi and Rajeesh Kumar (*editors*)
THE EUROZONE CRISIS AND THE FUTURE OF EUROPE
The Political Economy of Further Integration and Governance

Karen E. Young
THE POLITICAL ECONOMY OF ENERGY, FINANCE AND SECURITY IN THE UNITED ARAB EMIRATES
Between the Majilis and the Market

Monique Taylor
THE CHINESE STATE, OIL AND ENERGY SECURITY

Benedicte Bull, Fulvio Castellacci and Yuri Kasahara
BUSINESS GROUPS AND TRANSNATIONAL CAPITALISM IN CENTRAL AMERICA
Economic and Political Strategies

Leila Simona Talani
THE ARAB SPRING IN THE GLOBAL POLITICAL ECONOMY

Andreas Nölke (*editor*)
MULTINATIONAL CORPORATIONS FROM EMERGING MARKETS
State Capitalism 3.0

Roshen Hendrickson
PROMOTING U.S. INVESTMENT IN SUB-SAHARAN AFRICA

Bhumitra Chakma
SOUTH ASIA IN TRANSITION
Democracy, Political Economy and Security

Greig Charnock, Thomas Purcell and Ramon Ribera-Fumaz
THE LIMITS TO CAPITAL IN SPAIN
Crisis and Revolt in the European South

Felipe Amin Filomeno
MONSANTO AND INTELLECTUAL PROPERTY IN SOUTH AMERICA

Eirikur Bergmann
ICELAND AND THE INTERNATIONAL FINANCIAL CRISIS
Boom, Bust and Recovery

Yildiz Atasoy (*editor*)
GLOBAL ECONOMIC CRISIS AND THE POLITICS OF DIVERSITY

Gabriel Siles-Brügge
CONSTRUCTING EUROPEAN UNION TRADE POLICY
A Global Idea of Europe

Jewellord Singh and France Bourgouin (*editors*)
RESOURCE GOVERNANCE AND DEVELOPMENTAL STATES IN THE GLOBAL SOUTH
Critical International Political Economy Perspectives

Tan Tai Yong and Md Mizanur Rahman (*editors*)
DIASPORA ENGAGEMENT AND DEVELOPMENT IN SOUTH ASIA

Leila Simona Talani, Alexander Clarkson and Ramon Pacheco Pardo (*editors*)
DIRTY CITIES
Towards a Political Economy of the Underground in Global Cities

Matthew Louis Bishop
THE POLITICAL ECONOMY OF CARIBBEAN DEVELOPMENT

Xiaoming Huang (*editor*)
MODERN ECONOMIC DEVELOPMENT IN JAPAN AND CHINA
Developmentalism, Capitalism and the World Economic System

Bonnie K. Campbell (*editor*)
MODES OF GOVERNANCE AND REVENUE FLOWS IN AFRICAN MINING

Gopinath Pillai (*editor*)
THE POLITICAL ECONOMY OF SOUTH ASIAN DIASPORA
Patterns of Socio-Economic Influence

Rachel K. Brickner (*editor*)
MIGRATION, GLOBALIZATION AND THE STATE

Juanita Elias and Samanthi Gunawardana (*editors*)
THE GLOBAL POLITICAL ECONOMY OF THE HOUSEHOLD IN ASIA

Tony Heron
PATHWAYS FROM PREFERENTIAL TRADE
The Politics of Trade Adjustment in Africa, the Caribbean and Pacific

David J. Hornsby
RISK REGULATION, SCIENCE AND INTERESTS IN TRANSATLANTIC TRADE CONFLICTS

Yang Jiang
CHINA'S POLICYMAKING FOR REGIONAL ECONOMIC COOPERATION

Matthias Ebenau, Ian Bruff and Christian May (*editors*)
NEW DIRECTIONS IN COMPARATIVE CAPITALISMS RESEARCH
Critical and Global Perspectives

International Political Economy Series
Series Standing Order ISBN 978–0–333–71708–0 hardcover
Series Standing Order ISBN 978–0–333–71110–1 paperback
(*outside North America only*)

You can receive future titles in this series as they are published by placing a standing order. Please contact your bookseller or, in case of difficulty, write to us at the address below with your name and address, the title of the series and one of the ISBNs quoted above.

Customer Services Department, Macmillan Distribution Ltd, Houndmills, Basingstoke, Hampshire RG21 6XS, England

New Directions in Comparative Capitalisms Research

Critical and Global Perspectives

Edited by

Matthias Ebenau
Union Lecturer, IG Metall, Germany

Ian Bruff
Lecturer, University of Manchester, UK

Christian May
Research Fellow, Goethe University Frankfurt am Main, Germany

Editorial matter, selection, introduction and conclusion
© Matthias Ebenau, Ian Bruff and Christian May 2015
Individual chapters © Respective authors 2015

All rights reserved. No reproduction, copy or transmission of this publication may be made without written permission.

No portion of this publication may be reproduced, copied or transmitted save with written permission or in accordance with the provisions of the Copyright, Designs and Patents Act 1988, or under the terms of any licence permitting limited copying issued by the Copyright Licensing Agency, Saffron House, 6–10 Kirby Street, London EC1N 8TS.

Any person who does any unauthorized act in relation to this publication may be liable to criminal prosecution and civil claims for damages.

The authors have asserted their rights to be identified as the authors of this work in accordance with the Copyright, Designs and Patents Act 1988.

First published 2015 by
PALGRAVE MACMILLAN

Palgrave Macmillan in the UK is an imprint of Macmillan Publishers Limited, registered in England, company number 785998, of Houndmills, Basingstoke, Hampshire RG21 6XS.

Palgrave Macmillan in the US is a division of St Martin's Press LLC, 175 Fifth Avenue, New York, NY 10010.

Palgrave Macmillan is the global academic imprint of the above companies and has companies and representatives throughout the world.

Palgrave® and Macmillan® are registered trademarks in the United States, the United Kingdom, Europe and other countries.

ISBN 978–1–137–44460–8

This book is printed on paper suitable for recycling and made from fully managed and sustained forest sources. Logging, pulping and manufacturing processes are expected to conform to the environmental regulations of the country of origin.

A catalogue record for this book is available from the British Library.

Library of Congress Cataloging-in-Publication Data
New directions in comparative capitalisms research : critical and global
   perspectives / edited by Matthias Ebenau, Ian Bruff, Christian May.
      pages cm. — (International political economy series)
   Includes bibliographical references and index.
   ISBN 978–1–137–44460–8 (hardback)
   1. Capitalism.   2. Comparative economics.   I. Ebenau, Matthias, 1984–
   II. Bruff, Ian, 1978–   III. May, Christian.
   HB501.N39822 2015
   330.12′2—dc23   2014049662

In memory of Uwe Becker (1951–2014)

Contents

List of Tables and Figures	ix
Notes on Contributors	x
List of Abbreviations and Acronyms	xv

Introduction: Comparative Capitalisms Research and the Emergence of Critical, Global Perspectives 1
Matthias Ebenau, Ian Bruff and Christian May

Part I Comparing Capitalisms in the Global Political Economy

1 Varieties of Capitalism and 'the Great Moderation' 11
  David Coates

2 Fault and Fracture? The Impact of New Directions in Comparative Capitalisms Research on the Wider Field 28
  Ian Bruff, Matthias Ebenau and Christian May

3 Directions and Debates in the Globalization of Comparative Capitalisms Research 45
  Matthias Ebenau

Part II Critical Perspectives and Debates

4 Comparative Capitalisms and/or Variegated Capitalism 65
  Bob Jessop

5 Critical Institutionalism in Studies of Comparative Capitalisms: Conceptual Considerations and Research Programme 83
  Christian May and Andreas Nölke

6 Gender Inequalities in the Crisis of Capitalism: Spain and France Compared 101
  Julia Lux and Stefanie Wöhl

7 Social Structures of Accumulation: A Marxist Comparison of Capitalisms? 118
  Terrence McDonough

8 Entangled Modernity and the Study of Variegated
  Capitalism: Some Suggestions for a Postcolonial Research
  Agenda   134
  Ingrid Wehr

Part III Global Perspectives and Debates

9 Putting Comparative Capitalisms Research in Its Place:
  Varieties of Capitalism in Transition Economies   155
  Jan Drahokoupil and Martin Myant

10 State–Business–Labour Relations and Patterns of
  Development in Latin America   172
  Flavio Gaitán and Renato Boschi

11 All Varieties Are Equal… Contributions from Dependency
  Approaches to Critical Comparative Capitalisms Research   189
  Lucía Suau Arinci, Nadia Pessina and Matthias Ebenau

12 Decolonizing the Study of Capitalist Diversity: Epistemic
  Disruption and the Varied Geographies of Coloniality   207
  Lisa Tilley

Conclusion: Towards a Critical, Global Comparative Political
Economy   224
Christian May, Matthias Ebenau and Ian Bruff

Index   233

Tables and Figures

Tables

7.1	Comparing VoC and SSA frameworks	127
9.1	Varieties of capitalism and forms of integration	160
9.2	Indicators for principal forms of international integration: Countries representative of ideal types (2007, percentage of GDP)	162
11.1	Capitalist variegation between dominance and dependency	195

Figures

4.1	Compossibility and incompossibility	77

Contributors

Renato Boschi is Visiting Professor at the Institute of Social and Political Studies at Rio de Janeiro State University (IESP-UERJ), Brazil. His research interests include the relations among business and labour, as well as the patterns of development in Brazil and Latin America. His latest publications include the chapter 'Politics and Trajectory in Brazilian Capitalist Development' in the volume *The BRICs and Emerging Economies in Comparative Perspective* (2013, edited by Uwe Becker) and the edited book *Variedades de capitalismo, política e desenvolvimento na América Latina* (2011).

Ian Bruff is Lecturer in European Politics at the University of Manchester, United Kingdom. He has published widely on European varieties of capitalism, neoliberalism and social (especially historical materialist) theory and is currently researching the political economy of neoliberalism in Europe. With this volume, he completes a large cross-country project on the diversity of contemporary capitalism(s) with Matthias Ebenau, Christian May and Andreas Nölke, which also produced two German-language collections in 2013 (a volume with Westfälisches Dampfboot and a special issue of the journal *Peripherie*) and an English-language special issue (of the journal *Capital and Class*) in 2014.

David Coates holds the Worrell Chair in Anglo-American Studies in the Department of Politics and International Affairs at Wake Forest University in North Carolina, United States. His research interests lie in the broad fields of global and comparative political economy and include topics such as models of capitalism and patterns of empire, the history of labour politics and the nature of contemporary US/UK public policy. Among his recent publications are *Answering Back: Liberal Responses to Conservative Arguments* (2010) and *Making the Progressive Case: Towards a Stronger U.S. Economy* (2011).

Jan Drahokoupil is Project Director at the Mannheim Centre for European Social Research (MZES), University of Mannheim, Germany, and Senior Researcher at the European Trade Union Institute (ETUI) in Brussels, Belgium. He has published a number of books and journal articles on political economy, public policy and international business, particularly in the Eastern European context. He is also associate editor of *Competition and Change: The Journal of Global Business and Political Economy*. His publications include *Transition Economies: Political Economy in Russia, Eastern Europe, and Central Asia* (2011, with Martin Myant) and *Transition Economies after 2008: Responses to the Crisis in Russia and Eastern Europe* (2014, co-edited with Martin Myant).

Matthias Ebenau is Union Lecturer in Business and Political Economy at IG Metall's – the German metal workers' trade union – training centre at Beverungen. His research interests, situated in the fields of global and comparative political economy, focus on union and labour politics, global inequalities and North–South relations. Among his recent publications is the article 'Comparative Capitalisms and Latin American Neodevelopmentalism: A Critical Political Economy View' which forms part of a special issue on 'Critical Political Economy and Capitalist Diversity' of *Capital & Class* (volume 38, issue 1, 2014, co-edited with Ian Bruff).

Flavio Gaitán is Professor at the Federal University of Latin American Integration (UNILA) in Foz do Iguaçu, Paraná, Brazil. His research interests are in political economy and concern topics such as social policies, the role of elites and institutions, and patterns of development. His regional focus is especially on Argentina, Brazil, Mexico, Colombia and Chile. Among his recent publications is the volume *Instituições, Política e Desenvolvimento: America Latina frente ao século XXI* (2014, co-edited with Andrés del Río).

Bob Jessop is Distinguished Professor of Sociology at Lancaster University, United Kingdom. His research interests concern state theory, welfare state restructuring, post-war British politics, critical political economy and cultural political economy. His recent publications include *The Future of the Capitalist State* (2002), *Beyond the Regulation Approach* (2006, co-authored with Ngai-Ling Sum), *State Power* (2007) and *Towards a Cultural Political Economy* (2013, co-authored with Ngai-Ling Sum).

Julia Lux is Research Assistant and a PhD candidate at the Department of Political Economy in the Institute of Political Science at the University of Tübingen, Germany. Her research interests refer to Comparative Political Economy and gender issues, with a particular focus on Germany and France. Among her recent publications is the book chapter

'Wie "genderbar" ist der Varieties of Capitalism-Ansatz? Vergleichende Kapitalismusforschung aus einer Geschlechter-Perspektive', which forms part of the volume *Vergleichende Kapitalismusforschung: Stand, Perspektiven, Kritik* (2013, edited by Ian Bruff, Matthias Ebenau, Christian May and Andreas Nölke).

Christian May is Research Fellow in International Political Economy (IPE) at Goethe University, Frankfurt am Main, Germany. He is interested in the broad field of Global Political Economy, especially in the industrial and financial structures of emerging economies, as well as cultural approaches to political economy. He has published on large emerging economies and Comparative Capitalisms (CC), among other things as *Die großen Schwellenländer: Ursachen und Folgen ihres Aufstiegs in der Weltwirtschaft* (2013, with Andreas Nölke and Simone Claar) and *Vergleichende Kapitalismusforschung: Stand, Perspektiven, Kritik* (2013, with Ian Bruff, Matthias Ebenau and Andreas Nölke).

Terrence McDonough is Professor of Economics at the National University of Ireland, Galway. His research interests focus on globalization, stages of capitalism, social structures of accumulation, US-American and Irish economic history and economics education for labour and community groups. Among his recent publications is *Contemporary Capitalism and Its Crises: Social Structure of Accumulation Theory for the 21st Century* (2010, co-edited with Michael Reich and David M. Kotz).

Martin Myant is Head of the Unit for European Economic, Employment and Social Policy at the European Trade Union Institute in Brussels, Belgium. His research interests lie in the broad fields of European Political Economy and current economic policies. He has written widely on economic and political developments in Eastern and Central Europe, including *Transition Economies: Political Economy in Russia, Eastern Europe, and Central Asia* (2011, with Jan Drahokoupil) and *Transition Economies after 2008: Responses to the Crisis in Russia and Eastern Europe* (2014, co-edited with Jan Drahokoupil).

Andreas Nölke is Professor of International Relations and IPE at Goethe University Frankfurt, Germany. His research interests lie in the broad fields of global and comparative political economy and include topics such as the politics of financialization, accounting standards and transnational private self-regulation, capitalism in large emerging markets, southern multinational corporations, theories of CC, deep integration in North–South relations and the political economy of the Eurozone crisis. His recent publications include the edited volume *Multinational Corporations from Emerging Markets: State Capitalism 3.0* (Palgrave Macmillan, 2014) and a special issue on 'The Politics of Financialization' in *Competition and Change* (volume 17, issue 3, 2014, co-edited with Leo Bieling and Marcel Heires).

Nadia Pessina is Researcher and Lecturer in the Department of Political Science, Catholic University of Córdoba, Argentina, and a PhD candidate at the Centre of Advanced Studies at the National University of Córdoba. Her research interests include international relations and IPE.

Lucía Suau Arinci holds a degree in Political Science from the Catholic University of Córdoba, Argentina, and is currently working in the Migration and Decent Work research group at the University of Kassel, Germany. Her research interests lie in the area of political economy, with a regional focus on Latin America, and concern topics such as agricultural development, natural resources and economic policy. Recent publications include 'Zurück in die Zukunft: Dependenzperspektiven in der Analyse der Diversität des Gegenwartskapitalismus', *Peripherie* (volume 30, issue 130/131, 2013, co-authored with Matthias Ebenau and Facundo Parés).

Lisa Tilley is a double doctoral candidate at the University of Warwick, United Kingdom, and the Université Libre de Bruxelles, Belgium, funded by a GEM Erasmus Mundus fellowship. Her political economy research on the global South draws on both decolonial thought and critical geography.

Ingrid Wehr is Regional Coordinator at the Heinrich Böll Foundation's office for the Southern Cone in Santiago, Chile. Her academic work covers topics such as welfare regimes and social policy, democracy, the 'New' Left and inequality in Latin America, and development theory. Her most recent publication is *Entwicklungstheorien: Weltgesellschaftliche Transformationen, entwicklungspolitische Herausforderungen, theoretische Innovationen* (2014, co-edited with Cord Jakobeit, Franziska Müller, Elena Sondermann and Aram Ziai).

Stefanie Wöhl is Lecturer in Gender Studies and Political Science at the University of Vienna, Austria. Her research interests lie in global and regional governance and include topics such as the gendered political economy, state theory and democratic development within the European Union. Among her recent publications is 'The State and Gender Relations in International Political Economy: A State-Theoretical Approach to Varieties of Capitalism in Crisis' (*Capital & Class*, volume 38, issue 1, 2014).

Abbreviations and Acronyms

AFJP	Administradoras de Fondos de Jubilaciones y Pensiones (Pension and Retirement Funds Administrators, Argentina)
AkG	Assoziation für kritische Gesellschaftsforschung (Association for Critical Social Research)
APENOC	Asociación de Productores Noroeste de Córdoba (Producers' Association of Córdoba's Northwest, Argentina)
BISA-IPEG	British International Studies Association's International Political Economy Group
BNDES	Banco Nacional do Desenvolvimento (National Development Bank, Brazil)
BRIC(S)	Brazil, Russia, India, China (South Africa)
CARTEZ	Confederación de Asociaciones Rurales de la Tercera Zona (Confederation of Rural Associations of the Third Zone, Argentina)
CC	Comparative Capitalisms
CEE	Central and Eastern Europe
CEECs	Central and Eastern European Countries
CIS	Commonwealth of Independent States
CME	Coordinated Market Economy
CRA	Confederaciones Rurales Argentinas (Argentine Rural Confederations)
DFG	Deutsche Forschungsgemeinschaft (German Research Foundation)
DME	Dependent Market Economy
EMU	Economic and Monetary Union
EU	European Union
FDI	Foreign Direct Investment
GDP	Gross Domestic Product
HME	Hierarchical Market Economy
IBSA	India, Brazil, South Africa Dialogue Forum
IDA	Industrial Development Authority (Ireland)
IFSC	International Financial Services Centre
IMF	International Monetary Fund
INDEC	Instituto Nacional de Estadísticas y Censos (National Institute of Statistics and Censuses, Argentina)
IPE	International Political Economy

LME	Liberal Market Economy
LWT	Long Wave Theory
MAGyP	Ministerio de Agricultura, Ganadería y Pesca (Ministry of Agriculture, Animal Breeding and Fisheries, Argentina)
MNC	Multinational Corporation
NESC	National Economic and Social Council (Ireland)
NIE	New Institutional Economics
OECD	Organisation for Economic Co-operation and Development
PAH	Plataforma de Afectados por la Hipoteca (Platform of Those Affected of Mortgage Debt)
PEA	Plan Estratégico Agroalimentario y Agroindustrial (Strategic, Participatory, and Federal Agrarian and Agro-Industrial Plan, Argentina)
PT	Partido dos Trabalhadores (Workers' Party, Brazil)
PNR	Programme for National Recovery
RA	Regulation Approach
R&D	Research & Development
RLS	Rosa-Luxemburg-Stiftung
SEECs	Southeast European Countries
SME	State-permeated Market Economy
SSA	Social Structure of Accumulation
TINA	There Is No Alternative
TNC	Transnational Corporation
UATRE	Unión Argentina de Trabajadores Rurales y Estibadores (Argentine Union of Rural Workers and Porters)
UK	United Kingdom
USA	United States of America
VoC	Varieties of Capitalism
WTO	World Trade Organization
WZB	Wissenschaftszentrum Berlin (Berlin Social Science Center)
YPF	Yacimientos Petrolíferos Fiscales (State-owned Oilfields Company, Argentina)

Introduction: Comparative Capitalisms Research and the Emergence of Critical, Global Perspectives

Matthias Ebenau, Ian Bruff and Christian May

This volume's title centrally alludes to 'new directions' in Comparative Capitalisms (CC) research and thus sets the collective agenda for the multiple and diverse contributions it comprises. The shared point of departure across the chapters in this book is the observation that the CC field, which is centrally concerned with studying the differences, institutional and otherwise, between different localized 'models' or 'varieties' of capitalism, is going through several interwoven processes of rapid and consequential change:

- The dominance of Peter Hall and David Soskice's Varieties of Capitalism (VoC) approach, which occupied the centre of the broad CC field for almost a decade after its publication (Hall and Soskice, 2001) has gradually eroded in recent years, as a combined result of internal (intra-CC) and external critiques. Some of the most important criticisms concern VoC's underestimation of the really existing diversity of contemporary capitalism, its bias towards thinking in static terms and its economistic and functionalist predispositions (see, for example, Bruff and Ebenau, 2014b; Streeck, 2010). While this perspective is still influential, inspiring a 'second generation' of research projects framed in VoC terms, it has undoubtedly lost the dominant position it once held in CC debates.
- The latter has now passed to a broad, heterogeneous and rapidly evolving group of 'post-VoC' perspectives. These generally remain within the paradigmatic boundaries of neoinstitutionalism, the long-standing theoretical underpinning of CC research. Nevertheless, their proponents see the analytical problems which the dynamic 'VoC debate' unearthed during the 2000s as too relevant and too deeply

rooted to be resolved through limited modifications or extensions of this approach's 'relational view of the firm'. Rather, they turn (back) to the wider neoinstitutionalist paradigm, including its historical, sociological, discursive and statist variants for analytical guidance and, on this basis, elaborate new and innovative approaches for analysing the diversity of contemporary capitalism through a focus on institutions (see, for example, Becker, 2009; Crouch, 2005; Streeck, 2012). At the same time, neoinstitutionalist CC scholarship is increasingly being challenged by proponents of critical political economy (often Marxist) perspectives. These scholars argue that it is necessary to more fundamentally shift the coordinates of CC research if we are to make sense of the manifold forms in which we encounter contemporary capitalism around the globe and, crucially, of the huge and persistent social and economic inequalities which stretch across different 'types' of capitalism (see, for example, Albo, 2005; Bruff, 2011; Radice, 2000).

- This theoretical debate is accompanied – and, to a considerable degree, driven – by an expansion of the geographical scope of CC research, a process which may be described as an incipient 'globalization' of the field. Thus, more and more world regions, including Central and Eastern Europe, Latin America and, more recently, China, are coming into the horizon of CC scholars, while at the same time regional specialists increasingly draw on CC perspectives for enriching their own approaches (see, for example, Bohle and Greskovits, 2012; Huang, 2008; Schneider, 2013). This is certainly a welcome development, since it helps to bring down unhelpful disciplinary barriers to, among others, development and transition studies, but as with the wider field it is pervaded by intense debate on the best way forward in globalizing CC research.

Against this general background, the present volume seeks to make a series of more specific intellectual interventions. A first central objective is that of showcasing selected parts of the wide diversity of alternative institutionalist and critical-materialist approaches – the title's metaphorical 'new directions' – which have succeeded the VoC approach as cutting-edge forces in CC research. As such, the volume wishes to document a variety of novel and thus relatively less well-known ways of thinking about diversity within capitalism. A second, related aim is to intensify the dialogue between and across approaches associated with either of these two distinct, but at least partially compatible, strands of alternative CC theorizing. In this, the volume builds and expands upon an intuition expressed by David Coates a decade ago: that the majority of the best scholarship on capitalist diversity is produced precisely at the interface between left institutionalism and neo-Marxism, as well as other perspectives which are critical of capitalism. The virtue of these kinds of scholarship is that they

> probe two features... of different models that a focus on their institutional dynamics alone tends to obscure... the centrality of capital-labor tensions [and] the manner in which the interaction between capitalist models, and their shared experience of common global trends, has latterly corroded the viability of the particular internal settlements between classes on which the contemporary models rest.
>
> (Coates, 2005, p. 21)

It is our contention that these are qualities which, in today's context of global crisis and social turmoil, are more acutely needed than ever (for an interesting earlier collection along these lines, see Soederberg et al., 2005). Hence, the third important objective of this volume is that of advancing the globalization of the CC field while at the same time strengthening novel, critical approaches within the literatures that emerge from this process. Thus, it seeks to contribute to furthering our understanding of capitalism in parts of the world which previous generations of CC scholarship largely neglected, but which are becoming more important for understanding its development in different economic centres and on a global scale.

In a nutshell, the intellectual project which the present book pursues can be described as one of contributing to the development of a new generation of CC scholarship which is simultaneously conscious and critical of capitalism, and has a genuinely global horizon.

The structure of the book

The three chapters in Part I of the book – 'Comparing Capitalisms in the Global Political Economy' – describe in detail each of the processes of change identified at the start of this chapter. David Coates provides a critical overview of the intellectual-historical background to the emergence of debates on capitalist diversity. After reviewing the key tenets of the VoC approach, he turns to exploring, in a unique dialogue with protagonists of the field, the reasons behind its rise to dominance in CC debates during the 2000s, as well as those for its more recent decline in credibility. Subsequently, we (Ian Bruff et al.) simultaneously deepen and broaden the discussion begun by Coates. We return to the principal lines of the VoC debate and, subsequently, describe in general terms the 'new directions' which are unfolding and which are, in turn, vying for authority in shaping the present and future agenda of CC research. Matthias Ebenau, finally, reviews the ways in which these directions shape the globalization of the CC field and the chief issues of debate among scholars active in this process. Ebenau thus builds on Coates' intellectual-historical overview, and Bruff et al.'s enquiry into the conceptual foundations underpinning the evolution of the debate towards new directions, by explicitly focusing on the global dimensions to contemporary CC research.

Part II of the volume – *Critical Perspectives and Debates* – unites a group of contributions which continue the reinvigorated discussion of the fundamental *how* and *why* questions associated with research on capitalist diversity. In particular, the chapters are concerned with the ways in which different theoretical perspectives are competing for interpretative authority regarding *how* diversity is (re)produced in multiple ways around the world, and also with how fundamental questions concerning the *why* of investigations into the diversity, variety or variegation of contemporary capitalism are once again being asked. Accordingly, they present alternative theoretical outlooks which emerge from the engagement between a range of critical perspectives. Importantly, these alternative perspectives are not necessarily in agreement with each other. Thus, this part of the volume firstly showcases the range and vibrancy of debates among scholars advocating alternatives to the mainstream, and secondly invites readers to draw their own conclusions rather than viewing the different chapters as fixed templates for research.

Firstly, Bob Jessop uses the 'variegated capitalism' notion as a means of providing a conceptual alternative to a one-sided focus on VoC *and* to an equally narrow emphasis on capitalism as a single, integrated mode of production. Hence he makes the claim – rooted in Marx's critique of political economy – that we need to locate research on CC within a world market context. Jessop's suggestion that this entails a rather different way of conceptualizing the role of institutions is developed extensively by Christian May and Andreas Nölke who argue – to an extent against Jessop – that we ought to resist the temptation to discard or neglect institutionalist approaches for the comparative study of capitalism. Calling instead for a critical institutionalism, they show how the normative premises of critical social theory can reinvigorate institutionalist research.

Next, Julia Lux and Stefanie Wöhl highlight the often-ignored benefits of making use of feminist political economy scholarship for research on capitalist diversity. Using France and Spain as examples, they argue for the relevance of a focus on social reproduction and associated gender norms and inequalities, which in their view is essential for a more thorough critical approach to be realized. Terrence McDonough takes a different approach again, arguing for the relevance of the Social Structure of Accumulation (SSA) framework, which is particularly interested in how capitalism varies over time. In other words, 'capitalist diversity' is not just about differences across space, but also across different periods of history. Ireland's post-1945 trajectory is used to illustrate McDonough's case. Finally, Ingrid Wehr seeks to open up a debate on the Eurocentric and Orientalist tendencies which pervade contemporary CC scholarship, including many of its 'post-VoC' variants. After critically engaging with these tendencies, which she sees most clearly embodied in attempts to identify 'patrimonial' models or varieties of capitalism in the Global South, she suggests introducing into critical CC the insights from the debate on entangled modernity as a way of overcoming them.

The chapters assembled in Part III of the volume – *Global Perspectives and Debates* – are concerned with the development of, and debate between, different approaches for studying capitalism in world regions which have not traditionally formed part of the field's geographical purview. Crucially, they also cover the multiple forms of interaction between these different models and their global context. As such, they ask the *how* and *why* questions in a different manner to the authors in Part II, because they assume that the CC field has to undergo a fundamental reorientation if it is to acquire relevance in a global sense. Again, the chapters present alternative approaches while showing, in greater empirical detail than elsewhere in the book, what this means for the study of capitalism in a range of spatial and developmental contexts. As such, they offer a contrast to the critical-theoretical perspectives discussed in Part II, because these approaches are fundamentally rooted in a conception of capitalism as a developed system, which may understate some factors which are key for the study of low- or middle-income capitalisms.

Partly defending the VoC approach from its more radical detractors, Jan Drahokoupil and Martin Myant suggest that it is possible to recover some of the merits of the original CC debates about economic performance for the study of transition economies, whose specificities are often under-appreciated. Their fivefold typology accounts for the different types of international economic integration that characterizes transition in Russia, Eastern Europe and Central Asia. Flavio Gaitán and

Renato Boschi are similarly interested in economic performance and international economic integration, using a focus on Latin America to critique both CC contributions on the region and classical dependency approaches to argue that the potentially significant role of the state in the (semi-)periphery needs to be re-emphasized.

In contrast to these chapters, the next two chapters seek to show how a combination of critical-theoretical concerns can be brought to bear in the concrete study of capitalist diversity in non-Western contexts. Firstly, Lucía Suau Arinci et al. revise and update the insights of classical dependency approaches in order to show that situations of dependency, while not fixed for all time or the same in all countries/regions, are difficult to overcome. This is demonstrated through an analysis of post-2001 Argentina which covers several dimensions of dependence. Secondly, Lisa Tilley argues – utilizing the insights of post/decolonial scholarship – that most forms of CC research, critical or otherwise, tend to take 'national capitalism' as the starting point for analysis and to assume that non-Western countries increasingly emulate a Western 'model' the more they develop economically. Focusing on East Asia but also considering other parts of the world, she shows that this masks the material geographies of coloniality both within and across national borders, especially the relationship between accumulation in metropolitan areas and impoverishment and dispossession in rural regions.

This volume closes with a short chapter in which we (Christian May et al.) establish the main agreements and disagreements among the preceding chapters, and highlight a number of themes which emerge from the volume that will be important in shaping the future evolution of the CC field towards what we hope will be a critical, global, Comparative Political Economy. These themes are the re-appreciation of many classics of politico-economic thought for CC research; the interconnected issues of capitalist dynamics, crises and institutional change; establishing plausible connections between investigations into 'national' diversity and the constitutively relational, cross-border character of global capitalism; the need to redefine fundamental research parameters in order to appreciate the real diversity of capitalism on a global scale; and the politics of CC research.

This volume is the fourth and last publication that emerges from a larger international research project, 'Comparison, Analysis, Critique: Perspectives on the Diversity of Contemporary Capitalism(s)', which we conducted between 2011 and 2014 in partnership with Andreas Nölke of Goethe-University Frankfurt. The other publications were a German-language collection with Westfälisches Dampfboot, which for the first time sought to introduce critical CC perspectives into debates in the German-speaking countries (Bruff et al., 2013); a special issue, also in German, in the journal *Peripherie*, which contained various critical contributions on global capitalist diversity, especially regarding the global South (Ebenau et al., 2013); and, finally, a special issue of the British journal *Capital & Class*, which brought together a considerable number of critical political economy perspectives, both in the critique of conventional CC research and in the development of alternative approaches (Bruff and Ebenau, 2014a). The present collection brings this varied series to a close. We hope that it will be of use to seasoned researchers, but in particular to the younger generation of scholars in which we count ourselves and which will hopefully shape the future of CC research.

We are intellectually indebted to all of the colleagues who contributed to one or several of these publications and/or who presented at the kick-off event of our project held in Wiesbaden, Germany, in February 2012. We would also like to express our gratitude to the institutional sponsors of the project, the *Deutsche Forschungsgemeinschaft* (DFG), the *Rosa-Luxemburg-Stiftung* (RLS), the *Assoziation für kritische Gesellschaftsforschung* (AkG) and the British International Studies Association's International Political Economy Group (BISA-IPEG). At Palgrave Macmillan, we want to thank Timothy Shaw, Christina Brian and Ambra Finotello for their continued support and friendly cooperation.

Finally, this book is dedicated to the memory of Uwe Becker, who from the very beginning was very supportive of alternative approaches to comparing capitalisms. Uwe was with us at the initial workshop in Wiesbaden 2012 and, with his unique mixture of comradeship, dry wit and uncompromising intellectual attitude, he gave us enthusiastic support while being very critical of particular arguments and perspectives at the same time. He had agreed to write an endorsement for this collection but, due to his tragic and untimely passing a few days before the manuscript could be finalized, it is now up to us to write a tribute to him. As one of the forerunners of what in this book we call 'post-VoC' approaches, he was one of the first to point out that 'the emperor', the popular VoC approach, was in some regards 'naked'. But he also directed his critical energy towards the alternative institutionalist approaches which he himself favoured, as well as to self-professed critical perspectives. In developing further our work on critical, global CC research, which he had in part inspired, this guidance will be sorely missed. Also, doing this kind of research will now be less fun, since not only his wit but also his friendship will be missing. We cannot do more than to keep his intellectual spirit alive by occasionally asking ourselves how Uwe would have torn our arguments apart. And, of course, to acknowledge that sometimes even the best CC work has to wait when there is a good sports tournament going on.

Bibliography

Albo, G. (2005) 'Contesting the "New Capitalism"', in D. Coates (ed.), *Varieties of Capitalism, Varieties of Approaches* (Basingstoke: Palgrave Macmillan), 63–82.
Becker, U. (2009) *Open Varieties of Capitalism: Continuity, Change and Performances* (Basingstoke: Palgrave Macmillan).
Bohle, D. and B. Greskovits (2012) *Capitalist Diversity on Europe's Periphery* (Ithaca: Cornell University Press).
Bruff, I. (2011) 'What about the Elephant in the Room? Varieties of Capitalism, Varieties in Capitalism', *New Political Economy*, 16:4, 481–500.
Bruff, I. and M. Ebenau (eds.) (2014a) 'Critical Political Economy and Capitalist Diversity', special issue of *Capital & Class*, 38:1, 3–251.
Bruff, I. and M. Ebenau (2014b) 'Critical Political Economy and the Critique of Comparative Capitalisms Scholarship on Capitalist Diversity', *Capital & Class*, 38:1, 3–15.
Bruff, I., M. Ebenau, C. May and A. Nölke (eds.) (2013) *Vergleichende Kapitalismusforschung: Stand, Perspektiven, Kritik* (Münster: Westfälisches Dampfboot).
Coates, D. (2005) 'Conclusion: Choosing Between Paradigms – A Personal View', in D. Coates (ed.), *Varieties of Capitalism, Varieties of Approaches* (Basingstoke: Palgrave Macmillan), 265–71.
Crouch, C. (2005) *Capitalist Diversity and Change: Recombinant Governance and Institutional Entrepreneurs* (Oxford: Oxford University Press).
Ebenau, M., R. Kößler, C. May and I. Wehr (eds.) (2013) 'Die Welt des Kapitals', double special issue of *PERIPHERIE: Zeitschrift für Politik und Ökonomie in der Dritten Welt*, 33:130–1, 143–348.
Hall, P.A. and D. Soskice (eds.) (2001) *Varieties of Capitalism: The Institutional Foundations of Comparative Advantage* (Oxford: Oxford University Press).
Huang, Y. (2008) *Capitalism with Chinese Characteristics: Entrepreneurship and the State* (New York et al.: Cambridge University Press).
Radice, H. (2000) 'Globalization and National Capitalisms: Theorizing Convergence and Differentiation', *Review of International Political Economy*, 7:4, 719–42.
Schneider, B.R. (2013) *Hierarchical Capitalism in Latin America: Business, Labor, and the Challenges of Equitable Development* (Cambridge: Cambridge University Press).
Soederberg, S., G. Menz and P. Cerny (eds.) (2005) *Internalizing Globalization: The Rise of Neoliberalism and the Decline of National Varieties of Capitalism* (Basingstoke: Palgrave Macmillan).
Streeck, W. (2010) 'E Pluribus Unum? Varieties and Commonalities of Capitalism', *MPIfG Working Papers*, 10/12 (Köln: Max-Planck-Institut für Gesellschaftsforschung).
Streeck, W. (2012) 'How to Study Contemporary Capitalism?' *European Journal of Sociology*, 53:1, 1–28.

Part I
Comparing Capitalisms in the Global Political Economy

1
Varieties of Capitalism and 'the Great Moderation'

David Coates

When Peter Hall and David Soskice wrote their introduction to the now widely cited collection of essays they published in 2001 under the title *Varieties of Capitalism: The Institutional Foundation of Comparative Advantage*, they could hardly have known how important in the history of comparative political economy that introduction was going to be. True, they saw their own work as an important attempt to shift the goal posts – as 'a new approach to the comparison of national economies' – one that was capable in their mind of going beyond the 'three perspectives on institutional variation that [had] dominated the study of comparative capitalisms [CC] in the preceding thirty years' (Hall and Soskice, 2001, pp. v, 2). They saw themselves, that is, as challengers to the dominant approaches of the day in comparative political economy – challengers to the modernization paradigm, the neo-corporatism framework and the social systems of production approach. What they presumably did not see, as they drafted that introductory chapter, was the speed with which their approach would replace those three in dominance. This chapter, which draws heavily on correspondence with many of the key players involved, has been written to explain this unexpected rise to dominance and to evaluate the significance of its subsequent erosion (see also Bruff et al., in this volume).

Charting the rise

So what was it that Hall and Soskice said in that opening essay that turned out to be so incredibly influential? Essentially it came down to just five broad things.

(1) They saw themselves as introducing to the field of comparative political economy a new sense of how behaviour is shaped by

institutions, doing so by focusing on the strategic interactions central to the behaviour of economic actors. In ways in which the other three approaches had not, they put the firm at the centre of their analysis. They examined the behavior of firms in game-theoretic terms – establishing what they termed 'a relational view of the firm' by focusing on five spheres in which a successful profit-seeking company was necessarily obliged to coordinate its activity with other key players. The five spheres on which they chose to concentrate were industrial relations, vocational training and education, corporate governance and access to finance, inter-firm relations, and relations with their own employees.

(2) Hall and Soskice then argued that national economies could be compared with one another by how firms within them handled these coordination problems: a comparison that was possible and fruitful only because 'the incidence of different types of firm relationships varies systematically across nations' (ibid., p. 9). For them, 'the core resulting distinction' was one 'between two types of political economies, liberal market economies and coordinated market economies...ideal types at the poles of a spectrum along which many nations can be arrayed' (ibid., p. 8). 'Broadly speaking', they argued, 'liberal market economies are distinguished from coordinated market economies by the extent to which firms rely on market mechanisms to coordinate their endeavors as opposed to forms of strategic interaction supported by non-market institutions' (ibid., p. 33).

(3) Hall and Soskice then listed six liberal market economies ([LMEs] Australia, Canada, Ireland, New Zealand, the United Kingdom, the United States), detailing the United States as the exemplar; and they listed eleven coordinated market economies ([CMEs] Austria, Belgium, Denmark, Finland, Iceland, Germany, Japan, the Netherlands, Norway, Sweden, Switzerland), with Germany as the detailed case. They were adamant that they were 'not arguing here that one' model was necessarily 'superior to another' (ibid., p. 21), though they did recognize different capacities for innovation in each. LMEs, they said, were better at radical innovation, CMEs at incremental innovation, and they implied that other differential patterns of performance were likely.

(4) Hall and Soskice reinforced this core difference between polar types of national economy by emphasizing the consolidation within each of 'institutional complementarities', and the resulting 'comparative institutional advantage' enjoyed by economies in which

such complementarity was high. The existence of institutional complementarities then determined which set of public policies was likely to be effective in each: market-oriented policies that increased the autonomy of capital relative to labour in the case of LMEs, policies favoring a stronger element of social partnership in CMEs, and so on. As they put it, 'it follows that economic policies will be effective only if they are *incentive compatible*, namely complementary to the coordinating capacities embedded in the existing political economy' (ibid., p. 46; italics in original).

(5) Likewise, although Hall and Soskice recognized pressures common to both models from intensifying global competition – pressures pushing both towards more market-based forms of coordination – they nonetheless insisted that the depth of institutional complementarities within CMEs would blunt those pressures to a significant and persistent degree. Indeed it was their view that, contrary to the TINA ('there is no alternative') argument of many globalization advocates, their 'concept of comparative institutional advantage also suggests that many firms may exploit new opportunities for movement to engage in a form of *institutional arbitrage*' (ibid., p. 57; italics in original).

The argument presented in this essay was therefore relatively simple and brief, but the result was not. It was catalytic to an unprecedented outpouring of high-quality research and debate. The essay was initially published in the company of others by Kathleen Thelen, Torben Iversen, Margarita Estévez-Abe, Isabella Mares, Pepper Culpepper, Bob Hancké, Sigurd Vitols, Steven Casper, Stewart Wood and Orfeo Fioretos, on issues as different as varieties of labour politics, patterns of skill formation and attitudes to the European Union. It then quickly gave rise to: (i) a series of linked research initiatives; (ii) a flow of articles and monographs; and (iii) an eventually extensive body of reaction and critique. In the first category, think of the later work by many in that original volume (Thelen, 2004; Estévez-Abe, 2009; Iversen, 2005, 2010; Fioretos, 2011) and of the many subsequent collections of research data, including those edited by Hancké et al. (2007) and by Mahoney and Thelen (2009). In the second, think of the writings of, among many others, Colin Crouch (2005), Wolfgang Streeck (2006, 2009) and Bob Jessop (2011). In the third, think of the debates that regularly filled the pages of *Socio-Economic Review*; the steady drumbeat of critical doctoral theses, including, recently, that by Travis Fast (2012); and the critical collections edited by Coates (2005), Elsner and Hanappi (2008), Wood and Lane

(2011) and now this collection (see also Bruff et al., in this volume). No other essay published in comparative political economy in 2001 had anything like the impact of that first one. No other academic product published that year ended up triggering an industry of its own, as the Varieties of Capitalism (VoC) introductory essay certainly did.

Explaining the dominance

In modern social science, the dominance of a particular approach – however fleeting – is always ultimately a product of the approach's strength, where strength is understood as a potent mixture of intellectual coherence, conceptual clarity, explanatory force and contemporary relevance. The VoC approach had those strengths in abundance.

The academic and intellectual context

Peter Hall and David Soskice were both well-known and well-positioned scholars as they wrote the introduction to VoC: Peter Hall at the Center for European Studies at Harvard and David Soskice at the Wissenschaftszentrum Berlin (WZB). Years later, Bob Hancké remembered it all starting

> sometime between 1991, when David was giving talks at Harvard outlining for the first time the LME–CME distinction, and 1993, when a series of workshops were organized under the auspices of the programme for the study of Germany and Europe at Harvard, located in the Center for European Studies. In 1993 the programme had funding for joint workshops and for sending graduate students over to the WZB for anything between three and six months, to work with David. The reputation of the group grew quickly and others (especially graduate students from other top schools in the US) asked if they could join for a term or two, and the basic group was born.[1]

Vivien Schmidt's recollection is similar:

> VoC came together as a research project led by David Soskice and Peter Hall that drew in many talented young...doctoral students.... and in which participants presented their papers in many different venues. So call it a 'thought collective' that was creating an epistemic community around a project that was pretty exciting to

scholars, in particular younger ones, for normative, methodological and empirical reasons.[2]

What is now clear is that by 2001 the main arguments in the opening chapter had already been well-trailed over the near-decade that the project had taken to come to fruition, so that by the time the essay was published, the VoC approach had an audience waiting for its crystallization in published form. And then, because (as Ben Rosamond put it in private correspondence on the impact of that first volume) 'this was a big book by two of the big players',[3] it created substantial academic waves almost as soon as it appeared.

The intellectual context surrounding the publication of VoC was also critical. The essays in the original collection, and so many of the studies that followed, were able to draw on, and benefit from, the prior existence of a coherent body of literature, arguing that a full understanding of modern economies required the careful and extensive examination of institutions and their consequences. The big claim was that institutions mattered. Against this background, the original VoC collection, and particularly its opening essay, quickly became the flagship enterprise of an increasingly self-confident new institutionalist literature (see also Bruff et al. in this volume). Institutionalism was an approach to the study of modern economies and society that had already spawned its own – rational choice, historical and sociological – sub-divisions, whose relative strengths and weaknesses were being discussed in major academic journals from the mid-1990s onwards (Zysman, 1994; Hall and Taylor, 1996; Hodgson, 1996; Immergut, 1998; Thelen, 1999). The new institutionalists saw themselves as offering a superior approach to the understanding of modern capitalism to those currently available either from neo-classical economics or from conventional Marxism. They saw their analyses as inherently superior to conventional Marxism in their understanding of the role that institutions, and not just classes, play in the coordination of economic activity, an understanding that enabled new institutionalists to capture the fine grain of economic life in ways that academics deploying Marxist categories of analysis for the most part did not even choose to capture (for contrasting assessments, see Jessop and McDonough, in this volume). And they saw their approach superior to 'economics and its rational choice bridgeheads in social science', through its capacity to 'treat the preferences of actors as endogenous to the institutional settings in which they are acted out' (Streeck, 2006, p. 34).

To scholars persuaded of the intellectual superiority of the new institutionalism, the analysis of contemporary economies needed to be grounded neither in the methodological individualism beloved of modern economists nor in the historical materialism of mainstream Marxism. The first (the abstract modelling of individual rationalities) was too small a step to take in the pursuit of a full understanding of how modern economies functioned, and the second (the mapping of broad-class interests and the incompatibilities between them) was a step too far. The focal point of analysis, they argued, needed instead to remain at the level of dominant institutions, because it was the complementarity or otherwise of institutional patterns that gave broad comparative advantage to successful economies. Though epistemologically squeezed in between these two powerful paradigms, the new institutionalist scholarship was nonetheless from the outset internally divided. The initial approach had been predominantly historical in focus – Peter Hall's own work in the 1980s had certainly been that (Hall, 1986) – and stressed the importance of critical junctures, which were conceptualized as key moments in time that established patterns of institutional formation and interaction and then left those societies locked onto particular paths. But through the 1990s, Peter Hall appears to have moved towards a more rational choice-based form of institutionalism, one in which David Soskice's early work was already an important point of reference (Soskice, 1990).

In contrast to historical and sociological institutionalism, Peter Hall and Rosemary Taylor wrote in 1996, rational-choice institutionalism 'offer[ed] the greatest analytical leverage in settings where consensus among actors accustomed to strategic action and of roughly equal standing is necessary to secure institutional change' (i.e. CMEs) and in 'settings where intense competition among organizational forms selects for those with some kind of efficiency that is clearly specifiable *ex ante*, as in some settings of market competition' (i.e. LMEs) (Hall and Taylor, 1996, pp. 950–3). It was not that Peter Hall was here suggesting a break with historical institutionalism. He was not, and historical institutionalism continued to have strong support from colleagues with whom he carried on working, most notably from Kathleen Thelen (Thelen, 1999). It was rather that, by the late 1990s and cooperating closely with David Soskice, Peter Hall had become a powerful advocate of a creative dialogue between these various schools of institutionalism – not a blind synthesis, but the building of an understanding of the character and trajectory of modern economies that drew on them all (see also Hall, 2009). The opening essay in the VoC collection can in part be understood as an opening shot at that new and creative synthesis.

VoC and the earlier CC literatures

Peter Hall, David Soskice and their colleagues were not the first intellectuals to explore issues of institutional variation across national capitalisms. Nor were they the first to explore those issues from what they and we would now recognize as a broadly neo-Weberian background (cf. Bruff and Hartmann, 2014). That exploration goes back at the very least to the writings of Andrew Shonfield in the 1960s (Shonfield, 1965) and had already generated a number of bodies of relevant research material. This included not only the strands of new institutionalism surveyed by Hall and Taylor but also what Wolfgang Streeck later called 'the corporatist growth industry of the 1970s' (Streeck, 2006, p. 12), the extensive literatures on models of capitalism triggered by Michel Albert's distinction between Anglo-Saxon and Rhenish capitalism (Albert, 1993; Crouch and Streeck, 1997; Hollingsworth and Boyer, 1997), and even the developments on the edge of conventional Marxism through the work of French and US-American regulation theorists (Aglietta, 1979; Boyer, 1990; Kotz et al., 1994; see also McDonough in this volume). But, at least during the 1990s, what characterized much of that research was its existence in separate and largely uncoordinated debates. It was against that background that the Hall and Soskice essay then serendipitously provided the emerging sub-field of comparative political economy with a new and tighter unity, by generating an overarching conceptual framework that contained within it the seeds of a fertile and accessible research agenda.

By suggesting that comparative political economists should deploy a basic distinction between two polar opposites (LMEs and CMEs) and should understand each as clusters of related institutions centred on the capitalist firm, Peter Hall and David Soskice fired the starting gun on the race to explore continuity and change, complexity and convergence, in one advanced capitalist economy after another. The VoC gun was such a powerful catalyst to new research – and more powerful for a while than any of its competitors – because it managed to do two vital things simultaneously. It offered a basic distinction that was sharp enough to enable empirical data to be easily chopped into component bits, but one that was sufficiently nuanced internally as to facilitate the mapping of a number of major spheres of economic coordination within each institutional cluster. The basic bi-polar typology in the original Hall and Soskice essay, by its very paucity of options, invited the creation of sub-types and new types of capitalist models. Hall and Soskice's focus on just five key spheres of economic coordination invited the consideration of yet more spheres, and the interplay between an expanding typology and a proliferation of spheres then rapidly created a whole universe of possible interactions to be researched, catalogued and explained. By claiming to be simultaneously a typology and an explanation, the original VoC approach enabled a whole generation of young researchers to explore detailed economic developments in particular national contexts, inside a framework that facilitated the linking of their findings to parallel developments elsewhere (see also Drahokoupil & Myant, in this volume). As Cathie Jo Martin put it, the VoC model became 'a foundational work in comparative politics due to its elegance, parsimony, breadth, employer-centered theory of action, and preferential focus on the structural features of the political economy as determinants of cross-nation variation' (Martin, 2014, p. 68).

'The Great Moderation'

The timing of the VoC initiative was excellent for more than just its relevance for contemporary intellectual debates. It emerged at the height as what we can now see was 'The Great Moderation' – a two-decade span in which sustained economic growth in advanced capitalist economies became the norm rather than the exception. This was a period in which jobs were plentiful and living standards buoyant, and in which a whole slew of academic and political leaders could persuade themselves and others that the basic contradictions between capital and labour had been permanently transcended. The Great Moderation was a period in which, among other things, Robert E. Lucas could use his presidential address to the American Economic Association to declare that the central problem of macroeconomics – depression prevention – had for all practical purposes now been solved (Lucas, 2003); and the UK Finance Minister (Gordon Brown) could appear before the House of Commons and announce that the business cycle was now mastered. 'We will never return', he said, 'to the old boom and bust' (see Coates (2008) for more).

It was also a period in which, across the English-speaking world as a whole, the political forces of the Left were in retreat. They were in retreat politically before a revitalized conservatism. They were in retreat industrially before a revitalized employing class: and they were in retreat academically before a revitalized neo-classical liberalism – one reinforced in the United Kingdom by the broadly conservative consequences of the regular Research Assessment Exercises (Lee et al., 2013), and in the United States by the increasing professional dominance of 'fresh water' economists over 'salt water' ones (Krugman, 2009). Inside the academy, the once-plentiful flow of Marxist scholarship diminished in both volume and confidence as the crisis of the Left deepened, so that in the wake of what Wolfgang Streeck later called 'the neoliberal turn' (Streeck, 2006, p. 26), responsibility for slowing down the academic imperialism of methodological individualism fell, if only by default, from their shoulders onto those of the new institutionalists.

It was a responsibility that many of the academic networks operating within the VoC approach accepted consciously and willingly, arguing back against the TINA arguments of the neoliberals that there was indeed an alternative way of running a capitalist economy – namely a coordinated market one. As Hall and Soskice (2001, p. 53) put it, 'there are at least two viable ways of organizing a liberal capitalist economy'. There was both 'novelty and attractiveness', Geoff Hodgson recently wrote privately, in a literature on VoC 'that countered the traditional Marxist and market-fundamentalist notions that only one type of capitalism (or only one developmental track for capitalism) is feasible, normal or desirable'.[4] Thus, '[i]mplicitly (and sometimes explicitly)', Greg Albo said, 'the VoC approach has provided an important theoretical and ideological defense of social democracy. It suggests that states with strong social democratic histories and current political balance of forces with strong social democratic parties still govern themselves in important ways that are more egalitarian and less market-determined.'[5] Mark Blyth saw that early: 'implicitly then', he wrote in 2003, '*Varieties of Capitalism* argues *for* the CME alternative and thereby *for* the equalitarian distributions and outcomes typical of European political economies in the face of the neo-liberal onslaught' (Blyth, 2003, p. 217; italics in original).

However, the VoC rupture with TINA was never total. The approach was at best a 'Third Way' defence of managed capitalism, one heavily imbued with an orthodox understanding of basic market rationalities, and one that conceded the appropriateness of neoclassical economics as a guide to the inner workings of LMEs, if not to that of CMEs (Fast, 2012, p. 49). As Colin Crouch put it, 'its main message is that clearly the pure market economy (which Anglo-America is considered to be) is the more dynamic, innovative, future-oriented form of capitalism: but there is a kind of long-term future for the Germans and those like them, churning out high-quality but going-nowhere-new motor cars and similar things.'[6] The VoC defence of even German capitalism was not that it was as dynamic as UK-American capitalism – only that it was viable (Blyth, 2003); and it was a defence that took at face value conservative claims that US capitalism was both uncoordinated and strong-because-uncoordinated, claims that would turn out to be hollow in the wake of the financial crisis that engulfed both models in late 2008. But at the very least, key VoC scholars consistently held the front against those who insisted on the inevitability (and even desirability) of convergence towards some kind of Anglo-American capitalist model (see also Bruff et al., in this volume). As Peter Hall (2007, pp. 39, 82) put it: 'As Mark Twain might have said, rumours of the death of CMEs are greatly exaggerated...cross-national divergence in institutional practices and patterns of economic activity of the sort emphasized by VoC approaches persists over time.'

VoC and rival approaches

That defence of alternative capitalist models by writers deploying the VoC distinction between LMEs and CMEs took different forms with different audiences. Against the conservatism of mainstream economics departments, the VoC argument was just as solidly based on rational choice modelling as was its opponent's, insisting not that rational choice modelling be abandoned but only that it be garnished with a sensitivity to institutional context. A choice that was rational for profit-seeking firms in a LME was not necessarily the same as a choice that was rational in a coordinated market one: institutional variation made different choices rational in each. Against the radicalism of conventional Marxist understandings of capitalism and its limits, the VoC argument was that institutional differences within particular national capitalisms did make a genuine difference. Not all cats were grey in the dark: so it mattered whether capitalists were free to treat labour as a pure commodity or were constrained to treat labour as a commodity with rights. And against the prevailing wisdom in governing circles in both Washington and London that the future of capitalism was necessarily Anglo-American, the VoC response was the insistence that capitalism had more than one future. It had a German future as well as an American future; and it did so because institutional complementarity is a necessary source of strength, and because institutional clusters, once locked onto successful growth paths, are more likely to stay on those paths than they are to converge.

The result was a 20-year explosion of high-quality research solidly rooted in empirically grounded data sets. In consequence, we now know a lot more than we might otherwise have done about the internal workings of a string of mainly European economies, with that enhanced knowledge linked together by a shared concern with a mapping of the institutional variations and logics at play. The basic conceptual distinctions deployed in VoC-inspired research were so accessible and so easily applicable that an entire generation of doctoral students in comparative political economy was able to use them for its own purposes. Moreover, this generation was still able to find enough room in the imperfections of the fit between the original typology and the complexity of modern conditions for each of them to niche-market themselves as contributors to knowledge, while (in the United States in particular) simultaneously meeting the requirements of their examining committees that any contribution they make should be accomplished within the tight time constraints of the PhD programme. As Matthew Watson later put it in private correspondence on this issue, the attraction of the VoC approach was

> that it looked sufficiently complex in theoretical terms to be a really good antidote to the simplicities of rational choice theory, but it was by no means complex enough in political economy terms to put anyone off using it as an approach. Its appeal was that it was straightforward in intuitive terms (capitalism *does* come in many diverse forms, after all) and that those intuitions translated nice and simply to single or comparative empirical case studies.[7]

The very proliferation of such studies has then in its turn left more and more aspiring academics invested in the continued dominance of the approach they have made their own, and the governing requirement in contemporary academic life to continually reference sources has now given the VoC citation index a separate dynamic of its own. Kathleen Thelen described this as 'a multiplier effect'[8]: more and more studies citing the original not simply to support it but also to critique it. Mark Blyth wrote this in 2003:

> Perhaps it is simply a generational artifact, but every 10 years or so certain positions in the field of comparative political economy become canonical. I suspect that the VOC literature will do exactly that in the coming decade, framing more research projects than any other perspective, and shaping the way that an entire cohort of graduate students thinks about growth, employment, and the critical issues of institutional convergence and divergence in a globalized economy.
> (Blyth, 2003, p. 215)

As we have seen, that canonical status came quickly to the VoC approach, and in the process something else came quickly too – a fundamental change in the status of the original essay. Over time, it became less a direct source of inspiration and more an indirect source of legitimation – a touchstone now rather than a starting gun, in Vivek Chibber's striking imagery[9] – with the paradoxical implication that, in the years to come, the number of citations of the VoC approach will very likely continue to increase as the influence of the approach actually goes down. And it will very likely go down for the exact same reason that initially it went up. It will go down because the VoC approach was very much a product of its time, and because that time has now well and truly passed (see also Bruff et al., in this volume).

Reflecting on the dominance

In saying that the original VoC time is over – that we are now necessarily *post*-VoC – I mean no insult or criticism, just the reverse in fact. Everyone reading this now (and those of us writing now) are unavoidably aware that the Great Moderation came crashing down in the financial crisis of 2008. But in order to give the original VoC authors their due, it is vital to remember that, as late as 1 January 2008, virtually nobody of any intellectual persuasion – left/right/centre – saw that crash coming. A few sceptics and jeremiahs did, but they were as ignored then as they are hailed now. Instead the bulk of academia, no less than the politicians they studied, settled back – on the basis of a 20-year run – into assumptions about the likelihood of steady economic growth across the advanced capitalist world, with only incremental adjustments necessary to globalization and its associated new international division of labour, and therefore also into assumptions about the continued stability of different national economies (see also Ebenau, in this volume). In that intellectual and political climate, it made perfect sense to go on prioritizing as research questions issues of incremental institutional change, institutional complementarity, welfare state adjustments to new conditions and so on. It made sense not to probe deeper, beneath the institutional formations, because those formations seemed stable and any underlying capitalist contradictions seemed muted or gone. To be sure, there were things to worry about, including global imbalances between creditor and debtor nations, and persistent inequalities within core capitalisms; but technical problems of that kind (as they were by then increasingly being understood) invited simply technical solutions. No one saw the upcoming global crash and the wheels falling off the entire bus.

But then came the traumatic month – September 2008 – and the temporary seizing up of the credit flows between as well as within economies. With it, in rapid succession, came the Great

Recession – more than 50 million jobs gone worldwide – and the explosion of state aid to finance and industry (even in LMEs, and particularly in the two main LMEs), with every economy caught, to varying degrees, in the global whirlwind. So, just like the fall of the Berlin Wall transformed the status and relevance of everything written earlier on the Cold War, the end of the Great Moderation transformed the status and relevance of everything written earlier on VoC and their patterns of institutional change. In the wake of the collapse of Lehman Brothers, institutional variation still mattered – boring banking suddenly became a Canadian plus over an American negative – but even so, where the deckchairs stood on the deck of the *Titanic* suddenly mattered less than the fact that they were all going down on the same doomed ship. In calm waters, the difference between ships is fascinating. In storms, the only thing that matters is the weather. What had been ignored in the bulk of the VoC debate (underlying capitalist contradictions), and what had been marginalized (cross-national linkages between economies), suddenly in late 2008 moved centre-stage again, and a conceptual universe preoccupied with minute institutional variation could suffice no more (Bruff and Horn, 2012; Bruff and Ebenau, 2014).

That conceptual universe had already generated a powerful and coherent critique from many sources, including from the outset by Mark Blyth and more recently Wolfgang Streeck (Blyth, 2003; Streeck, 2006, 2009; also Schmidt, 2009; Martin, 2014; Peck and Theodore, 2007). From the get-go, Mark Blyth questioned whether Germany was in reality a CME, and whether US capitalism was economically superior in spite of its LME status. And long before the financial crisis, Streeck had seen weaknesses in the VoC approach – such as methodological nationalism, functionalism, economism and static comparativism – that persuaded him that it should be abandoned (Streeck, 2011, p. 435). It became his clearly stated view that the new institutionalism needed to be strengthened as an approach to the understanding of modern economies by bringing capitalism back in and taking VoC out (cf. Streeck, 2009). But what is also worth emphasizing is the extent to which both Peter Hall and David Soskice have now joined many other scholars, including myself, in recognizing that elements of our work prior to 2008 need to be reset. David Soskice in particular, while studiously continuing to deploy the LME–CME distinction, has now shifted his attention to the weaknesses of each revealed by the financial crisis and to the associated agendas of reform (Soskice, 2009). Even for Soskice, LMEs are clearly not as institutionally stable as they were once presumed to be (see also Bruff et al., in this volume on the 'post-VoC' generation).

So where does that leave us? My judgement would be this: we do not need to throw out the baby with the bathwater, and we should not. The new institutionalism has brought a level of understanding about the character of modern capitalism that needs to be both honoured and retained. What we should argue instead is that the greater strength of the new institutionalism lies in its historical-institutionalist and discursive variants rather than in its rational-choice one, and that accordingly the explanatory power of concepts like 'path dependency' and 'critical junctures' should not be discarded. After all, we are living through a critical juncture right now. But the comparative analysis of continuity and change, convergence and divergence in modern economic systems must now be subsumed into a deeper analysis of trends and processes operating below the level of institutions. Furthermore, since the basic nature of those trends and processes was first identified effectively by Marx and Engels, comparative scholars would do well to engage systematically once more with their intellectual legacy. It is time to replace an analysis of capitalism seen from above through the lens of its relational firms with an analysis of capitalism seen from below through the lens of its oppressed producers. It is time within the intellectual universe of the new institutionalism to move left – away from rational choice concerns to historical and discursive ones – and it is time for the rest of us to keep on moving left, fusing the best of the new institutionalism with the best of a reviving Marxism (Coates, 2007, 2014).

A fundamental intellectual realignment of this kind is both urgent and vital because only in that way will the academic left get an effective handle on what is actually going on around us, and so be in a position at long last to do something effective about it. Remember what the young Marx wrote in the 11th *Theses on Feuerbach*: 'The philosophers have only interpreted the world in various ways; the point however is to change it.' It is time for some of that youthful change again. It is time for New Directions.

Acknowledgements

The author wishes to thank the following friends and colleagues for help in preparing this chapter: Greg Albo, Mark Blyth, Phil Cerny, Vivek Chibber, Dan Coffey, Colin Crouch, Pepper Culpepper, Travis Fast, Orfeo Fioretos, Colin Hay, Geoffrey Hodgson, Geoff Ingham, Bob Jessop, Herbert Kitschelt, William Lazonick, Cathie Jo Martin, Matthias Mattijs, Leo Panitch, Jonas Pontusson, Ben Rosamond, Vivien Schmidt, Sven

Steinmo, Wolfgang Streeck, John Stephens, Kathleen Thelen, Carole Thornley and Matthew Watson. None are responsible for the content, only for protecting it from greater error.

Notes

1. Bob Hancké, in private correspondence, 9 December 2013.
2. Vivien Schmidt, in private correspondence, 30 November 2013.
3. Ben Rosamond, in private correspondence, 11 November 2013.
4. Geoff Hodgson, in private correspondence, 8 November 2013.
5. Greg Albo, in private correspondence, 22 November 2013.
6. Colin Crouch, in private correspondence, 11 November 2013.
7. Matthew Watson, in private correspondence, 11 November 2013.
8. Kathleen Thelen, in private conversation, 9 December 2013.
9. Vivek Chibber, in private conversation, 20 November 2013.

Bibliography

Aglietta, M. (1979) *A Theory of Capitalist Regulation: The US Experience* (London: New Left Books).
Albert, M. (1993) *Capitalism Against Capitalism* (trs. P. Haviland) (London: Whurr).
Blyth, M. (2003) 'Same as It Never Was: Temporality and Typology in the Varieties of Capitalism', *Comparative European Politics*, 1:2, 215–25.
Boyer, R. (1990) *The Regulation School: A Critical Introduction* (New York: Columbia University Press).
Bruff, I. and M. Ebenau (2014) 'Critical Political Economy and the Critique of Comparative Capitalisms Scholarship on Capitalist Diversity', *Capital & Class*, 38:1, 3–15.
Bruff, I. and E. Hartmann (2014) 'Neo-Pluralist Political Science, Economic Sociology and the Conceptual Foundations of the Comparative Capitalisms Literatures', *Capital & Class*, 38:1, 73–85.
Bruff, I. and L. Horn (2012) 'Varieties of Capitalism in Crisis?' *Competition & Change*, 16:3, 161–8.
Coates, D. (2005) 'Paradigms of Explanation', in D. Coates (ed.), *Varieties of Capitalism, Varieties of Approaches* (New York: Palgrave Macmillan), 1–25.
Coates, D. (2007) 'The Concept of Labour: Its Continuing Relevance in Social Theory', in A. Gamble, S. Ludlam, A. Taylor and S. Wood (eds), *Labour, the State, Social Movements and the Challenge of Neo-Liberal Globalization* (Manchester: Manchester University Press), 7–20.
Coates, D. (2008) ' "Darling, it is Entirely My Fault!" Gordon Brown's Legacy to Alistair and to Himself', *British Politics*, 3:1, 3–21.
Coates, D. (2014) 'Studying Comparative Capitalisms by Going Left and by Going Deeper', *Capital & Class*, 38:1, 18–30.
Crouch, C. and W. Streeck (eds.) (1997) *The Political Economy of Modern Capitalism: Mapping Convergence and Diversity* (London: Sage).
Crouch, C. (2005) *Capitalist Diversity and Change: Recombinant Governance and Institutional Entrepreneurs* (Oxford: Oxford University Press).

Elsner, W. and H. Hardy (eds.) (2008) *Varieties of Capitalism and New Institutional Deals: Regulation, Welfare and the New Economy* (Cheltenham: Edward Elgar).

Estévez-Abe, M. (2009) 'Gender Inequality and Capitalism: The Varieties of Capitalism and Women', *Social Politics*, 16:2, 182–91.

Fast, T. (2012) *The Profound Hegemony of Neoliberalism: Economic Theory, Public Policy and Capitalist Accumulation* (York University, Canada: Unpublished PhD thesis).

Fioretos, O. (2011) *Creative Reconstructions: Multilateralism and European Varieties of Capitalism After 1950* (Ithaca: Cornell University Press).

Hall, P.A. (1986) *Governing the Economy: The Politics of State Intervention in Britain and France* (Cambridge: Polity).

Hall, P.A. (2007) 'The Evolution of Varieties of Capitalism in Europe', in B. Hancké, M. Rhodes and M. Thatcher (eds.), *Beyond Varieties of Capitalism: Conflict, Contradictions and Complementarities in the European Economy* (Oxford: Oxford University Press), 39–88.

Hall, P.A. (2009) 'Historical Institutionalism in Rationalist and Sociological Perspective', in J. Mahoney and K. Thelen (eds.), *Explaining Institutional Change; Ambiguity, Agency and Power* (Cambridge: Cambridge University Press), 204–23.

Hall, P.A. and D. Soskice (2001) 'An Introduction to Varieties of Capitalism', in P.A. Hall and D. Soskice (eds.), *Varieties of Capitalism: The Institutional Foundations of Comparative Advantage* (Oxford: Oxford University Press), 1–68.

Hall, P.A. and R.C.R. Taylor (1996) 'Political Science and the Three New Institutionalisms', *Political Studies*, 44:4, 937–57.

Hancké, B., M. Rhodes and M. Thatcher (eds.) (2007) *Beyond Varieties of Capitalism: Conflict, Contradictions and Complementarities in the European Economy* (Oxford: Oxford University Press).

Hodgson, G. (1996) 'Varieties of Capitalism and Varieties of Economic Theory', *Review of International Political Economy*, 3:3, 380–433.

Hollingsworth, J.R. and R. Boyer (1997) *Contemporary Capitalism: The Embeddedness of Institutions* (Cambridge: Cambridge University Press).

Immergut, E. (1998) 'The Theoretical Core of the New Institutionalism', *Politics & Society*, 26:1, 5–34.

Iversen, T. (2005) *Capitalism, Democracy and Welfare* (Cambridge: Cambridge University Press).

Iversen, T. (2010) *Work, Women, and Politics: The Political Economy of Gender* (New Haven: Yale University Press).

Jessop, B. (2011) 'Rethinking the Diversity and Varieties of Capitalism: On Variegated Capitalism in the World Market', in G. Wood and C. Lane (eds.), *Capitalist Diversity and Diversity Within Capitalism* (London: Routledge), 209–37.

Kotz, D., T. McDonough and M. Reich (eds.) (1994) *Social Structures of Accumulation: The Political Economy of Growth and Crisis* (Cambridge: Cambridge University Press).

Krugman, P. (2009) 'How Did Economists Get It So Wrong?' *New York Times*, 9 September.

Lee, F., X. Pham and G. Gu (2013) 'The UK Research Assessment Exercise and the Narrowing of UK Economics', *Cambridge Journal of Economics*, 37:4, 693–717.

Lucas, R.E. (2003) *Macroeconomic Priorities* (Washington, DC: American Economic Association).

Mahoney, J. and K. Thelen (eds.) (2009) *Explaining Institutional Change: Ambiguity, Agency and Power* (Cambridge: Cambridge University Press).
Martin, C.J. (2014) 'Getting Down to Business: Varieties of Capitalism and Employment Relations', in A. Wilkinson, G. Wood and R. Deeg (eds.), *The Oxford Handbook of Employment Relations: Comparative Employment Systems* (Oxford: Oxford University Press), 65–85.
Peck, J. and N. Theodore (2007) 'Variegated Capitalism', *Progress in Human Geography*, 31:6, 731–72.
Schmidt, V.A. (2009) 'Putting the Political Back into Political Economy by Bringing the State Back in Yet Again', *World Politics*, 61:3, 516–46.
Shonfield, A. (1965) *Modern Capitalism: The Changing Balance of Public and Private Power* (London: Oxford University Press).
Soskice, D. (1990) 'Reinterpreting Corporatism and Explaining Unemployment: Coordinated and Non-Coordinated Market Economies', in R. Brunetta and C. Dell'Aringa (eds.), *Labour Relations and Economic Performance* (London: Macmillan), 170–214.
Soskice, D. (2009) 'Varieties of Capitalism, Varieties of Reform', in A. Hemerijck, B. Knapen and E. van Doorne (eds.), *Aftershocks: Economic Crisis and Institutional Choice* (Amsterdam: University of Amsterdam Press), 133–41.
Streeck, W. (2006) 'The Study of Organized Interests: Before "The Century" and After', in C. Crouch and W. Streeck (eds.), *The Diversity of Democracy: Corporatism, Social Order and Political Conflict* (Cheltenham: Edward Elgar), 3–45.
Streeck, W. (2009) *Re-Forming Capitalism: Institutional Change in the German Political Economy* (Oxford: Oxford University Press).
Streeck, W. (2011) 'E Pluribus Unum? Varieties and Commonalities of Capitalism', in M. Granovetter and R. Swedberg (eds.), *The Sociology of Economic Life* (3rd ed.) (Boulder: Westview Press), 419–55.
Thelen, K. (1999) 'Historical Institutionalism in Comparative Politics', *Annual Review of Political Science*, 2:3, 369–404.
Thelen, K. (2004) *How Institutions Evolve: The Political Economy of Skills in Germany, Britain, the United States, and Japan* (Cambridge: Cambridge University Press).
Wood, G. and C. Lane (eds.) (2011) *Capitalist Diversity and Diversity within Capitalism* (London: Routledge).
Zysman, J. (1994) 'How Institutions Create Historically Rooted Trajectories of Growth', *Industrial and Corporate Change*, 3:1, 243–83.

2
Fault and Fracture? The Impact of New Directions in Comparative Capitalisms Research on the Wider Field

Ian Bruff, Matthias Ebenau and Christian May

As David Coates notes in the previous chapter, we are currently in a paradoxical period. Peter Hall and David Soskice's (2001) Varieties of Capitalism (VoC) approach dominated the Comparative Capitalisms (CC) landscape for at least a decade after its 2001 publication, but is clearly the product of a period in time which is now in the past. Nevertheless, the earlier dominance may well ensure that it is even more widely cited in the coming years. In this chapter, we wish to broaden the scope of critique to encompass the CC field, within which the VoC approach sits. This is because (to quote Coates) the 'indirect source of legitimation' now provided by the VoC approach is, in our view, strongly tied to its innovative and creative reworking of the neoinstitutionalist paradigm which came to the fore in the 1980s and 1990s. In other words, although the specific form of *rationalist* neoinstitutionalism embodied in VoC is no longer at the cutting edge of CC research, the neoinstitutionalist paradigm more generally has remained relatively dominant in scholarship on capitalist diversity. However, this ought not to be the end of the story for the CC field, for many of the limitations inherent to the VoC approach characterize neoinstitutionalist CC scholarship more broadly. Thus, there is a need to develop more fundamentally 'new directions' in research on capitalist diversity.

This chapter will, after a brief reprise of the VoC debate, focus on how mainstream CC scholarship is now coming under pressure from a range of different sources. What unites these alternatives to the mainstream is their wish to engage in CC research in a different manner: conscious and critical of capitalism, but remaining aware of how it exists in multiple forms across the world. The current volume, in explicitly giving centre-stage to several of these new directions, is part of this desired shift towards alternative forms of CC scholarship. As will become clear in the present chapter as well as elsewhere in the volume, this does not entail either the abandonment of the study of institutions in regionally, nationally and locally specific contexts or of attempts to elaborate typological theories of capitalism. Rather, most authors acknowledge that a deep understanding of institutions, and the development of typologies as potentially powerful analytical tools, can help us to understand capitalist diversity on a global scale (see especially the chapters by May and Nölke, Wehr, and Drahokoupil and Myant). Nevertheless, the impact of these new directions as they begin to unfold – both through articulating their critique of mainstream CC perspectives and through developing alternative lines of research and theorization – will undoubtedly have other consequences for the field as it is presently constituted.

Hence the title of this chapter: *fault and fracture*. This can be conceived of as symbolic for the state of the art in the CC field: we are past the high watermark of VoC scholarship but the receding tide has left the previously subsumed rock – representing the neoinstitutionalist paradigm – standing in the seawater. This leaves the rock exposed to the cross-cutting forces that have been set in motion by the attempts to think about CC research in a different way. In consequence, over time the relatively unified field of CC research could, as a rock does under pressure from the elements and from new water currents, develop faults and fractures which gradually hollow out and weaken it. This scenario of 'fault and fracture' – which, as we outline below, is a very real possibility – would have significant implications for the study of the diversity of contemporary capitalism. Unless the insights of these new directions are taken more seriously, the neoinstitutionalist 'rock' will become ineffectual in the face of new developments, both theoretical and empirical, and crumble away. This would diminish the CC field as a whole, for its fragmentation into competing paradigms would reduce the potential for dialogue and thus for further advances in our understanding of capitalist diversity.

Before moving to the below discussion, it ought to be noted that the 'critical and global perspectives' that comprise the subtitle of this volume will largely be considered in two steps. Accordingly, this chapter focuses on what it means to conduct critical research on capitalist diversity, while the next by Ebenau considers the growing globalization of the field (this distinction is also used for parts II and III of the volume). Of course, in practice it is difficult to separate 'critical' and 'global' – not least because a critical view of capitalism lends itself to a more global understanding of how it functions and evolves – but this enables us here to concentrate on one of the key underlying tendencies in CC scholarship, which is to see itself as broadly progressive in nature and intent.

Reprise: The significance of the Varieties of Capitalism intervention for Comparative Capitalisms debates

Nowadays, when teaching debates on capitalist diversity, it becomes increasingly difficult to persuade students of why the VoC intervention was so important in the first place. Different developments have led this generation – who would have been quite young when *Varieties of Capitalism* was published in 2001 – to be more sceptical than in the past. Among them is the dying down of the post-Cold War 'hyper-globalist' discourse, whose protagonists had insisted that economies around the world would quickly converge upon a neoliberal, Anglo-American model of capitalism. Therefore, the 'enemy' of VoC scholarship is not so obvious nowadays. Another tendency relates to the resurgence of social conflict and political turmoil throughout the last years of economic crisis: this poses the question of transformative change in different ways to hyper-globalism, and thereby challenges the stability hypothesis inherent in VoC and similar perspectives. Hence, it is worth reminding ourselves of what the VoC intervention meant for the wider debates on capitalist diversity and models.

Two interrelated points of principle stand out. First, there was an explicit break with rival perspectives on the question of the future viability of national 'models'. In comparison to the earlier CC literatures, the VoC approach distinguishes itself for mounting an emphatic and rigorously argued challenge to the assumption that some national models of capitalism were more likely to succeed than others (hence the aforementioned antidote to hyper-globalism). Most earlier approaches had advocated a normative preference for social-democratic, corporatist, welfare or 'progressive' models of capitalism such as those found in Western Europe, but remained worried about their future existence (see, for example, Albert, 1993; Streeck, 1997a). In contrast, the VoC approach made a principled shift of focus which turned out to be vital for challenging such pessimism. Its proponents located the causes of capitalist success squarely in the national institutional environments and thus decisively moved the debate away from external 'imperatives' such as globalization, liberalization and so on, and towards the 'internal' quality of institutional arrangements and public policies.

This brings us to the second key point of principle which distinguished the VoC agenda from earlier CC approaches: the argument that firms may actively seek and create non-market forms of coordination within the given national economy and, concomitantly, that they may benefit from the resulting institutional arrangements (such as social and labour protection laws) just as much as trade unions and employees. This challenged both neoclassical-inspired approaches and non-VoC institutionalist contributions such as the power resources perspective, which was popular in comparative research on welfare states (Esping-Andersen, 1990). At the heart of this challenge was the assertion that firms do not possess a universal, intrinsic desire for market-oriented forms of coordination, always seeking the relative weakness of the state and trade unions in the wider political economy. Instead, their worldviews are seen as much more nationally specific and could be compatible with more socially and politically embedded forms of capitalism. In VoC's view, such an embeddedness does not necessarily hamper, but may in fact foster certain forms of economic efficiency and competitiveness.

In developing these arguments, the VoC approach provided a highly significant corrective to single-minded commentaries on the supposedly superior performance of 'free' markets, and also to the institutionalist pessimism on the future viability of 'progressive' capitalisms. As a result, this intervention opened the door to a wave of important research on capitalist diversity. Nevertheless, it came at a high price: as argued at length in Coates' chapter, the advantages wrought by the parsimonious and elegantly constructed conceptual apparatus led others to question whether too much was being neglected in VoC's firm-centred defence of the continued national differentiation of modern capitalism. The debate surrounding the approach mushroomed in the years following the publication of the original *Varieties of Capitalism* volume, and it exposed a considerable number of theoretical and empirical shortcomings. In the introduction to their *Beyond Varieties of Capitalism* collection, Bob Hancké and his co-authors provide a long – but far from complete – list of the objections raised on the grounds:

> that it is too static and focused on permanency and path-dependence, missing important dynamic elements of economic change; that it is functionalist; that it ignores the endogenous sources of

national system transformation and 'within-system' diversity; that it has a propensity to 'institutional determinism' in its mechanistic conception of institutional complementarities and neglect of underlying power structures, including social class; that it has a truncated conception of the firm as an 'institution-taker' rather than an autonomous, creative, or disruptive actor and neglects variation among firms within national models; that it divides the world into reified notions of LME [liberal market economies] and CME [coordinated market economies] archetypes and lacks the tools for moving beyond this bifurcation; that VoC theory is not built deductively, to create Weberian 'ideal-types' that could be used for the construction of hypotheses, but rather creates 'types' by reading back empirical information from the countries it seeks to make its paradigm cases – the USA and Germany; that it has a manufacturing bias and cannot deal with the presence of sizeable service sectors in CMEs; that it treats nation-states as 'hermetically sealed' and neglects the linkages between them and the forces of convergence and globalization; that it is 'apolitical', equilibrium-biased and downplays conflict; that it is 'sex-blind' and has problems understanding class inequalities among women and class differences in the nature and patterns of gender inequality; and that it neglects the role of the state.

(Hancké et al., 2007, pp. 7–8)

Despite the number and diversity of these criticisms a great many scholars sympathetic to the VoC agenda, including Hancké and his colleagues, continued insisting that the approach could, in principle, respond to the most relevant of these objections. Hence, there was no need to turn away from its fundamentals. Rather, they suggested that by relaxing, adapting or complementing its key premises the VoC approach could not only continue to contribute to our understanding of capitalist diversity in so-called advanced economies, but even expand its substantive and geographical scope of application (see also Ebenau, in this volume). These scholars' endeavours crystallized in what might be coined a 'second generation' of VoC scholarship. Examples include Orfeo Fioretos' (2010) attempt to make the approach fruitful for understanding international financial market regulation; Rhodes and Molina's (2007) suggestion to incorporate the economies of the European Mediterranean into the VoC universe as so-called mixed market economy hybrids somewhere on the continuum between liberal and coordinated market economies (LMEs and CMEs); or Margarita Estévez-Abé's (2005) efforts to elaborate a 'gendered' VoC perspective.

However, the questionings continued, and the aforementioned objections were quickly directed towards this second generation of VoC scholarship as well. Thus, it became increasingly clear that the perspective did not just suffer from many different, but *minor*, shortcomings which could be remedied without abandoning the approach. Recent critical contributions have shown that these shortcomings virtually always go back to one or another of a few more *fundamental* problems which are rooted in the specific brand of rational choice institutionalism advocated by its proponents (Bruff and Ebenau, 2014; Bruff and Horn, 2012). In this sense, the mounting critique identified four central flaws in both generations of VoC research:

- First, VoC scholarship assumes that a few institutional criteria, narrowly related to the corporate sphere, are decisive for the constitution of capitalist varieties across the globe. Thus, even where the original LME/CME typology is refined and/or expanded VoC unduly universalizes a focus which is derived from a small set of experiences of capitalism, leading to a limited grasp of the full scope of capitalist diversity on a global scale. For instance, it by and large fails to make sense of the preponderant economic role which the state plays in many world regions, including heavyweights such as Brazil and China (cf. Becker, 2013).
- Second, VoC approaches, even where they consciously set out to study institutional change, have severe difficulties with understanding contemporary processes of politico-economic change (Soederberg et al., 2005). This is especially the case where these processes transcend formal institutional appearances. A key example for such an omission would be the functional, but not formal, transformation of corporatist institutions such as the German works councils (*Betriebsräte*) system, whose gradual transformation into mere subordinate partners to capital in local competitiveness pacts is hardly ever discussed in VoC scholarship (cf. Bruff, 2015; Streeck, 2009).
- Third, due to its continued adherence to a strong assumption of a national constitution of capitalist diversity, associated with its methodological nationalism, VoC scholarship has an overwhelming tendency to neglect both intra-national variation and the transnationally relational character of capitalism. With regard to the former, we may point, for instance, to the lack of serious discussions of the role of the East German periphery within the 'coordinated market economy' of Germany; the latter aspect manifests itself, for example, in the one-sided treatment of transnational economic

integration as an outcome of preference formation rooted within particular national capitalist varieties (cf. Bluhm, 2010; Nölke, 2011).
- Fourth, as a corollary of VoC's firm and efficiency focus, approaches rooted in this tradition tend towards an excessive economism and functionalism. This means that they are generally unable to make sense both of class and group conflicts and of the structural crisis tendencies which have characterized the capitalist mode of production since its emergence. The former becomes obvious, for example, in the inability of VoC scholarship to understand and explain contemporary struggles surrounding the future of the so-called Nordic model in Scandinavia (Bieler, 2012). Without doubt, the central example of the latter is VoC's disappointing treatment of the most recent global economic crisis, a point to which we will return below.

The gravitational pull exerted by VoC's founding principles – the national focus and the firm and efficiency-centredness – thus remained strong, and this has undoubtedly restricted what the second generation of VoC scholarship could deliver. These authors regularly offered significant refinements of the original approach, but could not thoroughly remedy its more fundamental shortcomings. As a result, increasing numbers of neoinstitutionalist scholars began to recognize that, in order to advance further the project of an institution-centred analysis of capitalist diversity, it was necessary to leave this framework's confines behind and to articulate alternative perspectives more confidently.

'New directions' in Comparative Capitalisms research

As a result of this collective recognition, over time a body of scholarship on capitalist diversity began to take shape whose fundamental theoretical orientation is best described as 'post-VoC'. This process was led both by established proponents of rival institutional perspectives (such as Bruno Amable, Colin Crouch and Vivien Schmidt) and by scholars whose former sympathy for the VoC approach turned to more critical assessments (such as Wolfgang Streeck and Kathleen Thelen). Post-VoC research constitutes a serious attempt to retain the analytical focus on institutions while also significantly changing the field of study. It does so through broadening CC research in scope and by going 'deeper' into the fundamental questions associated with capitalist diversity which the debate on the VoC approach had brought to the fore.

Broadly speaking, post-VoC research distances itself from VoC's specific rendering of neoinstitutionalist theory and the associated research agenda. On the methodological plane, a highly significant intervention, whose general thrust is shared by most post-VoC scholarship, has come from Uwe Becker (2007, 2009). Becker has argued, in contrast to what proponents of the VoC approach have claimed, that typologies and categories can never be more than an *approximate* judgement of what is most important for the case study being considered, and that actually existing (national) political economies are always and necessarily 'hybrids' of different steering principles. Here, Becker explicitly abandons the quest for classificatory certainty that the VoC approach had foregrounded strongly, thus pointing to the need for much greater analytical openness. This means that, in 2015, it can safely be stated that post-VoC research is gradually overcoming the gravitational pull exercised by VoC, a fact which sets this 'new direction' positively apart from the 'second generation' literature just described.

Thanks to this and other theoretical and methodological developments in the post-VoC camp, we have now returned to broader and more robust definitions of 'institutions' and an understanding of the role of institutions in capitalist economies that goes beyond narrow efficiency-centred considerations (see, for example, Amable and Palombarini, 2009; see also May and Nölke, in this volume). We also benefit from greater reflection on the kinds and drivers of processes of politico-economic dynamism and change (Deeg and Jackson, 2007; Streeck and Thelen, 2005). There is now a more nuanced understanding of the issue of institutional convergence and/or divergence and, concomitantly, of the recent trajectories of different national political economies (Hay, 2004). We have new theoretical and methodological insights regarding the generation of typological analyses of the institutional diversity *within* as well as across different national 'models' (Crouch, 2005; Lane and Wood, 2009). The transnational interrelations among different models of capitalism have been analysed more profoundly than previously (Nölke, 2011). Finally, there is a clearer recognition of the commonalities and differences between these models on a global scale (Becker, 2013).

Perhaps the most prominent example of the greater distance between the cutting-edge of CC research and 'second generation' VoC scholarship can be found in the trajectory of Wolfgang Streeck's work. Over time, he has moved away from his original position, which lauded the ability of certain types of institutional arrangements to create 'beneficial constraints' on capital in the name of more socially just and economically efficient versions of capitalism (Streeck, 1997b). Thus, in his recent work, he problematizes much more strongly the potential for developments in global capitalism to have transformative consequences for the models or varieties in question. He substantiates this argument through an in-depth analysis of functional – rather than formal institutional – change in Germany, VoC's archetypical CME (Streeck, 2009). Crucially, Streeck argues that in the context of these processes the relationship between capitalism and democracy, especially democracy in countries which continue to affirm the 'social' elements of the political economy, is in danger of breaking down (Streeck, 2011). Therefore, through his comprehensive re-examination of the purpose of the study of capitalist diversity, Streeck's argument mirrors Becker's powerful discussions of methodology and research strategy. This has condensed into the claim that 'the subject... is *not institutions but capitalism.*' (Streeck, 2009, p. 3; original emphasis).

However, it is here, when examining the conceptualization of capitalism and institutions, that it becomes clear that even this strand of CC scholarship has (up to now) fallen short of making a full turn towards a more holistic approach, which would be necessary to make the most of the critiques aimed at the VoC approach. For instance, in the very next paragraph to the one just cited, Streeck declares capitalism to be merely 'an institutionalized social order' (ibid.), meaning that the apparent shift in emphasis signalled by 'bringing capitalism back in' becomes void. Similarly, Becker's remarks on how capitalism is defined by its 'competition-induced structural dynamic... [which] causes more or less permanent material change' (2009, p. 168) come across as afterthoughts rather than anything more central to his vision. This leaves us with the impression that even in its most radical and novel post-VoC guises, neoinstitutionalist CC scholarship fails to make a full break with the reductionist understanding of capitalism for which the VoC approach has been so often, and rightly, criticized.

In this regard, it is striking just how little its protagonists have engaged with literatures which frame the examination of specific institutional configurations in broader analyses of the development of capitalism, as found most prominently – but by no means exclusively – in Marxist-inspired scholarship (such as Coates, 2000, 2005a; Jessop, 2011). This is symptomatic of a persistent limitation in the study of capitalist diversity, associated with the almost unmitigated dominance of the neoinstitutionalist paradigm which cross-cuts virtually all strands of CC scholarship. Despite numerous attempts at a theoretical renewal of CC approaches, there is still a tendency in the field's mainstream, now occupied by the post-VoC literatures, to under-appreciate perspectives which investigate the issue of capitalist diversity and performance from a fundamentally different starting point than that suggested by neoinstitutionalism. In our view, there is thus a real risk of paradigmatic closure, which would be to the detriment of our capacity to understand contemporary capitalism as a whole. David Coates describes the risks associated with this scenario in the following terms:

> Unfortunately, it is often a feature of successful paradigmatic thought that in its moment of dominance it becomes invisible. Once established, those adhering to it often lose their understanding of the necessarily paradigmatic and relativistic nature of their own thought processes. They come to see the way that they think about the world as simply 'common sense': as a self-evident set of truths, and as the only possible set of methods for the understanding of social reality. They even come to think of people working outside their paradigm as not simply wrong but as either ill-trained or, yet worse, ill-conceived.
>
> (Coates, 2005b, p. 265)

As we explain in the following section, the danger of such closure is that, despite the emergence of the post-VoC generation of CC scholarship in its various incarnations, intellectual development becomes inert and ultimately unable to respond to the new theoretical and practical challenges which modern capitalism generates for those seeking to understand – and change – it. As stated above, it is partly to such a scenario that our image of a CC rock exposed to fault and fracture refers. We therefore suggest that there is an urgent need to reinvigorate the debate on capitalist diversity across different intellectual and paradigmatic worldviews. The new directions in *critical* and *global* CC research which are represented in this volume seek to contribute to this task.

'New directions' in *critical* Comparative Capitalisms research

We argue that the way in which the post-2007 world has been analysed and discussed in CC scholarship is a clear indicator not only of its inherent limitations but also of the risks of paradigmatic closure. The global crisis should thus be considered as a major warning shot for scholars active in the field. Protagonists of the neoinstitutionalist CC approaches were surprised by the crisis, but given that this happened to most other non-critical political economists, this fact is perhaps less noteworthy than the subsequent development of the CC debate on the crisis, which revealed an excessive degree of self-absorption. For instance, apart from a handful of exceptions, no major attempts were made to develop CC-based explanations for the *why* and *how* of the crisis, that is, the factors that combined to produce it and the specific ways in which it played out in different parts of the globe. Even where this was attempted (see, for example, Hall, 2012), virtually no attention was paid to anything outside the narrowly defined institutional aspects of this issue. Yet again, therefore, we are left with interesting but limited discussions of institutional evolution or of the ideas which dominate policymaking debates (examples include Jackson and Deeg, 2012; Blyth, 2013). The conditions in which these institutions and ideas emerge, evolve and acquire significance were, as in the CC literatures more generally, not enquired into.

Against this background, it is unsurprising that those scholars who did seek to evaluate the usefulness of CC theories for understanding the global crisis have come to mainly negative conclusions – whatever their initial intellectual persuasion (see, for example, Becker and Jäger, 2012; Myant and Drahokoupil, 2011; Heyes et al., 2012; Weber and Schmitz, 2011). What, however, constitutes an alarming sign of intellectual closure is that general CC debates continue to be quite unperturbed by these findings. Indeed, events that unfolded in recent years were viewed as problematic for *other* approaches, especially those focused on the 'virtues' of the free market (cf. Bruff and Horn, 2012; Bruff and Ebenau, 2014).

Of course, this is not the end of the story, given that recent years have seen the growth of more avowedly *critical* perspectives in debates on capitalist diversity. It is on these perspectives that the present volume principally builds and which it seeks to bring into a dialogue with the dynamic post-VoC literature. In our understanding, 'critical' should be viewed as a collective term that covers a rich, pluralistic and diverse range of perspectives and debates (cf. van Apeldoorn et al., 2010; Shields et al., 2011; Bruff et al., 2013). The focus of research on the diversity of contemporary capitalism is thus once again up for debate: discourses, class relations, gender relations, space and scale, colonial relations, the nation and so on. Accordingly, we identify three principal sources of inspiration for these new directions in the field of CC research, all of which are represented in this book.[1]

It ought to be stated here that we say a little less about Marxism because, as noted in our introduction to the volume, these perspectives have, up to now, been central to the critiques which have been articulated about the CC literatures. However, it is important to note that these arguments have not just been made on the assumption that all one needs to do is talk about capitalism as a global, single, system of production. On the contrary, Marxists do not deny the place for differentiation *within* capitalism, but they do emphasize the fundamental significance of class relationships for producing such differentiation (Gough, 2014). Varieties *of* capitalism are thus always also varieties *in* capitalism and, accordingly, institutions of all forms acquire their historical power because they privilege capital over labour on an everyday basis (Bruff, 2011; de Souza, 2014). In other words, the systemic production of differentiation across a range of spaces and scales is strongly connected to the systemically produced *inequalities* which are part of capitalism. This then allows the researcher to bring to the fore the roles played by social and political struggles over such inequalities, be they in the form of strikes against employers, fights against dispossession of land or other forms of human rights, or political protest against a range of institutions (Bailey and Shibata, 2014).

Like Marxists, feminist and post/decolonial scholars claim the need to foreground inequality and struggle, albeit with a different focus. For instance, feminists argue that a full understanding of capitalism is impossible without an appreciation of 'a whole host of [concealed] social relations and forms of work that are essential to the reproduction of people and communities' (Roberts, 2012, p. 96; Fraser, 2014). This concealment masks an artificial distinction between public labour ('productive') and household labour ('domestic') which is part of wider inequalities of power that are highly gendered (Bakker and Gill, 2003). The 'male breadwinner' worldview, for example, produces inequalities in the labour market, with women remaining under-paid in comparison to their male counterparts, in more precarious employment, and more likely to work in (low-paid) 'caring' industries (Rubery et al., 1999). This results in not only a gender pay gap across economies but also the diminished potential for the collective organization of female labour. Moreover, women are mostly responsible for the vast majority of social provisioning and reproduction within the household, including nursing of the very young, the infirm and the elderly, and social provisioning of the essentials of life.

As with Marxism, feminist scholars account for differentiation *within* capitalism by highlighting the significance of gendered relationships for producing such 'varieties of patriarchal capitalism' (Folbre, 2009; see also Walby, 2004). Within this frame, researchers question perspectives which, like the 'gendered' VoC approach mentioned above, reduce gender inequalities to a small and discrete set of institution-mediated labour market outcomes, and call instead for a broad-based renewal of research on capitalist diversity. Part of this investigation has to be, in this view, an analysis of how gender inequalities relate with class and other forms of inequality, and how such interrelations intersect and produce forms of capitalism that are distinctive and specific in the way that power materializes in the given context (Lux, 2013; Lux and Wöhl, in this volume).

It is in this self-set objective that feminist and post/decolonial perspectives meet. But where the primary focus of the former is on gender inequalities, the latter tend to concentrate more strongly on the asymmetric, often ethnically codified relations between North and South, the West and the 'rest', so-called advanced and so-called developing countries and so on. While the post- and decolonial direction so far has had little impact on CC research as such (this book contains some of the first forays onto this terrain), it clearly has much to contribute to the project of a critical and global renewal of scholarship on the diversity of contemporary capitalism (for potential sources of inspiration, see Blaney and Inayatullah, 2010; Chatterjee, 2010; Shilliam, 2012).

In the literature on *post*colonialism, true to the poststructuralist origins of a good part of it, there is a tendency to centre attention on issues such as the production of discourse and knowledge, rather than the immediate material conditions of human existence under capitalism. As such, a significant merit of postcolonial perspectives is their development of some of the most incisive critiques of the Eurocentrism which pervades many conventional approaches to the politico-economic analysis of contemporary capitalism, including some self-professedly 'critical' ones (Spivak, 1999; see also Wehr, in this volume). *De*colonial perspectives, broadly speaking, seek to bend the stick back the other way, by reconnecting this critique of Eurocentrism to the critique of the manifold material inequalities which cut through global capitalism – especially those which can be connected to colonial histories and the artificial construction of postcolonial 'nations', and thus the silencing of locally situated subaltern forms of knowledge about such inequalities (Grosfoguel, 2007; see also Tilley, in this volume).

Whichever point of entry one takes, post/decolonial approaches help us understand that the expansion of the geographical horizon of CC research needs to be accompanied by an appreciation of how world capitalism is characterized by a multiplicity of material and discursive inequalities which overdetermine the constitution and evolution of particular localized varieties or models. They also provide some of the necessary intellectual tools for assessing critically the extent to which CC perspectives meet their self-proclaimed objective of providing nuanced and context-sensitive frameworks for the study of specific instantiations of capitalism in different parts of the globe.

Conclusion

Inevitably, the rich and dynamic contributions to CC literatures cannot be covered in either their breadth or their depth in one chapter. Similarly, the scope and implications of the arguments made from more critical perspectives cannot be discussed in their entirety. Nevertheless, it is hoped that this chapter has provided a useful and informed overview of the evolution of debates on capitalist diversity and the key developments that have been part of such evolution. Moreover, we have sought to show that, for such debates to continue moving forward, it is essential that more critical perspectives are given their due place in the conversation. In this sense, the more focused and in-depth chapters found in Part II of this volume build upon the above discussion, as does the next chapter by Ebenau on the growing globalization of the field. We close by reiterating that the CC field needs to engage in greater self-reflection about its purpose and goals if it is not to fault and fracture into competing paradigms, and that this volume shows what more critical and global perspectives can contribute to our understanding of capitalist diversity.

Note

1. Through taking this approach we do not consider here the contributions made by critical geographers (for example, Peck and Theodore, 2007; Brenner et al., 2010; Birch and Mykhnenko, 2009), mainly because a number of these are already well integrated into the arguments made by critical CC researchers (see, for example, Bruff and Horn, 2012). Instead, we seek to highlight the broader thematic issues that critical perspectives point us towards.

Bibliography

Albert, M. (1993) *Capitalism Against Capitalism* (trs. P. Haviland) (London: Whurr).
Amable, B. and S. Palombarini (2009) 'A Neorealist Approach to Institutional Change and the Diversity of Capitalism', *Socio-Economic Review*, 7:1, 123–43.
Bailey, D. and S. Shibata (2014) 'Varieties of Contestation: The Comparative and Critical Political Economy of "Excessive" Demand', *Capital & Class*, 38:1, 239–51.
Bakker, I. and S. Gill (eds.) (2003) *Power, Production and Social Reproduction: Human In/security in the Global Political Economy* (Basingstoke: Palgrave Macmillan).
Becker, J. and J. Jäger (2012) 'Integration in Crisis: A Regulationist Perspective on the Interaction of European Varieties of Capitalism', *Competition & Change*, 16:3, 169–87.
Becker, U. (2007) 'Open Systemness and Contested Reference Frames and Change: A Reformulation of the Varieties of Capitalism Theory', *Socio-Economic Review*, 5:2, 261–86.

Becker, U. (2009) *Open Varieties of Capitalism: Continuity, Change and Performances* (Basingstoke: Palgrave Macmillan).
Becker, U. (ed.) (2013) *The BRICS and Emerging Economies in Comparative Perspective: Political Economy, Liberalisation and Institutional Change* (Abingdon: Routledge).
Bieler, A. (2012) 'Small Nordic Countries and Globalization: Analysing Norwegian Exceptionalism', *Competition & Change*, 16:3, 224–42.
Birch, K. and V. Mykhnenko (2009) 'Varieties of Neoliberalism? Restructuring in Large Industrially Dependent Regions across Western and Eastern Europe', *Journal of Economic Geography*, 9:3, 355–80.
Blaney, D. and N. Inayatullah (2010) *Savage Economics: Wealth, Poverty and the Temporal Walls of Capitalism* (Abingdon: Routledge).
Bluhm, K. (2010) 'Theories of Capitalism Put to the Test: Introduction to a Debate on Central and Eastern Europe', *Historische Sozialforschung*, 35:2, 197–217.
Blyth, M. (2013) *Austerity: The History of a Dangerous Idea* (Oxford: Oxford University Press).
Brenner, N., J. Peck and N. Theodore (2010) 'Variegated Neoliberalization: Geographies, Modalities, Pathways', *Global Networks*, 10:2, 182–222.
Bruff, I. (2011) 'What about the Elephant in the Room? Varieties of Capitalism, Varieties in Capitalism', *New Political Economy*, 16:4, 481–500.
Bruff, I. (2015) 'Germany: Steady as She Goes?' in R. Westra, D. Badeen and R. Albritton (eds.), *The Future of Capitalism after the Financial Crisis: The Varieties of Capitalism Debate in the Age of Austerity* (Abingdon: Routledge), 114–31.
Bruff, I., M. Ebenau, C. May and A. Nölke (eds.) (2013) *Vergleichende Kapitalismusforschung: Stand, Perspektiven, Kritik* (Münster: Westfälisches Dampfboot).
Bruff, I. and M. Ebenau (2014) 'Critical Political Economy and the Critique of Comparative Capitalisms Scholarship on Capitalist Diversity', *Capital & Class*, 38:1, 3–15.
Bruff, I. and L. Horn (2012) 'Varieties of Capitalism in Crisis?' *Competition & Change*, 16:3, 161–8.
Chatterjee, P. (2010) *Empire and Nation: Selected Essays* (New York: Columbia University Press).
Coates, D. (2000) *Models of Capitalism: Growth and Stagnation in the Modern Era* (Cambridge: Polity).
Coates, D. (ed.) (2005a) *Varieties of Capitalism, Varieties of Approaches* (Basingtoke: Palgrave Macmillan).
Coates, D. (2005b) 'Conclusion: Choosing Between Paradigms – A Personal View', in D. Coates (ed.), *Varieties of Capitalism, Varieties of Approaches* (Basingstoke: Palgrave Macmillan), 265–71.
Crouch, C. (2005) *Capitalist Diversity and Change: Recombinant Governance and Institutional Entrepreneurs* (Oxford: Oxford University Press).
de Souza, M.B. (2014) 'Variedades de, dentro e no capitalismo', *Ensaios FEE*, 35:1, 7–32.
Deeg, R. and G. Jackson (2007) 'Towards a More Dynamic Theory of Capitalist Diversity', *Socio-Economic Review*, 5:1, 149–79.
Esping-Andersen, G. (1990) *The Three Worlds of Welfare Capitalism* (Princeton: Princeton University Press).
Estévez-Abé, M. (2005) 'Gender Bias in Skills and Social Policies: The Varieties of Capitalism Perspective on Sex Segregation', *Social Politics*, 12:2, 180–215.

Fioretos, O. (2010) 'Capitalist Diversity and the International Regulation of Hedge Funds', *Review of International Political Economy*, 17:4, 696–723.
Folbre, N. (2009) 'Varieties of Patriarchal Capitalism', *Social Politics*, 16:2, 204–9.
Fraser, N. (2014) 'Behind Marx's Hidden Abode: For an Expanded Conception of Capitalism', *New Left Review*, 2:86, 55–72.
Gough, J. (2014) 'The Difference Between Local and National Capitalism, and Why Local Capitalisms Differ from One Another: A Marxist Approach', *Capital & Class*, 38:1, 197–210.
Grosfoguel, R. (2007) 'The Epistemic Decolonial Turn: Beyond Political-Economy Paradigms', *Cultural Studies*, 21:2–3, 211–23.
Hall, P.A. (2012) 'The Economics and Politics of the Euro Crisis', *German Politics*, 21:4, 355–71.
Hall, P.A. and D. Soskice (eds.) (2001) *Varieties of Capitalism: The Institutional Foundations of Comparative Advantage* (Oxford: Oxford University Press).
Hancké, B., M. Rhodes and M. Thatcher (2007) 'Introduction: Beyond Varieties of Capitalism', in B. Hancké, M. Rhodes and M. Thatcher (eds.), *Beyond Varieties of Capitalism: Conflict, Contradictions, and Complementarities in the European Economy* (Oxford: Oxford University Press), 3–38.
Hay, C. (2004) 'Common Trajectories, Variable Paces, Divergent Outcomes? Models of European Capitalism Under Conditions of Complex Economic Interdependence', *Review of International Political Economy*, 11:2, 231–62.
Heyes, J., P. Lewis and I. Clark (2012) 'Varieties of Capitalism, Neoliberalism, and the Economic Crisis of 2008-?' *Industrial Relations Journal*, 43:3, 222–41.
Jackson, G. and R. Deeg (2012) 'The Long-Term Trajectories of Institutional Change in European Capitalism', *Journal of European Public Policy*, 19:8, 1107–25.
Jessop, B. (2011) 'Rethinking the Diversity of Capitalism: Varieties of Capitalism, Variegated Capitalism, and the World Market', in C. Lane and G. Wood (eds.), *Capitalist Diversity and Diversity in Capitalism* (London: Routledge), 209–37.
Lane, C. and G. Wood (2009) 'Diversity in Capitalism and Capitalist Diversity', *Economy and Society*, 38:4, 531–51.
Lux, J. (2013) 'Wie "genderbar" ist der Varieties of Capitalism-Ansatz? Vergleichende Kapitalismusforschung aus einer Geschlechter-Perspektive', in I. Bruff, M. Ebenau, C. May and A. Nölke (eds.), *Vergleichende Kapitalismusforschung: Stand, Perspektiven, Kritik* (Münster: Westfälisches Dampfboot), 148–62.
Myant, M. and J. Drahokoupil (2011) *Transition Economies: Political Economy in Russia, Eastern Europe, and Central Asia* (Hoboken, NJ: Wiley-Blackwell).
Nölke, A. (2011) 'Transnational Economic Order and National Institutions: Comparative Capitalism Meets International Political Economy', *MPIfG Discussion Papers 3/11* (Cologne: Max-Planck-Institut für Gesellschaftsforschung).
Peck, J. and N. Theodore (2007) 'Variegated Capitalism', *Progress in Human Geography*, 31:6, 731–72.
Rhodes, M. and O. Molina (2007) 'The Political Economy of Adjustment in Mixed Market Economies: A Study of Spain and Italy', in B. Hancké, M. Rhodes and M. Thatcher (eds.), *Beyond Varieties of Capitalism: Conflict, Contradictions, and Complementarities in the European Economy* (Oxford: Oxford University Press), 223–52.

Roberts, A. (2012) 'Financial Crisis, Financial Firms...and Financial Feminism? The Rise of "Transnational Business Feminism" and the Necessity of Marxist-Feminist IPE', *Socialist Studies*, 8:2, 85–108.

Rubery, J., M. Smith and C. Fagan (1999) *Women's Employment in Europe: Trends and Prospects* (London: Routledge).

Shields, S., I. Bruff and H. Macartney (eds.) (2011) *Critical International Political Economy: Dialogue, Debate and Dissensus* (Basingstoke: Palgrave Macmillan).

Shilliam, R. (2012) 'Forget English Freedom, Remember Atlantic Slavery: Common Law, Commercial Law and the Significance of Slavery for Classical Political Economy', *New Political Economy*, 17:5, 591–609.

Soederberg, S., G. Menz and P. Cerny (eds.) (2005) *Internalizing Globalization: The Rise of Neoliberalism and the Decline of National Varieties of Capitalism* (Basingstoke: Palgrave Macmillan).

Spivak, G.C. (1999) *A Critique of Postcolonial Reason: Toward a History of the Vanishing Present* (Harvard: Harvard University Press).

Streeck, W. (1997a) 'German Capitalism: Does It Exist? Can It Survive?' *New Political Economy*, 2:2, 237–56.

Streeck, W. (1997b) 'Beneficial Constraints: On the Limits of Rational Voluntarism', in J.R. Hollingsworth and R. Boyer (eds.), *Contemporary Capitalism: The Embeddedness of Institutions* (Cambridge: Cambridge University Press), 197–219.

Streeck, W. (2009) *Re-Forming Capitalism: Institutional Change in the German Political Economy* (Oxford: Oxford University Press).

Streeck, W. (2011) 'The Crises of Democratic Capitalism', *New Left Review*, 2:71, 5–29.

Streeck, W. and K. Thelen (eds.) (2005) *Beyond Continuity: Institutional Change in Advanced Political Economies* (Oxford: Oxford University Press).

van Apeldoorn, B., I. Bruff and M. Ryner (2010) 'The Richness and Diversity of Critical IPE Perspectives: Moving Beyond the Debate on the "British School"', in N. Phillips and C. Weaver (eds.), *International Political Economy: Debating the Past, Present and Future* (Abingdon: Routledge), 215–22.

Walby, S. (2004) 'The European Union and Gender Equality: Emergent Varieties of Gender Regime', *Social Politics*, 11:1, 4–29.

Weber, B. and S.W. Schmitz (2011) 'Varieties of Helping Capitalism: Politico-Economic Determinants of Bank Rescue Packages in the EU during the Recent Crisis', *Socio-Economic Review*, 9:4, 639–69.

3
Directions and Debates in the Globalization of Comparative Capitalisms Research

Matthias Ebenau

This chapter reviews a number of recent attempts to geographically expand the Comparative Capitalisms (CC) agenda. Its point of departure is the observation that CC – traditionally focused on some so-called 'advanced' capitalist countries – has begun to broaden its horizon to include other world regions, in particular Central and Eastern Europe (CEE) and Latin America. As in the wider CC literature, it is useful to divide the approaches associated with this intellectual process into three broad groups or – to stick with the metaphor in this book's title – 'directions'. The first group refers affirmatively to the emblematic Varieties of Capitalism (VoC) perspective and, consequently, seeks to broaden its scope of application; the second, more diverse set of alternative ('post-VoC') perspectives partly distance themselves from VoC but remain within the frame of the wider neoinstitutionalist paradigm; and, finally, the third, smaller group of approaches draws principally on the critical-materialist paradigm and thus begins to introduce imperialism and dependency approaches, among others, into the CC canon.

The chapter is divided into four sections. The first is dedicated to a brief review of the form and significance of the traditional (self-)limitation and current 'globalization' of CC research. The following three sections then discuss the promises and shortcomings of the respective directions taken by different scholars in their endeavours to expand the field. The chapter's core arguments are, first, that mere extensions of the VoC perspective repeat and partly even aggravate the problems associated with it; second, that the post-VoC approaches represent analytically powerful alternatives, which nevertheless are prone to some problems commonly associated with neoinstitutionalist political economy, in particular its microeconomic bias and its theoretical nationalism; and third, that the promise of approaches pertaining to the critical-materialist group for the project of 'globalizing' the CC field lies in their potential provision of important correctives to these problems.

From self-limitation to globalization

Even a cursory analysis of the historical development of the CC field reveals that its focus has, until recently, remained concentrated on only a remained concentrated on only a few world regions. This is true for a considerable and diverse number of approaches, quite regardless of the theoretical and empirical metamorphoses which CC underwent (see also Bruff et al., in this volume). Thus, a handful of so-called advanced capitalist economies, in particular the United States, Japan and some Western European countries – the 'Triad', in short – have long constituted virtually the only empirical points of reference (see, for example, Albert, 1993; Amable, 2003; Coates, 2000; Hall and Soskice, 2001; see also the collection of central texts of 1980s/1990s CC research in Coates, 2002). This way, significant parts of the world and, as a consequence, important dimensions of the variegation of capitalist political economies remained outside the focus of CC researchers and scarcely fed into their typologies and theories. This was the case especially for regions which did not form part of the core of the capitalist world economy, such as South and Southeast Asia, Latin America and Africa, and also the former Soviet and CEE states after the collapse of actually existing socialism (on the latter, see Drahokoupil and Myant, in this volume).

Politico-economic debates which centred on these regions were for the most part confined to the more specialist fields of development and transition studies, despite the fact that they often revolved around very similar substantial problems. From the early 1990s onwards, these included particularly the debate on an alleged necessity of distinct institutionalized forms of capitalist development to converge on a (neo)liberal, Anglo-American model which was supposedly better adjusted to the exigencies of global capitalism after the Cold War (cf. Bruff, 2005). Also with regard to the dominant theoretical coordinates, the neoinstitutionalist turn constituted an important similarity between CC research on the one hand and development and transition studies on the other (see, for example, Coates, 2005; Saad-Filho, 2005; Streeck, 2010). Nevertheless, connections between CC and these latter fields remained rare, with the only major exception to this being the debates in the 1980s and 1990s on the industrialization of the East Asian 'tigers' (see, for example, Wade, 1990; Weiss, 1998; for a critical view on this, see Tilley, in this volume).

It is all the more significant that in recent years CC scholars have turned their attention increasingly towards some of these previously neglected world regions, while more and more researchers from these areas have begun drawing on and situating themselves within said literatures. To be sure, as of yet this is still an incipient development: CC studies on important emerging economies such as China and India are still few and far between (see, for example, ten Brink, 2010; McNally, 2007; Peck and Zhang, 2013; and the contributions in a 2013 special issue of *Socio-Economic Review* on 'Asian Capitalisms'); similar engagements with capitalism in Africa are virtually non-existent, apart from some isolated discussions of the South African case (Nattrass, 2014; and the contributions in a 2013 special issue of *Transformation* on 'South African Capitalism Before and After 1994'). However, these literatures are growing both in theoretical sophistication and empirical saturation. What is more, there are two previously ignored world regions where CC theories and approaches can be said to have laid down roots over the last five to ten years: CEE and Latin America. Crucially, debates on these regions have each produced sets of alternative perspectives with developed typological components (see also Drahokoupil and Myant, and Gaitán and Boschi, in this volume).

Generally speaking, this opening of the field can only be welcomed since it helps to break with the often problematic disciplinary and geographical separation between related fields of knowledge. In such a context, the reflexive application of established analytical perspectives on new subject matters can serve to promote theoretical development and thus improve our understanding of worldwide capitalist variegation. The globalization of CC research also means that significant political problems come into focus, which until now had been largely ignored in the field's mainstream, with its focus on performance differences among 'advanced' economies. Perhaps the most important of these issues is the persistence of massive socio-economic inequalities on a global scale, a problem to which both development and transition studies have so far only given unsatisfactory answers (cf. Ebenau, 2012). Against this background, the expanding CC-inspired literatures on capitalism in Latin America and CEE and the vividness of the ensuing debates serve as proof of the fresh energy which the mutual opening and the increasing articulation between CC research, development and transition studies can bring to many long-standing debates on the distinctive trajectories of capitalism in different parts of the world. However, as the following

48 *Comparing Capitalisms in the Global Political Economy*

sections will document, moving forward in these debates remains a challenging task and the CC approaches developed thus far are not problem-free (see also Wehr, in this volume).

Expectedly, one of the main drivers behind the expansion of CC is the popularity boost which this field has received from the development of Hall and Soskice's VoC approach (see also Coates, in this volume). This is why a considerable number of researchers have sought to widen and partly adapt this perspective so as to deal with an ever broader range of capitalist variegation. However, the persistent criticism to which standard VoC theory has been exposed is also finding resonance in this 'second generation' context. Hence, a second group of perspectives has developed out of a certain distancing from and in a critical interaction with VoC. This is a highly heterogeneous group of approaches, which can jointly be described as an expression – and one of the motors – of the neoinstitutionalist 'post-VoC convergence' among manifold emerging alternative perspectives in the institutionalist camp (see also Bruff et al. and Drahokoupil and Myant, in this volume). Finally, there is a third, smaller group of studies which seek to continue the growing globalization of CC research by drawing more strongly on explicitly critical-materialist perspectives, in particular imperialism and dependency approaches. As indicated in the introduction to this chapter, the following three sections will consider each of these groups in turn.

VoC perspectives on capitalism in CEE, Latin America and beyond

Early on, Hall and Soskice's neat distinction between 'liberal' and 'coordinated market economies' led sympathizers and critics of VoC alike to debate whether the underlying idea of a one-dimensional continuum along which different 'varieties' could be meaningfully arrayed would permit an adequate grasp of capitalist variegation beyond VoC's flagship cases (see, for example, Goodin, 2003; Martin, 2005). This problem became more acute once scholars started taking an interest in applying the approach outside its usual Triad purview. While initially some sought to expand the reach of the original liberal market economy (LME)/coordinated market economy (CME) typology beyond the cases for which it had first been developed, in more recent years it seems to have become widely accepted, even among those who praise VoC's analytical parsimony, that understanding distinct forms of capitalism would also require infusing more complexity into its trademark dichotomy.

One early attempt of transposing the dichotomous VoC typology was undertaken by Magnus Feldmann, who seeks to characterize Estonia and Slovenia respectively as CEE variants of LMEs and CMEs (Feldmann, 2006). Following the established categories, he identifies 'market-based' and 'strategic' coordination as dominant forms of intermediation of firm action and thus as decisive principles of politico-economic organization. Other countries in CEE, he argues, would likely have to be positioned along the continuum between the two ideal types. However, subsequent studies on the institutional configurations of capitalism in post-socialist contexts have rendered highly contradictory results regarding the possible classification of a great many country-cases, and have thus cast doubt on the applicability of the dichotomous typology (Knell and Srholec, 2007; Lane, 2007). By now, the position that the one-dimensional, bipolar axis underlying the standard LME/CME typology cannot simply be transferred to other contexts seems to have imposed itself on most comparativists, including those who remain committed to the VoC perspective as such (though see Adam et al., 2009; Feldmann, 2013).

Thus, in order to understand through VoC lenses the variegation of capitalist economies outside the Triad, many have taken to elaborating new ideal-typical models via a more inductive application of the approach's 'relational view of the firm'. One of the most well known of these new analytical proposals has been developed by Ben Ross Schneider and a number of colleagues, including David Soskice, and refers to the so-called hierarchical market economies (HMEs) of Latin America (see particularly Schneider and Karcher, 2010; Schneider and Soskice, 2009; Schneider, 2009, 2013). With respect to the economies of the region, these authors identify a characteristic form of 'hierarchical' coordination, dominated by Transnational Corporations (TNCs) and domestic business groups. The basis of their argument is that this mode of coordination is less efficient than both its LME and CME equivalents, since it is not propitious for generating sound institutional solutions for a great many collective action problems, particularly in the areas of research and development (R&D) and of education and skills. The consequences for Latin American economies, according to these authors, are weak innovative capacities, a forced concentration on activities less likely to generate quality employment and, in the last instance, structurally low economic growth rates and high levels of social inequality. However, past reform efforts in both a (neo)liberal and a (neo)developmentalist direction have been thwarted by the 'negative complementarities' – driven by TNC and business group dominance, low skills and atomized labour relations – which cross-cut and interconnect the HME institutions in a dysfunctional but resilient whole (Schneider, 2013, pp. 32–9, 191–7).

The fundamental merit of the efforts of Schneider and his colleagues, as well as similar new applications of the VoC approach which detach themselves from the constitutive typological dichotomy (see, for example, Nattrass, 2014), arguably lies in having brought Latin America and other previously neglected world regions into the orbit of mainstream CC research. Thus, *pace* most of the development and transition literatures, they implicitly or explicitly recognize that these regions possess distinctive, fully formed capitalist models which must be analysed in their own right. Nevertheless, in transposing rather uncritically VoC's rationalist and business-centred framework, these analytical efforts remain beset by many of the known deficits of this approach, often in an exacerbated form (see also Bruff et al., in this volume). For one thing, the HME analysis has been once again criticized for neglecting the significant breadth of capitalist diversity. Ilán Bizberg, for instance, has argued that by trying to characterize the wide diversity of Latin American economies by means of a single ideal type of 'hierarchical capitalism', Schneider and his colleagues neglect the considerable differences with regard to their inward or outward orientation and the more or less proactive role of government (Bizberg, 2012).

The latter line of argument has been developed further by scholars working within the parameters of state-centred institutionalism, such as Renato Boschi and Flavio Gaitán, who fault the HME analysis for ignoring the potentialities for overcoming the deficits attributed to hierarchical capitalism that lie in the recuperation of (neo)developmentalist thinking and action in considerable parts of the Latin American region, particularly Brazil (Boschi, 2011; see also Gaitán and Boschi, in this volume). Moreover, different scholars have criticized Schneider's arguments for failing to appreciate the fundamental importance which transnational political and economic relations have for the very constitution of capitalism in Latin America. In this view, Schneider and his colleagues ignore the manifold ways in which basic socio-economic features, such as the composition of the local corporate sector, are (re)produced in a dialectical interplay with 'external' factors, for instance the insertion of a specific economy in transnational trade and investment networks (see, for example, Ebenau et al., 2013; Ebenau, 2012; Fernández and Alfaro, 2011; see also Suau Arinci et al., in this volume).

Against the background of these and similar criticisms of attempts at 'globalizing' the CC research agenda by means of adapting and expanding the reach of Hall and Soskice's VoC framework, a large and heterogeneous group of scholars has turned to elaborating alternative, post-VoC approaches based on different strands of institutionalist political economy. A selection of them will be discussed in the next section.

Alternative institutionalist approaches to globalizing CC research

Within this second group, historical, sociological, discursive and state-centred variants of institutionalism take precedence over the rationalist meta-theory underpinning the VoC approach. The latter perspective is received critically, for the most part, but not normally rejected outright. Rather, the protagonists of this post-VoC agenda of globalizing CC research generally criticize VoC for what they perceive to be undue conceptual simplifications, but they do share the basic objectives of this approach – explaining the economic and social performance of national-level institutions – and its fundamental theoretical outlook (for more, see Drahokoupil and Myant, in this volume).

An example of such an approach which has received considerable attention of late is found in the recent works of Uwe Becker, who seeks to analyse institutional change and performance in the BRIC countries and other large emerging economies (Becker, 2013a). Building on a moderate critique of VoC, Becker argues for a more 'open' approach in which 'institutional complementarities will be stressed much less and differently' and 'the distinction between ideal types and empirical cases of capitalism will give space to grasp nuances and gradual change' (Becker, 2013b, p. 4). In this sense, Becker operates on the basis of a more complex typology of five ideal types of capitalism, variously labelled liberal, statist, corporatist, meso-communitarian and patrimonial. Hence, it is argued that the actually existing institutional configuration of a given economy needs to be understood through identifying their specific 'mixtures' of the characteristics which these labels describe, rather than by bluntly lumping them together in categories. The BRIC countries, according to these scholars, have all undergone liberalization processes – some more, some less wide-ranging – in recent years, but patrimonial and/or statist influences remain important throughout most of them.

Another example of an alternative institutionalist perspective on capitalist variegation outside CC's traditional purview is that elaborated by

Ilán Bizberg and a Mexican-French group of collaborators for understanding capitalism in Latin America (Bizberg and Théret, 2012; Bizberg, 2011, 2012). Their approach is based on the institutionalist variant of régulation theory which is known in mainstream CC debates through the works of the likes of Bruno Amable (2003) and Robert Boyer (2005). Following from their critique of the typological oversimplification inherent in VoC's business-centred perspective, Bizberg and his colleagues propose a framework which differentiates national types of capitalism according to three dimensions, which they hold to be neglected or treated merely in a fragmentary manner in rationalist institutionalism: the articulation with the international economy, the degree and kind of state intervention, and the sphere of unions, industrial relations and welfare regimes. On this basis, they identify several distinctive types of capitalist economies in Latin America. These include a state-led model oriented towards the internal market (Brazil, Argentina); a model which is more outwardly oriented but still counts with a considerable degree of state regulation (if not direct intervention) (Chile); and finally a model of passive international integration and non-intervention, which they label 'international subcontracting capitalism' (Mexico).

Other alternative institutionalist perspectives add to the sense of heterogeneity already apparent from the above sketch of Becker's and Bizberg's approaches, including those represented in this book with their diverse theoretical references – ranging from the historical institutionalist branch of mainstream CC research to Karl Polanyi's classic analysis of capitalism to Latin American (neo)developmentalism (see also Drahokoupil and Myant, and Gaitán and Boschi, in this volume). This multiplicity of approaches complicates any attempt at providing a summary evaluation of their respective strengths and weaknesses in the frame of a globalizing CC agenda. Nevertheless, the remainder of this section presents some general considerations on their promises and potential pitfalls from a critical political economy viewpoint; they are to be read, of course, with the mentioned heterogeneity in mind.

When measured against the criticisms which have been aimed at the extended VoC perspectives (see also Bruff et al., in this volume), the analytical proposals presented above and their post-VoC institutionalist cousins undoubtedly represent important advances. First of all, their differences notwithstanding, they all share a predisposition towards greater conceptual and methodological breadth and flexibility. This means that their analytical frameworks are normally more complex, nuanced and sensitive to change. Obviously, this means that they renounce much of VoC's simplicity, let alone the ambition to develop one powerful theory of capitalist diversity which is simultaneously conceptually parsimonious and geographically encompassing. Nevertheless, in order to respond effectively to the points raised by the critics of said theory and to facilitate a more precise understanding of the variegation of capitalism on a global scale, this seems to be an inevitable compromise of scholarly ambitions. For even if we were to accept VoC's underlying assumption that capitalism in the so-called advanced countries can be analysed without looking at government actors, organized labour or the global insertion of any specific local economy, the same is evidently more problematic for other geographical contexts where politico-economic relations are often ordered very differently.

For example, in many non-core regions the state still plays a preponderant role in steering the capitalist trajectory (see Gaitán and Boschi, and Drahokoupil and Myant, in this volume), class conflicts are much more open and produce frequent and deep-reaching institutional reconfigurations, and the processes 'within' any given social formation are often more or less openly overdetermined by 'external' structures (see also Suau Arinci et al. and Tilley, in this volume). Alternative institutionalist perspectives on global capitalist variegation are therefore to be credited with focusing attention on dimensions which are neglected in standard VoC theory, and thus with tackling the problems of excessive simplification and bias towards institutional stasis that are inherent in this approach. Still, to many critical-materialist scholars there are other potential analytical and normative problems to which not only VoC but also many of the institutionalist alternatives are prone. In these scholars' reading, the problems in question do not go back merely to VoC's specific rationalist rendering of institutionalism, but to the very theoretical fundamentals shared across the perspectives which constitute this paradigm (see, for example, Bieling, 2014; Bruff, 2011; Coates, 2014a). Two in particular shall be mentioned here, since they are especially relevant to a globally oriented CC: the perceived economistic and functionalist biases inherent to most neoinstitutionalist perspectives, and the disembedding of the national level from its context (generally, see Bruff et al., in this volume).

Neoinstitutionalist CC's microeconomic bias may be understood to result from its basic orientation towards the creation and maintenance of an institutional basis for a hypothesized 'capitalism at its best', loosely understood as a regime of accumulation which enables dynamic and stable economic growth, technological innovation and low levels of social inequality (see Bohle and Greskovits, 2012). Similarly, many

CC approaches continue to draw a relatively unproblematic line of causality from business competitiveness to macroeconomic success and the well-being of the population of a given country, as long as this can be made compatible with labour relations and the economy's global insertion (see, for example, Becker, 2009; Boschi, 2011). As already discussed in the introduction to this volume, this is a proposition which must appear questionable to critical-materialist scholars who emphasize the contradictory and conflicted nature of capitalist reproduction (cf. Bruff and Ebenau, 2014; Bruff, 2011).

Researchers concerned with transnational political and economic relations have added a 'global' dimension to this interpellation by arguing that in projecting notions akin to that of 'capitalism at its best' as normative or performance objectives, the protagonists of neoinstitutionalist approaches tend to ignore that the conditions for approximating such an ideal are very unequally distributed between actors anchored in different territories. In this perspective, behind such inequalities is the fact that due to their dominant positions in the global distribution of labour and regulatory forums, the dominant forces in some spaces are capable of spatially displacing the costs and crisis tendencies of capitalist reproduction while others are forced to absorb them (cf. Becker and Jäger, 2012; Domingues, 2012; Fernández and Alfaro, 2011). The political capabilities of generating 'institutional fixes' for sustaining continued capitalist accumulation thus tend to be inferior in non-core spaces than in the world regions CC has traditionally been concerned with (Jessop, 2014; see also Jessop, in this volume). In the view of critical-materialist scholars, neoinstitutionalist approaches are hardly able to elucidate these inequalities and their deeper causes, and hence run the danger of lapsing into an uncritical, problem-solving orientation.

This ties in with the second of the two problems mentioned above, namely the isolation of the national level, or what critics call neoinstitutionalist CC's theoretical nationalism (see also Wehr, in this volume). Post-VoC approaches are mostly much more sensitive to local (sub-national) differentiations than standard VoC theory, and their proponents also claim to pay greater heed to the global (transnational) embeddedness of different capitalist 'varieties'. However, in the eyes of many critical-materialist scholars, particularly this latter ambition is, at best, realized incompletely (cf. Peck and Theodore, 2007). Even where related issues are analysed for typological purposes or for measuring performance, they remain unduly neglected, the critics argue, as causal mechanisms which influence the very socio-economic constitution of the 'variety' in question. Thus, the fact that the balance of domestic social forces and their interests is overdetermined by the global insertion of specific territories, and that these territories' potential development trajectories are often narrowly circumscribed, goes without due consideration in neoinstitutionalist CC research (cf. Coates, 2014b; Fernández and Alfaro, 2011; Radice, 2000, 2008).

In view of these perceived shortcomings, including the post-VoC incarnation of neoinstitutionalist research, many of their critics have themselves become protagonists in the elaboration of a third set of approaches, which have their main theoretical reference points in the critical-materialist paradigm and which shall be considered in the following section.

Critical-materialist perspectives for a global comparative political economy

Again, the critical-materialist group is a heterogeneous one. Its smallest common denominator is that its protagonists seek to introduce perspectives such as imperialism and dependency approaches, which they see as particularly well placed to respond to the above-mentioned problems of neoinstitutionalist attempts at globalizing the field and, simultaneously, to expose the fundamental problems of the capitalist mode of production. The differences within this group are principally associated with the question of whether such critical-materialist theoretical perspectives are brought in as complements or as alternatives to neoinstitutionalism.

One of the most widely discussed examples of a complementary approach is Andreas Nölke's and Arjan Vliegenthart's analysis of the economies of the Visegrád group (Poland, Hungary, the Czech Republic and the Slovak Republic) as 'dependent market economies' (DMEs) (Nölke and Vliegenthart, 2009; Vliegenthart, 2010). 'Dependency', in these authors' reading, refers to the fact that politico-economic relations in these countries are strongly influenced by the cross-border hierarchical structures within TNCs. The latter hold the controlling positions in the Visegrád economies, due to their subordinated insertion – mainly as industrial 'assembly platforms' – into Western European networks of investment, production and trade. On this basis, the authors argue, the countries in question have reached a temporary institutional equilibrium, giving rise to a considerable period of relatively good economic and social performance, especially in comparison to other parts of CEE and a great many post-Soviet economies (see also Drahokoupil and Myant, in this volume). However, they also point out that the stability of this equilibrium is strongly conditioned by the preferences of external actors, implying that it is bound to remain structurally fragile. Thus, the authors argue, the current trajectories of the Visegrád countries are best characterized as contemporary incarnations of the classical situation of 'dependent development'.

While Nölke and Vliegenthart advocate a 'mix and match approach' which infuses the classical notion of dependency into an analytical framework that is otherwise adapted from VoC's business and nationally orientated heuristic, other scholars have taken to elaborating analytical approaches which are more firmly rooted in critical-materialist theory. For instance, Ramiro Fernández and Belén Alfaro have developed an economic-geographical perspective that strongly draws on Latin American structuralist thought and, in this way, seeks to make sense of the differential trajectories of regional development (Fernández and Alfaro, 2011). These authors' approach focuses on three factors which they consider key influences on specific capitalist trajectories. The first is the differential constitution of localized 'cores of accumulations': while some may be described as 'endogenous and dynamic', controlled by locally anchored actors and characterized by learning and upgrading processes, others are to be understood as 'exogenous and rent-oriented' – that is, to an important degree controlled by external actors and with a weak basis for sustaining continued accumulation. The second dimension concerns the 'politics of scale' to which any localized trajectory is subjected. For the political actors in peripheral spaces, the dynamics of sub- and supra-nationalization often imply the 'confiscation' of regulatory and steering instruments and, conversely, reinforce the power of external players, such as TNCs. The third factor, finally, is the role of the state. State actors in different spaces, Fernández and Alfaro argue, come with differential capacities for influencing the formation of the local cores of accumulation and the politics of scale, giving those from dominant spaces more policy leeway than those from the global periphery. Fernández and Alfaro thus present a holistic approach which attributes structures of dependency a fundamental role in the analysis.

In comparing the two perspectives, possible lines of dissent within the group of critical-materialist scholars and between them and their alternative institutionalist colleagues become apparent. Nölke and Vliegenthart's somewhat eclectic framework – and along with it other attempts at blending institutionalist and materialist perspectives – may seem insufficient to more radical proponents of a critical-materialist turn in the globalization of CC. For instance, in adapting VoC's firm-centredness, the DME perspective downplays other channels through which global and regional relations of dependency and domination influence more specific localized trajectories, such as the asymmetrical transnationalization of the state (for example, through the creation of multilateral trade and investment regulation frameworks), which, in turn, shape the arena in which business operates (cf. Becker and Jäger, 2012; Bieling, 2014). Also, the DME conceptualization seems to suggest that such relations are important merely for understanding the development of those economies which – like the Visegrád Four – occupy subaltern or peripheral positions in the global capitalist system. In contrast, many proponents of imperialism, dependency and similar perspectives argue that the trajectories of the core economies, which stand in the centre of attention of mainstream CC research, can also not be understood without reference to their transnational dominance or centrality (cf. Coates, 2014b; Panitch and Gindin, 2005; Wehr, in this volume).

Conversely, Fernández and Alfaro's analytical proposal – again, alongside other similarly structuralist-oriented approaches – could be faulted for bending the stick too far the other way when seeking to re-insert the analysis of specific varieties or models of capitalism into a holistic perspective on capitalism as a global system. They might thus be seen as abolishing the epistemologically and methodologically privileged terrain of institutional analysis. In a similar vein, due to its breadth and generality this framework, on its own, seems hardly able to guide the elaboration of genuine typological theories which are often considered one of the most attractive features of neoinstitutionalist CC (see also Drahokoupil and Myant, in this volume).[1]

It is here that fundamental differences in research strategies and objectives between (even) alternative institutionalist and critical-materialist approaches come to the fore. Whether these will eventually be combined in a new creative synthesis of critical, global CC research basically depends not only on the disposition and willingness of scholars to maintain and deepen their dialogue, but also on which of the underlying paradigms turns out to be more useful in empirical terms.

Concluding remarks

This chapter has discussed the form and significance of the growing globalization of the CC field, and it has reviewed and discussed different contributions to this process. These have been tentatively grouped in three 'directions': attempts at extending the emblematic VoC perspective; alternative, post-VoC institutionalist approaches; and contributions building on theories from the critical-materialist family. My comparative and critical discussion permits me to draw the following conclusions:

- First, it seems that not only the moment for Hall and Soskice's VoC approach has passed, as David Coates argues in his contribution to this volume. In addition, the examination of some major attempts at widening its geographical scope of application has revealed that it appears fundamentally unsuited for grasping the variegation of capitalism on a global scale. Some specific merits notwithstanding, these attempts reproduce many of the known problems of standard VoC theory, especially its excessive typological simplification, microeconomic bias, overemphasis on institutional stasis, and theoretical nationalism, often even in an exacerbated form.
- Second, post-Hall-Soskice institutionalist approaches, which are both broader and conceptually more flexible, appear as powerful alternatives to VoC theory. They generally do a much better job at grasping the specificities of particular cases, as well as the multiplicity of factors influencing their institutional constitution and socio-economic performance. Still, these perspectives seem prone to reproducing some of the problems pointed out previously, in particular a microeconomic, problem-solving bias and an undue disembedding of the national level of analysis. These appear to be associated with the theoretical fundamentals of the neoinstitutionalist paradigm itself, rather than VoC's specific rationalist rendering of it.
- Third, critical-materialist theories and perspectives hold promise for overcoming these problems and thus improving our understanding of capitalist variegation on a global scale. Regarding theory development, there are those who suggest that the best way forward is attempting creative syntheses between institutionalist and critical-materialist perspectives, while others advocate a more radical turn towards the latter.

In any case the debate recounted in this chapter is only just beginning. Its continuation is likely to constitute one of the most exciting strands of the development of CC research over the coming years. The proof of many of the proverbial theoretical puddings served here will lie, as usual, in their eating: in their empirical application, substantiation and questioning.

Note

1. This volume contains a new contribution to the critical-materialist 'direction' of globalizing CC research, written by Lucía Suau Arinci, Nadia Pessina and myself (chapter 11). We elaborate and apply an analytical frame which combines an encompassing, structuralist vision with a more fine-grained focus on specific local institutions. Whether this overcomes the identified shortcomings of neoinstitutionalist CC approaches while rescuing their methodological merits is, of course, for others to judge.

Bibliography

Adam, F., P. Kristan and M. Tomšic (2009) 'Varieties of Capitalism in Eastern Europe (with Special Emphasis on Estonia and Slovenia)', *Communist and Post-Communist Studies*, 42:1, 65–81.
Albert, M. (1993) *Capitalism Against Capitalism* (trs. P. Haviland) (London: Whurr).
Amable, B. (2003) *The Diversity of Modern Capitalism* (Oxford: Oxford University Press).
Becker, J. and J. Jäger (2012) 'Integration in Crisis: A Regulationist Perspective on the Interaction of European Varieties of Capitalism', *Competition & Change*, 16:3, 169–87.
Becker, U. (2009) *Open Varieties of Capitalism. Continuity, Change and Performances* (Basingstoke: Palgrave Macmillan).
Becker, U. (2013a) 'Measuring Change of Capitalist Varieties: Reflections on Method, Illustrations from the BRICs', *New Political Economy*, 18:4, 503–32.
Becker, U. (2013b) 'Introduction', in U. Becker (ed.), *The BRICs and Emerging Economies in Comparative Perspective: Political Economy, Liberalization and Institutional Change* (Abingdon: Routledge), 1–26.
Bieling, H.-J. (2014) 'Comparative Analysis of Capitalism from a Regulationist Perspective Extended by Neo-Gramscian IPE', *Capital & Class*, 38:1, 31–43.
Bizberg, I. (2011) 'The Global Economic Crisis as Disclosure of Different Types of Capitalism in Latin America', *Swiss Journal of Sociology*, 37:2, 321–39.
Bizberg, I. (2012) 'Types of Capitalism in Latin America', *Interventions économiques*, 47, 1–26.
Bizberg, I. and B. Théret (2012) 'La diversidad de los capitalismos latinoamericanos: los casos de Argentina, Brasil y México', *Noticias de la regulación*, 61, 1–22.
Bohle, D. and B. Greskovits (2012) *Capitalist Diversity on Europe's Periphery* (Ithaca: Cornell University Press).
Boschi, R.R. (2011) 'Instituições, trajetórias e desenvolvimento: uma discussão a partir da América Latina', in R.R. Boschi (ed.), *Variedades de capitalismo, política e desenvolvimento na América Latina* (Belo Horizonte: Editora UFMG), 7–30.
Boyer, R. (2005) 'How and Why Capitalisms Differ', *Economy and Society*, 34:4, 509–57.
ten Brink, T. (2010) 'Strukturmerkmale des chinesischen Kapitalismus', *MPIfG Working Papers*, 10/1 (Köln: Max-Planck-Institut für Gesellschaftsforschung).

Bruff, I. (2005) 'Making Sense of the Globalisation Debate When Engaging in Political Economy Analysis', *British Journal of Politics and International Relations*, 7:2, 261–80.

Bruff, I. (2011) 'What about the Elephant in the Room? Varieties of Capitalism, Varieties in Capitalism', *New Political Economy*, 16:4, 481–500.

Bruff, I. and M. Ebenau (2014) 'Critical Political Economy and the Critique of Comparative Capitalisms Scholarship on Capitalist Diversity', *Capital & Class*, 38:1, 3–15.

Coates, D. (2000) *Models of Capitalism. Growth and Stagnation in the Modern Era* (Cambridge: Polity Press).

Coates, D. (ed.) (2002) *Models of Capitalism: Debating Strengths and Weaknesses* (Cheltenham: Edward Elgar).

Coates, D. (2005) 'Paradigms of Explanation', in D. Coates (ed.), *Varieties of Capitalism, Varieties of Approaches* (Basingstoke: Palgrave Macmillan), 1–25.

Coates, D. (2014a) 'Studying Comparative Capitalisms by Going Left and by Going Deeper', *Capital & Class*, 38:1, 18–30.

Coates, D. (2014b) 'The UK: Less a Liberal Market Economy, More a Post-Imperial One', *Capital & Class*, 38:1, 171–82.

Domingues, J.M. (2012) 'Development and Dependency, Developmentalism and Alternatives', in R.R. Boschi and C.H. Santana (eds), *Development and Semi-Periphery: Post-Neoliberal Trajectories in South America and Central Eastern Europe* (London: Anthem Press), 83–101.

Ebenau, M. (2012) 'Varieties of Capitalism or Dependency? A Critique of the VoC Approach for Latin America', *Competition & Change*, 16:3, 206–23.

Ebenau, M., F. Parés and L. Suau Arinci (2013) 'Zurück in die Zukunft? Dependenzperspektiven in der Analyse der Diversität des Gegenwartskapitalismus', *Peripherie: Zeitschrift für Politik und Ökonomie in der Dritten Welt*, 33:130/131, 220–42.

Feldmann, M. (2006) 'Emerging Varieties of Capitalism in Transition Countries: Industrial Relations and Wage Bargaining in Estonia and Slovenia', *Comparative Political Studies*, 39:7, 829–54.

Feldmann, M. (2013) 'Varieties of Capitalism and the Estonian Economy: Institutions, Growth and Crisis in a Liberal Market Economy', *Communist and Post-Communist Studies*, 46:4, 493–501.

Fernández, V.R. and M.B. Alfaro (2011) 'Ideas y políticas del desarrollo regional bajo variedades del capitalismo: contribuciones desde la periferia', *Revista Paranaense de Desenvolvimento*, 120, 57–99.

Goodin, R.E. (2003) 'Choose Your Capitalism?' *Comparative European Politics*, 1:2, 203–13.

Hall, P.A. and D. Soskice (eds.) (2001) *Varieties of Capitalism: The Institutional Foundations of Comparative Advantage* (Oxford: Oxford University Press).

Jessop, B. (2014) 'Capitalist Diversity and Variety: Variegation, the World Market, Compossibility and Ecological Dominance', *Capital & Class*, 38:1, 45–58.

Knell, M. and M. Srholec (2007) 'Diverging Pathways in Central and Eastern Europe', in D. Lane and M. Myant (eds.), *Varieties of Capitalism in Post-Communist Countries* (Basingstoke: Palgrave Macmillan), 40–62.

Lane, D. (2007) 'Post-State Socialism: A Diversity of Capitalisms?' in D. Lane and M. Myant (eds.), *Varieties of Capitalism in Post-Communist Countries* (Basingstoke: Palgrave Macmillan), 13–39.

Martin, C.J. (2005) 'Beyond Bone Structure: Historical Institutionalism and the Style of Economic Growth', in D. Coates (ed.), *Varieties of Capitalism, Varieties of Approaches* (Basingstoke: Palgrave Macmillan), 47–62.

McNally, C. (2007) 'China's Capitalist Transition: The Making of a New Variety of Capitalism', in L. Mjøset and T.H. Clausen (eds.), *Capitalisms Compared* (Bingley: Emerald), 177–93.

Nattrass, N. (2014) 'A South African Variety of Capitalism?' *New Political Economy*, 19:1, 56–78.

Nölke, A. and A. Vliegenthart (2009) 'Enlarging the Varieties of Capitalism: The Emergence of Dependent Market Economies in East Central Europe', *World Politics*, 61:4, 670–702.

Panitch, L. and S. Gindin (2005) 'Euro-Capitalism and American Empire', in D. Coates (ed.), *Varieties of Capitalism, Varieties of Approaches* (Basingstoke: Palgrave Macmillan), 139–59.

Peck, J. and N. Theodore (2007) 'Variegated Capitalism', *Progress in Human Geography*, 31:6, 731–72.

Peck, J. and J. Zhang (2013) 'A Variety of Capitalism...with Chinese Characteristics?' *Journal of Economic Geography*, 13:3, 357–96.

Radice, H. (2000) 'Globalization and National Capitalisms: Theorizing Convergence and Differentiation', *Review of International Political Economy*, 7:4, 719–42.

Radice, H. (2008) 'The Developmental State Under Global Neoliberalism', *Third World Quarterly*, 29:6, 1153–74.

Saad-Filho, A. (2005) 'From Washington to Post-Washington Consensus: Neoliberal Agendas for Economic Development', in A. Saad-Filho and D. Johnston (eds.), *Neoliberalism: A Critical Reader* (London: Pluto), 113–19.

Schneider, B.R. (2009) 'Hierarchical Market Economies and Varieties of Capitalism in Latin America', *Journal of Latin American Studies*, 41:3, 553–75.

Schneider, B.R. (2013) *Hierarchical Capitalism in Latin America: Business, Labour, and the Challenges of Equitable Development* (Cambridge: Cambridge University Press).

Schneider, B.R. and S. Karcher (2010) 'Complementarities and Continuities in the Political Economy of Labour Markets in Latin America', *Socio-Economic Review*, 8:4, 623–51.

Schneider, B.R. and D. Soskice (2009) 'Inequality in Developed Countries and Latin America: Coordinated, Liberal and Hierarchical Systems', *Economy and Society*, 38:1, 17–52.

Streeck, W. (2010) 'E Pluribus Unum? Varieties and Commonalities of Capitalism', *MPIfG Working Papers*, 10/12 (Köln: Max-Planck-Institut für Gesellschaftsforschung).

Vliegenthart, A. (2010) 'Bringing Dependency Back In: The Economic Crisis in Post-Socialist Europe and the Continued Relevance of Dependent Development', *Historical Social Research/Historische Sozialforschung*, 35:2, 242–65.

Wade, R.H. (1990) *Governing the Market. Economic Theory and the Role of Government in East Asian Industrialization* (Princeton: Princeton University Press).

Weiss, L. (1998) *The Myth of the Powerless State: Governing the Economy in the Global Era* (Cambridge: Polity).

Part II
Critical Perspectives and Debates

4
Comparative Capitalisms and/or Variegated Capitalism

Bob Jessop

> All those laws developed in the classical works on political economy, are strictly true under the supposition only, that trade be delivered from all fetters, that competition be perfectly free, not only within a single country, but upon the whole face of the earth. These laws, which A. Smith, Say, and Ricardo have developed, the laws under which wealth is produced and distributed – these laws grow more true, more exact, then cease to be mere abstractions, in the same measure in which Free Trade is carried out... Thus it can justly be said, that the economists – Ricardo and others – know more about society as it will be, than about society as it is. *They know more about the future than about the present.*
>
> (Marx, [1847] 1976, p. 290; italics added)

This quotation from a lecture in 1847 by Marx on free trade will frame my critical appreciation of the Comparative Capitalisms (CC) literatures. I argue that it *knows less about the present than about the past* of capitalism – and is even less insightful about its future. This is because CC tends to adopt a disaggregative approach to diversity in the world market. This is useful for some theoretical and practical purposes and provides one possible 'first cut' analysis of the overall diversity of the capitalist landscape. But it marginalizes the emerging logic and constraining power of a world market that is becoming more tightly integrated through differential accumulation and the relative

---

This chapter has benefited from the careful reading of the editors, especially Matthias Ebenau; it draws on work conducted in 2010–2013 during an Economic and Social Research Council Professorial Fellowship (RES–051–27–0303).

success of specific strategic initiatives. Some of my earlier contributions to the critique of political economy shared these problems (Jessop and Sum, 2006), and, in response, I have recommended taking variegated capitalism in the world market as an alternative 'first cut' entry-point.

This does not posit a pre-existing world system with a pre-given, trans-historical logic; nor does it entail that, whether gradually or at some definite turning point, a single hyper-global or supra-imperialist capitalism has developed. It does mean that the world market increasingly not only provides the ultimate *horizon* of competition about differential accumulation (something familiar to mainstream accounts of globalization), but also generalizes and intensifies the contradictions of capital (something less often acknowledged, if at all, in these accounts). The importance of this second aspect becomes apparent only through consistent engagement with such contradictions and the attempts made to harmonize, defer or displace them at different scales and sites up to and including the world market. In short, the more integrated the world market becomes and, hence, the more capital's contradictions are generalized to the global level, the harder it becomes to analyse capitalism through a series of discrete case studies or broader comparative typologies, especially if the types are identified with national (or other territorially demarcated) economies. The inability to remove or suspend the incompressible contradictions of capital accumulation is self-evident from neoliberal globalization, the efforts to displace and defer the consequences of the North Atlantic Financial Crisis and its repercussions in emerging markets.

This chapter undertakes four tasks. It first outlines the theoretical framework for my analysis of variegated capitalism in an emerging world market that coexists with, and is structurally coupled to, a pluralistic world of states. Second, it endorses Marx's argument that the world market is both the presupposition and posit (result) of differential accumulation and indicates its increasing relevance as diverse obstacles to integration are overcome through the interaction of emergent structural logics and situated strategic action. Third, by examining the interaction between the world of states and the emerging logic of the world market, it indicates one justification for research on CC but, insofar as this research neglects the integration of different varieties of capitalism into the world market, also indicates the limits of such research. Fourth, on this basis, it suggests some new directions in critical research on CC based on the concept of variegated capitalism in a world market, in which some varieties are more influential than others.

Theoretical preliminaries

The strategic-relational approach was developed to study the dialectic of structure and agency. It is implicit in Marx's proposition that capital is not a thing but 'a relation between persons established by the instrumentality of things' (1967a, p. 537). In general, for this approach structure consists in differential constraints and opportunities associated with specific social relations and their emergent properties that vary by agency; agency in turn involves the differential deployment of strategic capacities that vary by structure as well as the actors involved. In the context of a concern with CC, this indicates a concern with the basic forms of the capital relation, their differential instantiation in different periods and types of capitalism and the accumulation strategies and state projects oriented to securing the expanded reproduction of capitalism and political order on different scales and terrains despite the contradictory, crisis-prone nature of capitalist social formations. This calls for historically specific analyses of changing forms of the capital relation, their role in shaping the balance of forces, their reproduction and transformation through struggles that also depend on changes in the organization, strategy and tactics of specific forces, as well as their embedding in wider social formations (see also Kannankulam and Georgi, 2014).

In addition to key categories of Marx's critique of political economy, I draw on four compatible bodies of regulationist work to develop this agenda: (i) the Parisian School's initial emphasis on the inherent contradictions and antagonisms of capital considered as a social relation and, hence, the need for partial, temporary and provisional fixes for accumulation to continue, at least for a time and in a given spatio-temporal framework; (ii) the Grenoblois emphasis on the plurinational and core–periphery character of economic-cum-political blocs, within which differential accumulation is more or less regulated, regularized, or 'fixed' and between which are more anarchic inter-bloc relations; (iii) the Amsterdam School's interest in how transnational power blocs seek to organize transnational accumulation, guided by comprehensive concepts of control that tend to privilege either profit-producing or interest-bearing capital; and (iv) German work on the changing form and functions of the state in regularizing-governing differential accumulation and, especially, its growing internationalization in response to world market integration.

Space constraints preclude a thorough explication of these schools' relevance to CC research (for details, see Jessop and Sum, 2006).

Nonetheless I hope to show that combining them can illuminate: (i) how the inherently fragile and crisis-prone capital relation is regularized-cum-governed through (ii) a historically variable set of partial, unstable and provisional institutional, spatio-temporal and semantic fixes at different sites and scales, below and above the national, that are (iii) promoted not only by national capitals in one or another guise but also by transnational power blocs and that, in addition, (iv) rely both on various kinds of state intervention and/or distinctive forms of political capitalism as well as the anarchic logic of profit-oriented, market-mediated accumulation. While institutional and spatio-temporal fixes are increasingly familiar terms in critical political economy, 'semantic fix' merits a brief comment. It refers here to the sedimentation of a social imaginary that (i) combines an accumulation strategy and state project such that a given accumulation regime and its mode of regulation are naturalized as objects of observation, calculation, management, governance, or guidance; and that thereby (ii) frames the competition, rivalries and struggles that occur within its parameters. Such fixes are never, of course, fully closed or sedimented: even hegemonic economic imaginaries are contested within the power bloc, often depend on complementary sub-hegemonic imaginaries with different social and spatio-temporal bases of support and are vulnerable to counter-hegemonic economic challenge. Like institutional and spatio-temporal fixes, semantic fixes are only ever partial, provisional and temporary. They work best when they connect different spheres, scales and sites of social action and have in-built sources of redundancy and flexibility that can be mobilized in the face of instability or crisis (for the general analytical framework, see Sum and Jessop, 2013).

Provided that one does not treat these fixes as permanently resolving (rather than displacing and/or deferring) contradictions and antagonisms, this approach can help to examine the diversity and varieties of accumulation regimes and their modes of regulation, including how they co-evolve in an ecology of self-organizing modes of growth that, in aggregate, constitute the world market and, through their interaction, shape its dynamic. This is a fractal process that is not confined to any particular scale of territorial organization. Indeed, a full account of the world market should refer to the changing articulation of territory, place, scale and flows across time and space. This occurs in more or less self-similar ways, with similarities due to the overall logic of capital and differences to the circumstances in which this logic plays out. This excludes both a one-sided focus on varieties of capitalism and a one-sided concern with the logic of a world market that pre-exists these varieties (for details, see Jessop, 2011, 2013, 2014). I will elaborate on this remark in my conclusions.

The world market as presupposition and posit of differential accumulation

Like Smith, Say and Ricardo before him, Marx knew more about the future than about his present. His critique of political economy is more relevant today than in the 1840s–1880s, because the world market is now even less 'fettered' by limits to trade, to investment flows and to rational organization of capitalist production on a world scale. As Marx and Engels noted in *The German Ideology* (written in 1845–1846):

> The movement of capital, although considerably accelerated, still remained, however, relatively slow. The splitting up of the world market into separate parts, each of which was exploited by a particular nation, the exclusion of competition among themselves on the part of the nations, the clumsiness of production itself and the fact that finance [*Geldwesen*] was only evolving from its early stages, greatly impeded circulation.
>
> (1976, p. 56n)

They added that this limitation was partly overcome by the rise of big industry, which 'universalized competition, established means of communication and the modern world market, subordinated trade to itself, transformed all capital into industrial capital and thus produced the rapid circulation (development of the financial system) and the centralization of capital' (ibid., p. 57). In the 170 years since Marx and Engels consigned these lines to 'the gnawing criticism of the mice', barriers to the movement of capital have been further removed in an uneven process involving, *inter alia*, technological change, time-space distantiation and compression, resort to force and political pressure, legislative and regulatory reform, ruptural crises and reversals. In the last 40 years, moreover, digital information and communication technologies, financialization (including securitization and derivatives) and neoliberalization have also steadily weakened remaining obstacles to completion of the world market. This has intensified the search for competitive advantage and has generalized capital's inherent contradictions and diverse crisis tendencies.

Thus, even if 'the splitting up of the world market into separate parts', each of which has national or other peculiarities, might once

70 *Critical Perspectives and Debates*

have justified a comparative analysis of diverse capitalisms *considered in isolation from each other*, this is less and less justified as the world market tends towards greater integration, whether through its emerging laws of motion or targeted strategic action. However, this does not warrant hyper-globalist or supra-imperialist claims that there is now just one, friction-free, capitalism that is integrated through the invisible but efficient hand of the market or guided by the hand of a more or less unified transnational class and its political allies. It does imply that varieties *of* capitalisms are also varieties *in* capitalism (Bruff, 2011) and should therefore be studied in terms of their covariation, structural coupling and co-evolution as well as attempts to transform and steer this process.

To develop this research agenda it would be helpful to elaborate, at least in spirit, Marx's 'six-book' plan for *Capital*. As Shortall (1994, p. 144) has noted:

> In the first three books – the books on capital, landed property and wage-labour – Marx intended to expose the objective, historically given, economic and material conditions on which the three great classes of bourgeois society are based. In the fourth book, the book on the state, Marx would have then sought to show how the contradictions between these three classes are held within the political unity imposed by the state. In the fifth book, the book on foreign trade, Marx would have been able to examine the economic relations between different states which would then prepare the way for the sixth and final book, the book on the world market and crises.

While the proposed themes of books four and five are crucial to CC research, the topic of the last book indicates the eventual need to situate varieties of capitalism within the world market. Only then, as Marx noted, would production be 'posited as a totality together with all its moments ... within which, at the same time, all contradictions come into play' (1973a, p. 227).

Shortall's comment indicates that a complete analysis of capital must, in Marx's words, extend to 'the concentration of bourgeois society in the form of the state', the role of taxes (and, one should add, tax competition), relations among national currencies and world money, the roles of public debt and state credit, colonies, international relations, diplomacy and war. Marx also mentions the international division of labour, development of foreign trade, exchange rates and so forth (1973b, p. 108). This partial list of economic and extra-economic forms, institutions, practices and events points well beyond any general economic tendencies or other 'commonalities of capitalism' to diverse factors that generate continuing differences.

The first steps in the development of the world market occurred in the context of the breakup of feudalism, the spread of a monetary economy and the expansion of regional, national and international commerce (Reinert, 2007; Wood, 2003; see also McDonough, in this volume). Thus the world market was the historical presupposition of capitalism during and after the mercantilist period *and* would also be changed through the rise of big industry (Marx, 1973a, pp. 407–10). Differences among pre-capitalist states shaped forms of primitive accumulation, the creation of a home market, the development of commerce and the opening of foreign markets. In its classic form in England, mercantilism rested on 'a systematical combination [of different moments of primitive accumulation], embracing the colonies, the national debt, the modern mode of taxation, and the protectionist system' (Marx, 1967a, p. 528). More generally, the shape of the emerging world market is related to 'the particular pre-existing territorial features of the pre-capitalist system of reproduction and the structure of its administrative apparatus of rule' (von Braunmühl, 1978, p. 167; cf. Gerstenberger, 2007).

Mercantilism was followed by a phase based on industrial (or, more generally, profit-producing) rather than commercial capital, with an expansionary logic that required ever more extensive markets to allow profits to be realized in the face of insufficient domestic demand (Marx, 1967b, pp. 245–58). Marx related uneven development in the world market in this phase to differences in the national intensity and productivity of labour, the relative international values and prices of commodities produced in different national contexts, the relative international value of wages and money in social formations with different degrees of labour intensity and productivity, the incidence of surplus profits and unequal exchange and so on (for instance, see Marx, 1967b, pp. 317–25). Such issues still matter today, as exemplified in the Eurozone crisis, which is often attributed to just these factors as well as to legal and other limits to compensatory devaluation by the 'less competitive' European member states. Unsurprisingly, then, from the mercantilist period onwards state power has been deployed to promote primitive accumulation, open or protect markets (depending on the competitiveness of the relevant capitals), organize the global division of labour and shape international monetary, credit and currency systems.

While early stages in Marx's critique analysed the circuits of capital on the simplifying assumption that it occurs in a unified economic (and political) space, this assumption must be relaxed to allow for uneven development in and across a plurality of states. Failure to relax it would, as Rosenberg (2007, p. 425) argues in another context, externalize 'the international' and open 'an unbridgeable gulf between a theory of capitalist development and its actual shape as a historical process'. This has obvious implications for the analysis of variegated capitalism (or, from some perspectives, variegated imperialism) in the world market. Yet, as Wood observed, 'we have yet to see a systematic theory of imperialism designed for a world in which all international relations are internal to capitalism and governed by capitalist imperatives. That, at least in part, is because a world of more or less universal capitalism... is a very recent development' (Wood, 2003, p. 127). Marx provides many concepts to develop this theory, showing how well he, more than Smith, Say or Ricardo, knew the future.

The rational kernel of CC research

The tendential integration of the world market (*Weltmarkt*) exists alongside a world of states (*Staatenwelt*). This has significant consequences for differential accumulation on a world scale. First, the world market constitutes *both* the ultimate strategic horizon for individual capitals in the profit-oriented, market-mediated competition for differential accumulation *and* the actually existing point of intersection of these capitals. This leads to a contingent dynamic that emerges from the interaction of competing strategies and thereby limits the scope for different strategies. In other words, the world market is tendentially unified and integrated through the logic of profit-oriented, market-mediated competition based on trade, financial flows and (capitalist) commodity production. Second, and conversely, we still find a 'motley diversity' of states that are often rivals, if not deadly enemies. These states have quite varied sizes, resources, commitments and abilities to promote and govern accumulation, whether on the part of their respective domestic capitals operating at home and abroad and/or on the part of foreign or transnational capitals whose activities impinge on domestic economic and political interests. They no more exist in unchanging mutual isolation, however, than do local, regional, national or international markets. Thus the nature of varieties of capitalism at one or another scale must be linked to the interaction of the world market and the world of states.

This interaction is shaped by the forms and extent of separation between the profit-oriented, market-mediated dimension of accumulation and its crucial extra-economic supports in, *inter alia*, the legal and political system and, notwithstanding this variable institutional separation, by the continued reciprocal interdependence of 'market' and 'state' as complementary moments of the capital relation. This interdependence is partly recognized in CC work on the extent and modes of state involvement in providing general external conditions of production – allocating money, credit and resources to different activities – and organizing production, distribution and trade in rational capitalism. Such concerns characterize CC work from Shonfield's analysis of modern capitalism to refinements of the Hall–Soskice dichotomy between liberal and coordinated market economies (Shonfield, 1965; Hall and Soskice, 2001; Becker, 2009). It is also informs research on state capitalism, developmental states and post-socialist economies (for instance, Woo-Cumings, 1999; Nölke and Claar, 2013; Myant and Drahokoupil, 2011).

In contrast to the state's role in rational capitalism, far less interest has been shown in the specificities of 'political capitalism' (for an exception, see Karadag, 2010). Weber (1961) distinguished three modes of orientation to gain (*Erwerbsorientierung*) with a 'political' character. These concern gains from: (i) force and domination, exemplified in efforts to secure access to key resources, to control foreign markets and, more recently, to constrain how foreign states govern their economies; (ii) the financing of political ventures, parties, key legislators or top executive branch members, government officials and advisers, and other political gatekeepers or veto holders, with a view to shaping legislation, regulation, spending, taxation and so on; and (iii) 'unusual deals with political authorities', enabling odious debt, unjust enrichment, corrupt contracts, privatization bargains and other forms of accumulation through dispossession. As ideal types, such orientations may not be instantiated as specific varieties of capitalism (although they may be significant in some empirical cases); but they matter because they may modify more familiar varieties, contribute to the core–periphery differentiation of the world market, help to sustain imperialist domination (especially in resource-rich extractivist economies), create obstacles to the integration of the world market, legitimate the imposition of political conditionalities in return for aid during crises and so on. In general, the existence of 'political capitalisms' or hybrid forms of rational and political capitalism indicates, as Karadag (2010) notes, the limits of the institutional separation of the economic and political that is so often taken for granted in mainstream CC research.

Another neglected aspect of states' roles at different scales in constituting varieties of capitalism is their enrolment in organizing the institutional and spatio-temporal fixes that seek to stabilize accumulation regimes and modes of regulation by managing their contradictions and displacing and/or deferring their costs elsewhere and/or into the future. These fixes, where they exist, are always partial, provisional and unstable and, sooner or later, break down. In general, periods of relative stability are characterized by complementary institutional hierarchies and institutionalized compromises that correspond to the prevailing accumulation strategies and modes of regulation within the overall framework of the world market. These may break down when the weight of different contradictions and/or their respective poles alters in ways that undermine previous displacement and deferral mechanisms and/or because there is growing resistance to the patterns of exploitation and domination once sustained by these fixes (for more details and some examples, see Jessop, 2013). In turn, periods of instability involve disruptive institutional hierarchies and struggles to roll back past compromises and establish new ones (see also McDonough, in this volume). In both cases, thanks to the presence of multiple contradictions and dilemmas, agents are forced, willingly or not, to prioritize some over others. This is not a neutral technical matter. It is essentially political and often contested, especially in periods of economic crisis.

Together, state intervention in 'rational capitalism' based on trade in free markets and the rational organization of capitalist production, plus the above-noted 'irrational' forms of 'political capitalism', suggest that variable state forms and functions and the specific modalities of state power are important causal factors in the differentiation of capitalism(s) within a world market framework. Indeed, this is a significant source of the tensions and conflicts inherent in the coexistence of a tendentially singular world market and the survival of a plurality of diverse states that shapes the character and development of varieties of capitalism within the world market framework. This is reflected in the tangled, unevenly developing hierarchy of local, regional, national, transnational and supranational markets that correspond to a greater or lesser degree with the territories controlled by particular states in a world of states.

This can be related in part to Harvey's contrast between the (strategic) logic of capital (in general) and the territorial (strategic) logic of particular states. While the former aims to reduce obstacles to the movement of capital, the latter aims to fix capital in place to maximize revenues for a particular local, regional, national or larger territorial unit, and/or to mobilize state power to control territory to promote geo-political interests. This results in a tension between (i) potentially mobile capital's interests in reducing its place-dependency and/or liberating itself from temporal constraints and (ii) state interests in fixing (allegedly beneficial) capital in its own territory and rendering capital's temporal horizons and rhythms compatible with statal and/or political routines, temporalities and crisis tendencies. Harvey further notes that each logic generates contradictions that must be contained by the other, leading to a spiral movement as contradictions are displaced to and fro between them. This is reflected in different forms of uneven geographical development, geopolitical struggles and imperialist politics, and in different kinds of crisis. Thus, if the territorial logic blocks that of capital, economic crisis may result; if capitalist logic undermines territorial logic, there may be a political crisis (Harvey, 2003, p. 140).

This indicates that world market formation and integration is hyper-complex. Rather than a 'flat world', we have an uneven terrain with uneven flows, differential frictions and uneven power with varying capacities for time-space compression and distantiation to exploit the opportunities offered by the formation of the world market. It is here, I suggest, that we can locate the rational kernel to the analysis of varieties of capitalism. Regardless of any specific ontological or methodological biases that might promote a one-sided concern with national varieties of capitalism considered in isolation from their integration into the world market, it remains the case that world market integration is incomplete, that important obstacles to this are rooted in the survival of a world of states as well as in the brute facts of physical geography and the path-dependent effects of historical modes of insertion into the global division of labour and the hierarchy of states in a world of states. Work on varieties of capitalism can help us to make sense of these complex dynamics.

From varieties of capitalism to variegated capitalism

In the previous section, I attempted to 'bend the stick in the other direction'. Against the overall line of critical argument in my recent work on this topic, I have argued that there is a rational kernel to the study of varieties of capitalism. However, while the notions of a 'flat world' of separate but equal national varieties of capitalism each with its own niche in an integrated global economy or, alternatively, of a mosaic of regional economies with variable geometries and growth potential have some appeal, the world market still remains hierarchically ordered (see also Suau Arinci et al. in this volume). Some 'spaces of flows', some territorial states (for example, the United States, the People's Republic of China, Germany), some places (for example, global cities), some scales of economic and political action (for example, the European Union (EU)), are more important than others. To study these differences requires more than a case-by-case comparison of varieties of capitalism considered in isolation.

Indeed, if we explore variation primarily in terms of the instantiation of different kinds of capitalism in particular territorial units, many other dimensions of capitalist variation get ignored. World market integration emerges from interactions in many sites and at many scales, including peripheral and semi-peripheral as well as central locations. Moreover, the contingent logic of the world market results from a complex dialectic between changes in the organization of the space of flows and the organization of territory reflected variously in the rise of multinational companies and transnational banks, the internationalization of economic spaces through growing penetration (inward flows) and extraversion (outward flows), global city network-building, the integration and competition among triad, cross-border region formation, international localization, glocalization and so on. This reorders economic, political and socio-cultural differences and complementarities across territories, scales, places and networks, and produces new forms of uneven development. These changing complexities also offer new opportunities for rescaling, jumping scales and so on; and for supranational, national and local states to attempt to shape these differences and complementarities. This is reflected in shifts among 'national economies' and in the rise and fall of regions, new forms of 'north-south' divide and so on. Thus, in addition to diverse regional spaces, we find a mosaic of cross-border alliances organized within and across regions and continents, sometimes based on intergovernmental cooperation, sometimes on the pooling of sovereignty and sometimes on more or less hidden forms of imperial or neo-imperial domination.

So one can also study the world market as a self-organizing ecology of varieties of capitalism that are structurally coupled and co-evolving and, moreover, are coupled not only through their territorial instantiation (their articulation to states within a world of states) but also through their entanglement at different scales and through networks (their relation respectively to the spatial division of labour and to spaces of flows). This means that they cannot be accorded *equal analytical weight as so many theoretically possible, empirically observable and more or less internally coherent, harmoniously functioning individual instances of capitalism*. Rather, varieties of capitalism should be studied in terms of their *asymmetrical, differential integration into an evolving world market that sets limits to compossible combinations and implies that some 'varieties' are more equal than others*, that is, cause more problems (or create more 'disharmonies') for other varieties than they can cause for it (cf. Suau Arinci et al., in this volume).

On this basis, I now propose a concern with variegated capitalism as a necessary complement to critical work on CC. This term refers to the *co*existence and *com*possibility of 'varieties of capitalism' within a tendentially singular (but not necessarily unified, let alone harmonious) world market. Once we consider issues of compossibility, the limits on persistent variation appear much greater than most of the CC literatures envisage. Figure 4.1 illustrates what is at stake. Some varieties cannot exist in isolation. An example would be an export-oriented economy without export markets; but it could nonetheless be part of a wider set of economies. We can also distinguish between neutral or benign compossibility (classically, the 'win-win' Ricardian international division of labour) and pathological compossibility (for example, 'Chimerica' as the increasingly dysfunctional interdependence of China and the United States). Finally, latent incompossibility, exemplified in the intensification of dysfunctions and tensions in a pathologically compossible system, such as the Eurozone from 2008 onwards, could lead to structural crises or other breakdowns.

Thinking in these terms also makes it easier to explain interconnections among the respective contradictions and crisis tendencies of the different varieties of capitalism, whether these are considered in idealtypical terms or in terms of actually existing (empirical) cases. This highlights the uneven scope and distribution of capacities for strategic

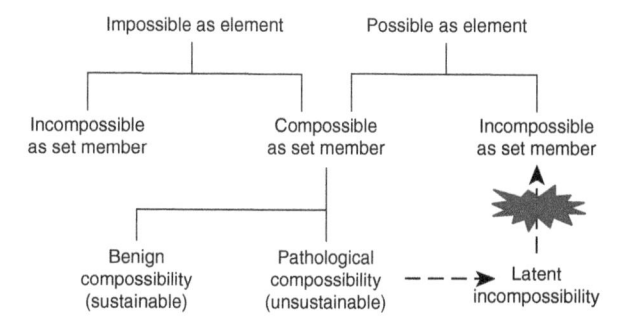

Figure 4.1 Compossibility and incompossibility

action oriented to ordering, reordering and stabilizing this variegation in the context of a changing world market as well as to regularize, govern or manage individual varieties through institutional, spatio-temporal and semantic fixes.

An important aspect of variegated capitalism is the issue of 'ecological dominance'. This refers in general to how far and how, in a self-organizing ecology of self-organizing systems or institutional orders, one system or order is a problem-*maker* for the others rather than a problem-*taker*. This can be related to the relative weights of different 'varieties of capitalism' and/or the uneven impact of different circuits of capital. These weightings are not automatic, mechanical outcomes of market forces but also derive from the clash of specific economic and political strategies, which may include force as well as market rigging. In these terms, we could study the uneven development and structural coupling of capitalist regimes in a regional or global division of labour, such as the Rhenish, Nordic and liberal market models in Europe or the global dominance of the liberal market model; or, again, the weight of commercial, industrial or financial capital in capitalist circuits at different scales.

The world market is not a static presupposition of capital accumulation but a hyper-complex, emergent result of the interaction of actually existing varieties of capitalism and different economic and political strategies to modify their articulation. As the world market expands, becomes more extensive and more tightly integrated, capital's fundamental contradictions are generalized and become harder to displace or defer in the medium to long term without significant 'blowback' effects. On the one hand, increasing integration offers clear benefits to capital in general. It enhances capital's capacity to defer and/or displace its internal contradictions by increasing the scope of its operations on a global scale; reinforcing its capacities to disembed certain of its operations from local material, social and spatio-temporal constraints; enabling it to deepen the spatial and scalar divisions of labour; creating more opportunities for moving up, down and across scales; commodifying and securitizing the future; and re-articulating different time horizons. It helps to emancipate the profit-oriented, market-mediated moment of capital accumulation from extra-economic and spatio-temporal constraints, increases the emphasis on speed, acceleration and turnover time, and enhances capital's capacity to escape the control of other systems insofar as these are still territorially differentiated and fragmented. And it enhances the economic and political power of capital, insofar as it weakens the capacity of organized labour to resist economic exploitation through concerted subaltern action in the economic, political and ideological fields and for which the 'multitude' alone is not an effective substitute. On the other hand, these enhanced capacities greatly reinforce tendencies to uneven development as the search continues for new spatio-temporal fixes which move the costs of capitalist contradictions elsewhere and/or into the future to create local zones of stability. It undermines state capacities to regulate economic activities within mainly national frameworks and thereby challenges both the territorial sovereignty and temporal sovereignty of states to make decisions about economic, political and social priorities and policies according to their own rhythms, routines and rules. And, insofar as it decreases the power of the working class, it increases inequalities of income and wealth, strengthens the potential for overproduction and weak demand, and, as is now widely recognized in critical political economy, creates the potential for financialization and finance-dominated accumulation as a driving force of even further – but destabilizing – world market integration. As the ultimate limit to capital is capital itself, the expansion and integration of a relatively unfettered (or disembedded) world market enhances the scope for its contradictions to be realized as well as for resistance to become global.

One reason for this is that, as the world market becomes ever more tightly integrated, the less scope there is to resolve crises by extending capitalist relations into previously marginal economic zones. This removes one of the classic spatial fixes that Harvey analysed in *The Limits of Capital* (1982). Thus crises will

> become more frequent and more violent, if only because, as the mass of production, and consequently the need for extended markets, grows, the world market becomes more and more contracted, fewer and fewer [new] markets remain available for exploitation, since every preceding crisis has subjected to world trade a market hitherto unconquered or only superficially exploited.
> (Marx, 1978, p. 228)

Some new directions

I have suggested that Marx's critique of political economy is more relevant to the present world and, hence, to critical CC research than many believe, especially those who regard Marx as 'a second-rate neo-Ricardian' or, at best, an acute observer and theorist of early industrial capitalism. The arc of Marx's planned six-book work on *Capital* would have moved from the abstract unity of the capital relation through factors making for its economic and political diversity in and across time-space to the world market as a totality with all of its interrelated moments. This indicates three possible forms of one-sided analysis: emphasis on abstract commonalities, institutional variation and pre-given laws of a closed world system.

CC research helps to sidestep the first analytical risk by focusing on the distinguishing features and dynamics of different economic regimes examined on a type-by-type or case-by-case basis; and it is particularly justified when major obstacles prevent the full integration of the separate parts of a world market that therefore exists more as the presupposition and horizon of capital accumulation than as a posited (realized) totality with its own emergent, totalizing dynamic. The downside of this middle-range focus is that it may forget that varieties *of* capitalism are varieties *in* capitalism. Moreover, the more these obstacles are attenuated, the more important it is to examine these parts in terms of their insertion into the emerging logic of a changing global political economy. Key issues here include their relative ecological dominance, hierarchical ordering, core–periphery linkages, relations of dependency and domination, embedding or decoupling, and patterns of adhesion and exclusion. Critical CC research deals with this in terms of the factors that shape international competitiveness and/or abilities to profit from global value chains. It also converges towards the variegated capitalism approach when it considers dependency relations and other forms of coupling and co-evolution.

Building on these studies and reconnecting them to the commonalities of capitalism can provide one means to go beyond CC research, critical or not, to consider the emerging dynamics of variegated capitalism in a world market. A final step in this movement, indicated in Marx's sixth book, would be to study whether, how and how far world market integration generalizes capital's basic contradictions, expands the potential scope and intensity of crises and makes it harder to overcome them. Even here critical CC research may help to explain the specific aetiology of crises, their uneven impact, the differential capacities to displace and/or defer crises and the different capacities for struggle and resistance.

Bibliography

Becker, U. (2009) *Open Varieties of Capitalism: Continuity, Change and Performances* (Basingstoke: Palgrave Macmillan).

Bruff, I. (2011) 'What about the Elephant in the Room? Varieties of Capitalism, Varieties in Capitalism', *New Political Economy*, 16:4, 481–500.
Gerstenberger, H. (2007) *Impersonal Power: History and Theory of the Bourgeois State* (Leiden: Brill).
Hall, P.A. and D. Soskice (eds.) (2001) *Varieties of Capitalism: The Institutional Foundations of Comparative Advantage* (Oxford: Oxford University Press).
Harvey, D. (1982) *The Limits to Capital* (Oxford: Blackwell).
Harvey, D. (2003) *A Brief History of Neoliberalism* (Oxford: Oxford University Press).
Jessop, B. (2011) 'Rethinking the Diversity of Capitalism: Varieties of Capitalism, Variegated Capitalism, and the World Market', in G. Wood and C. Lane (eds.), *Capitalist Diversity and Diversity within Capitalism* (London: Routledge), 209–37.
Jessop, B. (2013) 'Revisiting the Regulation Approach', *Capital & Class*, 37:1, 5–24.
Jessop, B. (2014) 'Capitalist Diversity and Variety: Variegation, the World Market, Compossibility and Ecological Dominance', *Capital & Class*, 38:1, 43–56.
Jessop, B. and N.-L. Sum (2006) *Beyond the Regulation Approach: Putting the Economy in Its Place in Political Economy* (Cheltenham: Edward Elgar).
Kannankulam, J. and F. Georgi (2014) 'Varieties of Capitalism or Varieties of Relationships of Forces? Outlines of a Historical Materialist Policy Analysis', *Capital & Class*, 38:1, 59–71.
Karadag, R. (2010) *Political Capitalisms: Power, Elites and the Economy in Turkey and the Philippines*, PhD dissertation (Cologne: University of Cologne).
Marx, K. (1967a) *Capital, Volume 1* (London: Lawrence & Wishart).
Marx, K. (1967b) *Capital, Volume 3* (London: Lawrence & Wishart).
Marx, K. (1973a) *Grundrisse: Foundations of the Critique of Political Economy (Rough Draft)* (Harmondsworth: Penguin).
Marx, K. (1973b) 'Introduction to the Contribution to the Critique of Political Economy'. In idem, *Grundrisse* (Harmondsworth: Penguin), 88–111.
Marx, K. (1976) 'Speech of Dr Marx on Protection, Free Trade, and the Working Classes', in *Marx-Engels Collected Works*, 6 (London: Lawrence & Wishart), 287–90.
Marx, K. (1978) *Wage Labour and Capital*, in *Marx-Engels Collected Works*, 9 (London: Lawrence & Wishart), 197–228.
Marx, K. and F. Engels (1976) 'The German Ideology'. In idem, *Marx-Engels Collected Works*, 5 (London: Lawrence & Wishart).
Myant, M. and J. Drahokoupil (2011) *Transition Economies: Political Economy in Russia, Eastern Europe, and Central Asia* (Hoboken, NJ: Wiley-Blackwell).
Nölke, A. and S. Claar (2013) 'Varieties of Capitalism in Emerging Economies', *Transformation: Critical Perspectives on Southern Africa*, 81/82, 33–54.
Reinert, E.S. (2007) *How Rich Countries Got Rich... and Why Poor Countries Stay Poor* (London: Constable).
Rosenberg, J. (2007) 'International Relations – the "Higher Bullshit": A Reply to the Globalization Theory Debate', *International Politics*, 44:4, 450–82.
Shonfield, A. (1965) *Modern Capitalism* (Oxford: Oxford University Press).
Shortall, F.C. (1994) *The Incomplete Marx* (Aldershot: Ashgate).
Sum, N.-L. and B. Jessop (2013) *Towards a Cultural Political Economy: Putting Culture in Its Place in Political Economy* (Cheltenham: Edward Elgar).

von Braunmühl, C. (1978) 'On the Analysis of the Bourgeois Nation State Within the World Market Context', in J. Holloway and S. Picciotto (eds.), *State and Capital: A Marxist Debate* (London: Arnold), 160–77.

Weber, M. (1961) *General Economic History* (New York: Collier).

Woo-Cumings, M. (ed). (1999) *The Developmental State* (Ithaca: Cornell University Press).

Wood, E.M. (2003) *The Empire of Capital* (London: Verso).

5
Critical Institutionalism in Studies of Comparative Capitalisms: Conceptual Considerations and Research Programme

Christian May and Andreas Nölke

Despite the criticisms to which institutionalist approaches in Comparative Capitalisms research (CC) have been exposed in recent years (see Coates and Bruff et al., in this volume), it would be unfortunate, in our view, to discard them altogether for the comparative analysis of capitalism. Instead of 'throwing out the baby with the bathwater', we suggest that building upon established concepts within institutional research and further developing them in a critical spirit is a fruitful way of finding 'new directions' for CC scholarship. To argue this point, and to show how it might be accomplished, is the purpose of this chapter.

In order to do so, we first clarify basic concepts such as 'institutions' and 'institutionalism' (in the first section); subsequently, we develop a critical-institutionalist CC research programme (in the second section); finally, we highlight some issues for empirical study (in the third section). We thereby seek to demonstrate that a critical, global CC agenda is able to respond to parts of the criticism articulated, in this volume without ignoring the rich results of the last two decades of institutionalist-inspired comparison of different models within modern capitalism. In contrast, we assume that particularly the combination of 'post-VoC' (Varieties of Capitalism) institutionalist and critical approaches makes for a valuable research programme (see also Gaitán and Boschi, in this volume). Saying that we wish to outline a research agenda means that we do not propose a particular method or theory, and nor do we seek to make specific empirical statements. Rather, we suggest which historical periods, countries, institutions and specific research questions should be addressed within a critical institutionalist framework, and why.

Institutions and institutionalism: Conceptual foundations from a critical perspective

Why, then, should we study institutions within the framework of a critical, global CC agenda?

- First, institutions enable us to grasp the structure of a particular economic order. They allow for a specific analysis of developments in capitalism, which is unfeasible on the systemic level. For instance, even if many observers agree that concepts such as 'financialization' can describe important features of early 21st-century capitalism, it often remains unclear how exactly these concepts materialize in reality (see Heires and Nölke, 2011). Institutionalist approaches make such broad-brush concepts more tangible, for example by linking them to specific institutions such as accounting standards (Nölke and Perry, 2007).
- Second, institutionalist approaches stake out a fruitful middle ground between the methodological extremes of holism and individualism. Holistic approaches (such as World System Theory) have a point when they argue that systems should be studied as wholes, rather than as mere ensembles of parts. However, they suffer from the problem of articulating research questions and research designs on specific issues. Individualistic approaches (such as neo-classical economics), in turn, are open to the reductionist fallacy of assuming that everything can be explained by going back to the properties of individual actors.
- Third, institutions constitute an auxiliary concept which is suitable for building a link between fundamental theories of the societal order and empirical research focused on specific cases. While the latter are often limited to descriptive accounts that do not help us to develop more general accounts of economy, politics and society, the former need to be 'translated' for being amenable to specific empirical studies. Institutions are a highly useful translation device.
- Fourth, and finally, regarding our more specific purpose of furthering critical research on the diversity of capitalism, the focus on institutionalist approaches has the advantage of making it possible to contribute to the body of knowledge already established in CC

scholarship (rather than discarding it altogether in a shift to, say, regulation theory, which represents a different combination of critical thinking and concern for institutions). Conversely, the results of the productive research activities of the last decade in the CC field can thus also be put to use for critical research projects.

In order to establish a critical-institutionalist CC research programme, however, it is necessary to critically inspect the theoretical baggage that comes with mainstream institutionalism and, where necessary, to develop alternative parameters that are in line with a critical understanding of research on capitalist diversity. Subsequently, we will do so by clarifying the notions of institutions, of institutionalism, of core capitalist institutions and of the usefulness of a comparative study of these institutions. We will put a specific focus on their proximity to some fundamental notions put forward by critical thinkers such as Marx.

What are institutions?

For the most part, existing institutionalist research does not pay much attention to theorizing the notion of institutions. Particularly more recent studies on institutional change (for example, Blyth, 2002; Mahoney and Thelen, 2010; Schmidt, 2010) treat institutions mostly as black boxes. Given this state of affairs it makes sense to take another look at some basic issues of institutionalist thought.

Institutions are, in the first instance, solutions to social coordination problems. This refers particularly to problems with the coordination of the societal division of labour (Berger and Luckmann, 1969). The notion of the division of labour refers to two fundamental aspects: first, humans are always social beings whose existence is mutually interdependent. Explanations of human action based on individual motives, as in neoclassical and rational choice models (including their 'institutionalist' versions), therefore constitutes what Marx (1974, p. 615) described as 'Robinsonades' which are part of bourgeois ideology. Second, the purpose of the division of labour lies in production and reproduction as 'basis of all social existence' (Cox, 1987, p. 1). In this context, people are not only able to maintain their reproduction but also to plan for the future and to improve their livelihood. Institutions help to stabilize this cyclical and dynamic process. For instance, they make sure that basic inputs are available, credit is being provided, and production works in a reliable manner.

Institutions therefore generate *typical* behaviour and people appear as *types* in the division of labour. The social division of labour assigns roles according to the position in the process of production and reproduction: 'The functions performed by the capitalist are only the functions of capital itself performed with consciousness and will... The capitalist functions only as capital personified... just as the worker only functions as the personification of labour' (Marx, 1976, p. 990). Typical patterns of behaviour become institutions when they are objectified as social facts, as the 'consolidation of our own product into an objective power over us' (Marx, 1973, p. 33). This enables the integration of new members of a society into the division of labour.

In most cases, typification and habitualization solve the most relevant coordination problems. Yet, we know of situations in which the problem of coordination is less a practical but rather a strategic one. Such problems of coordination often hamper collective action, which is, however, required for the division of labour. In these cases, action therefore has to be institutionalized by way of explicit rules of procedure. Such special instances of institutions can be modelled along game-theoretical lines and the different 'designs' can be assessed with respect to their efficiency (Scharpf, 1997).

What is institutionalism?

These two conceptions of institutions, the socio-theoretical and the game-theoretical, underlie different kinds of economic reasoning about institutions. The latter, more formal concept of institutions forms the backbone of 'new institutional economics' (NIE), which, especially through the work of Oliver Williamson, has had a strong influence on mainstream CC research (see, for example, Hall and Soskice, 2001, pp. 6–21). NIE subscribes to a rational choice perspective on institutions. Its conceptual apparatus, which includes notions such as transaction costs, bounded rationality, asset specificity and so on, treats institutions principally as contextual factors for the rational conduct of economic actors. The primary purpose of institutions, in this understanding, is to reduce uncertainty for cost-sensitive actors. VoC's framing of firms as economic actors (the 'relational view of the firm') translates this theoretical perspective into CC research. In a neo-classical, Walrasian logic capitalist forms achieve a state of equilibrium when their institutions provide actors with decisional confidence.

While NIE treats institutions as rules or organizations which constrain economic actions (see North, 1990), 'old institutional' or evolutionary economics conceives of them as historically and socially developed ways to manage real economic complexity, as 'settled habits of thought common to the generality of men' (Veblen, 1909, p. 626). In this perspective, institutions emerge from the practice of economic agents. The economy does not just consist of an ensemble of rational transactions but also represents a complex system, brought about by the multiple and contradictory developments in the process of growth (Veblen, 1998 [1898]). Hodgson (2006) referred to these two understandings of institutions as 'agent sensitive' vis-à-vis 'agent insensitive institutions' which form the base for a 'weak' and 'strong institutionalism' respectively (see also Coriat and Dosi, 1998). More importantly, the latter approach to institutions follows from a socio-theoretical perspective on the economy.

Which institutions are to be studied?

The old (or 'strong') institutionalism helps us to overcome some of the deficiencies of neo-classical game-theoretic concepts, but it does not, on its own, allow us to identify the specific capitalist institutions to be studied in the frame of a critical CC agenda. Rather, in this regard, we refer to basic social theory, in particular the critique of political economy developed by Marx. In contrast to the 'ascending' paradigm of neo-classical economics, Marx argued that economic reality is not produced by economic actors. Rather, he maintained that the actors themselves are constituted by the relations of production. To understand the economy, one must therefore study these relations. Marx suggested a focus on six dimensions: 'capital, landed property, wage-labor; the State, foreign trade, world market' (Marx, 1974, p. 7; see also Jessop, in this volume).

These dimensions comprise the fundamental institutional dimensions of capitalism, and they have become increasingly complex since the end of the 19th century (Cox, 1987). For instance, companies developed different forms of organization, in particular through the division of ownership and control. Moreover, the Great Depression highlighted the mutual dependency of capital and labour for continuing productivity and led to the rise of organized capitalism. Above all, capitalism came to require an institutionalized organization of productivity growth, both regarding constant capital (through technological innovation) and variable capital (through education and training). Thus, the institutional spheres on which VoC or late Regulation Approaches (RAs) choose to focus – corporate governance, financing of investments, industrial relations, innovation transfer, education and training regimes – are indeed historically grounded differentiations of the 'capital, landed property, wage-labour' triad identified by Marx. Yet, this reference also permits us to acknowledge that the dimensions which occupy centre-stage in conventional CC research do not exhaust the full spectrum which an institutional analysis of capitalism, in line with the critique of political economy, would require. Rather, they should be complemented by a focus on the institutions of the world economy and those of the state ('state, foreign trade, world market') (see Nölke, 2011a; May et al., 2014).

Why should we compare institutional configurations?

Why does it make sense analytically to divide capitalism into different institutional categories? Following the preceding remarks, the answer is relatively straightforward: because these institutions provide 'answers' to different problems. Institutions have causal effects of their own. However, what works in one institutional sphere might not necessarily work in another. The main reason for this is the real complexity of social and economic systems as such. Institutions are not isolated phenomena but always appear in the company of other institutions, and their effectiveness depends on how they work in concert. An institutionalist approach thus has to take the interrelation between parallel working institutions into account in order to make meaningful propositions about real-world phenomena.

One analytical concept to assess the causal effect of institutional configurations is that of *complementarity*, which refers to the functional 'fit' of institutions. Complementarity is an important institutional feature, because institutions can never be fully perfect or efficient. As soon as the problem to which they respond is tentatively solved, there is no need for further institutionalization – until new problems of coordination emerge (Berger and Luckmann, 1969; Schütz, 1962). Institutions thus help to solve problems in the short to medium term, but they cannot address problems that are yet to unfold, let alone the long-term problems that might evolve as a corollary side-effect of those shorter-term solutions. From a holistic perspective, institutions are always deficient; they are 'necessarily impure' (Hodgson, 1998, pp. 224–6). Their function depends crucially on their interaction with other institutions.

The nature of complementarity is hotly debated within CC circles (see Crouch et al., 2005). For example, Crouch distinguishes three ideal types, according to which institutions are complementary if they either compensate each other's deficits, are similarly organized, or if they mutually reinforce each other (Crouch, 2010). However, these are ideal-typical abstractions, often construed without reference to actually existing politico-economic institutions. We therefore reserve the notion of complementarity for functional interactions, rather than expanding it to comprise uniformity or isomorphism. What unifies both forms is a fundamentally institutional logic: institutions have an effect that is relatively independent from political or economic actors (Archer, 1995; Fleetwood, 2008). To conclude, institutionalism is an analytical approach in which institutions regularly exert causal powers upon economic structures. The differentiation of varying models of modern capitalism entails a degree of complexity in which institutions are functionally interrelated (Amin and Hausner, 1997; see also Jessop, in this volume). Institutionalism thus offers an explanatory model that is different from actor-centred theories. Its critical version understands institutionalization as a socializing mechanism which produces functional relations and dependencies that reach beyond individuals' horizons of action. From this perspective, the economy constitutes an 'open system' of institutional spheres, which goes beyond the reductionist conceptions of capitalism as 'market economies' (see Becker, 2009). Of special importance are the categories for the analysis of the relations of production, as well as those for the analysis of the complementarities between the institutions that govern those relations.

Foundations of critical institutionalism

Our promotion of a critical institutionalist research programme follows the common eponymous practice to label all institutional analyses as institutional*ism*, without therefore claiming to offer a full-fledged social theory. Such a programme should be critical in two respects: *internally*, by addressing the restrictions of contemporary institutionalist CC research, particularly with regard to its (i) temporal, (ii) cultural and (iii) spatial scope; and *externally*, by rejecting the liberal assumptions of the institutionalist mainstream and, based on the normative premises of a critical social theory, viewing capitalist political economies as founded upon asymmetrical power relations while also calling for a prominent role for the issues of equality (iv) and domination (v) in research agendas. These five demands will now be discussed in greater detail.

The temporal dimension: Historical emergence instead of institutional change

The concept of institutions helps to understand why, despite the vast array of potential actions, often the same actions are chosen again and again. The explanation of such forms of social stability is the main goal of any institutional analysis. Yet, many institutional analyses tend to obscure the fact that social structures – and the institutions that are part of them – are results of social practices. Instead, they treat them as 'objective' facts, and society merely appears as a given set of institutions. As a consequence, an overly static picture of our world emerges. This picture is problematic because it tends to universalize and extrapolate existing stabilities. It is not a consequence of the institutionalist approach as such, but of an almost completely ahistorical social theory that underpins many of its concrete manifestations.

Traditional institutional analyses interpret the possibilities for action and choice beyond institutionally established paths as mere results of their disruptions. Contemporary attempts to develop 'general' models of institutional change (see Mahoney and Thelen, 2010) are problematic because (radical) political action appears as 'disruption' and not as a social practice, which could and should be analysed with (other) scientific concepts and theories. We should not forget that societal dynamics are usually not explained by way of institutional theories, but with theories of power, conflict, action, stratification, and so on. Contemporary approaches to institutional change, however, attempt to explain social dynamics from *within* institutionalism at any cost, which results in overly descriptive and hermetically closed models. It is obviously insufficient to explain change though external shocks only. But if in contrast change is fully endogenized into institutionalist models, institutional theory is hyperbolized to a general social theory. This comes at the cost of obfuscating processes of socialization and their associated power relations.

We therefore call for an institutionalism that focuses more strongly on the differential emergence of institutions. Mainstream institutionalist CC research – just like its role models, neo-classical and institutional economics – cares relatively little about the historical emergence of institutions, let alone the conditions that gave rise to them. Yet, one must not forget that institutions are structural phenomena which are irreducible to actor preferences and strategies, and that these properties are results of successful socialization. For this reason, a critical institutionalist CC agenda should engage with the historical emergence of particular capitalist formations. Here, not only the development of different national formations matters, but also the stages of capitalist development that have a decisive influence on these various national formations (see Nölke and May, 2013). For this purpose, we find inspiration not only in the well-known economic anthropology of Polanyi (1978), but also within evolutionary economics (Veblen, 1998; Nelson and Winter, 1982; O'Hara, 2006; McDonough, in this volume), régulation theory (Boyer, 1990), and the classical theories of organized capitalism formulated by the likes of Hilferding, Naphtali and Sombart (Höpner, 2003; Nölke, 2012).

The cultural dimension: Ideology and habitus instead of ideas and discourses

Contemporary attempts to make institutionalist CC research more 'dynamic' (for example, Deeg and Jackson, 2007) often introduce some sort of liberal pluralism which not only contradicts the foundations of institutionalism but also abets a blurred vision of existing power relations. This tendency becomes particularly evident in recent works within what is termed 'constructivist' or 'discursive' institutionalism (for example, Blyth, 2002; Schmidt, 2010). Proponents of this orientation accuse existing institutional approaches of using models which are too static and thus account for change only by way of external shocks (Schmidt, 2010, p. 2). But they themselves *exclusively* deal with the phenomenon of institutional change, not with institutions or their configurations as such. Hence, institutions seem void of causal powers; they appear as neutral entities that can be shaped by political actors at random. For instance, in Mark Blyth's work ideas are reduced to 'policy ideas' or the ideas of epistemic communities or, more bluntly, of knowledge-producing elites. Colin Hay (in Bell, 2011, p. 906) rightly refers to such accounts as cases of 'voluntary idealism' that largely omit material conditions. It is this feature that makes these approaches largely unsuitable for critical institutional analyses of capitalism.

From our perspective, ideas and discourses should themselves be considered as institutions and therefore constitute subjects of critical institutional analysis (Searle, 2005). As seen above, institutions are always results of objectivation and, therefore, tend to hide their original purposes, including the associated problems and conflicts. Part of a critical analysis is therefore to unmask their genesis that occurred within a particular social relationship of forces (see also Kannankulam and Georgi, 2014). In a critical institutional perspective, ideas and discourses are analysed to lay bare the cognitive patterns, parlances and worldviews that are effective within an institutional arrangement. The critical institutionalist research programme can thereby draw inspiration from many approaches to ideology within the materialist tradition. According to these views, it is necessary to understand language and ideas as social products and less as individual resources for action. Here, more holistic approaches to discourse as well as theories of culture and ideology are of special utility. Subjective ideas are not 'free' but reflect relations of power

92 *Critical Perspectives and Debates*

and domination (Bourdieu, 1998). Ideologies and cultures give rise to logics of action that involve particular path dependencies and therefore have an enormous coordinative capacity. Ian Bruff, for instance, shows in his analysis of the changes in German and Dutch capitalism how a particular 'common sense' left only a small range of economic policies as meaningful options (Bruff, 2008).

The spatial dimension: Transnational dynamics and 'peripheral' capitalism instead of container comparison of Western societies

As little as the thesis of a uniform global capitalism holds true, the imagination of national economies as completely hermetic 'containers' that can only be shaken by external forces as a whole is equally misleading. In contrast, critical CC research treats capitalism as a 'multi-scalar' social relation. It follows that comparative research has to take the transnational dimension increasingly into account (see also Jessop, Wehr and Suau Arinci et al., in this volume). Transnational permeation – for example, through multinational enterprises – is especially important in peripheral capitalist formations. For this reason, critical institutionalism calls for looking beyond the capitalist centres and to turn the attention to the institutional particularities of non-Western capitalism (see also Ebenau, and Gaitán and Boschi, in this volume). This also has consequences for the choice of institutions to study.

A large part of institutionalist CC analyses dealt with traditional governance mechanisms in the fields of corporate governance, industrial relations and, more recently, skill formation (see, for example, Thelen, 2004), whereby they generally construed a limited variety of institutional options. This selection of institutions and the corresponding theoretical-analytical specialization was not least based on the researchers' preference for analysing developed economies in which the co-dependence between capital and labour had given rise to highly organized forms of capitalism. Beyond the centres, however, organized industrial relations are mostly less relevant. Even where they are not, they are often counterbalanced by large informal sectors, among other things. Moreover, even though peripheral capitalisms are for the most part to be considered genuine market economies, the market mechanism is often sidelined or limited in its reach by other modes of coordination such as reciprocity. Similar caveats apply for the role of the state, which is largely neglected in mainstream CC analyses of the capitalist centres but which is highly important for many peripheral economies (Nölke, 2011b; May et al., 2014). A critical institutionalism which seeks to account for actually existing models of capitalism beyond the centres of the world economy should therefore widen the spectrum of the institutions it studies and refrain from taking their concrete forms as givens.

Not only have the global economic balances changed over recent decades; the transnational dimension of modern capitalism has also greatly increased in importance, particularly through the increased impact of foreign direct investment on the development of national capitalist institutions (see also Drahokoupil and Myant, in this volume). Another important development has been the increase in importance of international institutions, especially the European Union (Wigger and Nölke, 2007; Nölke, 2008; Höpner and Schäfer, 2008). Until recently, these aspects have been by and large ignored by CC research. This situation reflects the long-established but highly problematic division between the Comparative and International Political Economy (IPE) subfields. Unlike CC, IPE engages much more with the development of capitalism beyond the centres, with cross-border relations of dominance and global economic institutions. Indeed, even mainstream institutionalist studies in International Relations and IPE have addressed the emergence and development of these institutions, although in doing so they have remained quite narrowly government-centred. This means that they have looked primarily at government preferences and intergovernmental negotiations in international institutions, an orientation which is hardly compatible with the aims of CC research. Transnationally oriented IPE studies which deal not only with intergovernmental but also private institutions appear much more useful (Wigger and Nölke, 2007; Nölke, 2008). But although the latter have been analysed extensively over the last years, the study of their effects on national capitalist systems continues to be neglected. Accordingly, we advocate a research agenda that brings CC and IPE back together, with a focus on transnational relations, to compensate for this particular weakness of institutionalist CC research (Nölke, 2011a; Bieling, 2014; see also Soederberg et al., 2005).

Equity instead of regulative efficiency

An institutionalism that pledges itself to a critical social science has to ask about the purpose of research: for which reason do we study institutions? Here we clearly depart from basic 'new institutional economics' assumptions that are inherent to much contemporary CC research. The reason is that, as stated above, we do not consider institutions necessarily as rational solutions which lead to the reduction of transaction costs. On the contrary: institutions are always imperfect entities and the results of political compromises (Amable, 2003, pp. 9–10). Critical theory, in contrast to problem-solving theory, examines the conditions that foster the emergence or construction of particular problems (Cox, 1981). Both regime theory and governance research adhere to the view that an intelligent design of institutions would facilitate efficient regulation and, therefore, the solution to 'global problems' (see critically Brand et al., 2000). Also within the CC field, especially in NIE-inspired perspectives, an approach to optimization is explicitly directed to the exploration of efficient institutional arrangements in terms of economic growth. Thus, by applying such a narrow focus regarding the 'outcomes' of institutions, mainstream CC work not only tends to exaggerate the success stories of capitalism, but also generalizes the standards for evaluating different forms of capitalism while ignoring questions of distributive equity. Nevertheless, the latter can in principle be studied within an institutionalist framework (see Lazonick and Mazzucato, 2013).

A critical perspective on institutions therefore asks the *cui bono?* question and stresses the relations of forces which form the core of institutions and their distributive function. Hence the question of social equity is part and parcel of a critical social science view of institutions (Berger and Luckmann, 1969, p. 127; Bourdieu, 1998), but has been insufficiently addressed in mainstream CC work (Jackson and Deeg, 2008, p. 693). Critical institutionalism takes a clear normative stance: since institutions preserve existing relations of forces, they can contribute to a problematic consolidation or even deepening of social inequalities. This becomes more of a problem when CC scholars deal with capitalisms in peripheral economies and their particularly dramatic relations of inequality (see Nölke, 2011b; Nölke and Vliegenthart, 2009; see also Gaitán and Boschi, and Suau Arinci et al., in this volume).

Power and domination: Institutional hierarchies instead of equilibrium analytics

Critical institutionalism is also a critique of power relations. In contrast to the creed of harmonious equilibria, it assumes that resources – and therefore creative possibilities – are unequally allocated: between capital and labour (see also Jessop, in this volume), between men and women (see also Lux and Wöhl, in this volume), or between the inhabitants of different world regions (see also Suau Arinci et al., in this volume). It is not least the 'stickiness', that is the relatively persistent organizational quality of institutions, which keeps such inequalities in place. Since the emergence of institutions takes place under conditions of socio-economic and political inequality, structural asymmetries exist within and between them. Therefore, following régulationist approaches (Boyer, 1990; Amable, 2003; see also McDonough, in this volume), we assume that institutional hierarchies always characterize political economies and must play an important role in CC research. As the historical development of capitalism has often brutally shown, stable economic orders do not necessarily depend on well-balanced institutions: rather, accumulation is very often sustained by sheer power (see also Wehr, in this volume). Thus, actors do not follow a supposed objective common good (such as growth), and there are fundamental lines of conflict between groups of actors. Within CC research, Bruno Amable stresses the central importance of the 'dominant social bloc' for the maintenance of an institutional order that reflects that bloc's interests (Amable, 2003, pp. 11–12; Amable and Palombarini, 2009). By defining the rules of the game, institutions always work to the advantage of a particular group – they always entail a concentration of power. Since they establish typical modes of behaviour, institutions make sure that the actions of the dominated remain calculable. Power and conflicts over the distribution of institutional advantages have to be accounted for in critical institutional analysis, but without turning into the pluralist opposite of assuming a constant yet ultimately undirected struggle over institutions. Institutions and the behaviour of the state depend on social relations of power and class relations. Practically, this implies an imperative to determine the functional units of state apparatuses, as well as to identify the relevant class fractions (see Nölke, 2011b, 2012; May et al., 2014).

Institutions and the analysis of capitalism: A research agenda

Contemporary CC research risks losing sight of its subject matter (Streeck, 2011). It is, however, in the fortunate position of being able to determine its subject very clearly: the capitalist mode of production. It constitutes the overarching order to which all institutional analysis must refer (Esser, 2000, p. 48). As Bohle and Greskovits (2009, p. 373) point out, a comparative analysis of capitalism has to be based upon a good theory of capitalism. A piecemeal institutionalism that only deals with a segment (such as the education system) must at least clarify its relation to the general capitalist system. Typologies are also merely analytical tools and should not become a subject on their own. For instance, whether Germany nowadays still constitutes a 'coordinated

96 *Critical Perspectives and Debates*

market economy' is less important than the fact that the fundamental relations of power within the German political economy have drastically shifted (Höpner, 2003; Bruff, 2015). Therefore, both the internal and the external critique of CC have to be developed further and to be linked up with relevant academic and socio-political discussions. In lieu of a summary, we formulate four theses for a critical research agenda and point to some of our own work, where we have tried to realize the agenda developed above in empirical research:

- Critical institutionalism must be *relevant*. Instead of ever more comparative studies of recent developments in the United Kingdom, Germany and Sweden on the basis of well-known OECD data, we call for the investigation of important contemporary problems, especially in transnational and historical perspective, in order to overcome the spatial and temporal limitations of existing CC research that were highlighted above. Studies furthering this perspective include the work on capitalisms beyond the OECD (May and Nölke, 2013; May et al., 2014), on the changes in finance capitalism after 2007–2008 (Nölke, 2009) and on the future of the Euro-capitalist project (Nölke, 2013).
- Critical institutionalism must be *accessible*. There is little purpose in artificially separating it from neighbouring disciplines if these actually pursue similar research interests. Here, we have heterodox, evolutionary and post-Keynesian economics, IPE, and parts of economic and financial sociology in mind, in particular when discussing the interaction between broad, long-term economic tendencies such as financialization with specific capitalist institutions on the national level (May, 2013; Heires and Nölke, 2014). At the same time, we call for a stronger reorientation towards classical political economy and its critique in the tradition of Marx, Veblen, Sombart, Hilferding, Schumpeter, Polanyi and others, particularly when moving from the international to the intertemporal comparison of organized capitalism and its alternatives (Nölke, 2012; May and Nölke, 2013).
- Critical institutionalism should know its *limitations*. The 'institution' has no significant ontological status. Its concrete manifestations – rules, norms, roles, organizations, or, within CC, corporate control, banking regulation, co-determination, the welfare state, and so on – do. For this reason, we call for mid-range theories as the objective of critical-institutional research. Institutions can, but must not, be turned into a concept to explain all social phenomena; nevertheless, combined with other theoretical elements such as the second image

perspective developed in IPE, CC concepts can help us understand, say, the foreign economic policies of emerging powers (Nölke, 2015).
- It follows that critical institutionalism aims to link CC back to *critical social theory*. Capitalism as such is the decisive subject matter to be explained. A critical institutionalism ideally acts as an 'auxiliary science' asking: 'What can we learn from the comparison of different capitalisms about capitalism as a social system?' For this, it is necessary to (again) place the above-mentioned key concepts of critical social science (power, domination, ideology, equity) much more prominently in comparative research, for instance when dealing with capitalism in large emerging markets (May, 2013; May et al., 2014).

Bibliography

Amable, B. (2003) *The Diversity of Modern Capitalism* (Oxford: Oxford University Press).
Amable, B. and S. Palombarini (2009) 'A Neorealist Approach to Institutional Change and the Diversity of Capitalism', *Socio-Economic Review*, 7:1, 123–43.
Amin, A. and J. Hausner (eds.) (1997) *Beyond Market and Hierarchy: Interactive Governance and Social Complexity* (Cheltenham: Edward Elgar).
Archer, M. (1995) *Realist Social Theory: The Morphogenetic Approach* (Cambridge: Cambridge University Press).
Becker, U. (2009) *Open Varieties of Capitalism: Continuity, Change and Performances* (Basingstoke: Palgrave Macmillan).
Bell, S. (2011) 'Do We Really Need a New "Constructivist Institutionalism" to Explain Institutional Change?' *British Journal of Political Science*, 41:4, 883–906.
Berger, P. and T. Luckmann (1969) *The Social Construction of Reality: A Treatise in the Sociology of Knowledge* (London: Penguin).
Bieling, H.-J. (2014) 'Comparative Analysis of Capitalism from a Regulationist Perspective Extended by Neo-Gramscian IPE', *Capital & Class*, 38:1, 31–43.
Blyth, M. (2002) *Great Transformations: Economic Ideas and Institutional Change in the Twentieth Century* (Cambridge: Cambridge University Press).
Bohle, D. and B. Greskovits (2009) 'Varieties of Capitalism and Capitalism Tout Court', *European Journal of Sociology*, 50:3, 355–86.
Bourdieu, P. (1998) *Practical Reason: On the Theory of Action* (Stanford: Stanford University Press).
Boyer, R. (1990) *The Regulation School: A Critical Introduction* (New York: Columbia University Press).
Brand, U., A. Brunnengräber, L. Schrader, C. Stock and P. Wahl (2000) *Global Governance* (Münster: Westfälisches Dampfboot).
Bruff, I. (2008) *Culture and Consensus in European Varieties of Capitalism: A 'Common Sense' Analysis* (Basingstoke: Palgrave Macmillan).
Bruff, I. (2015) 'Germany: Steady as She Goes?' in R. Westra, D. Badeen and R. Albritton (eds.), *The Future of Capitalism after the Financial Crisis: The Varieties of Capitalism Debate in the Age of Austerity* (Abingdon: Routledge).

Coriat, B and G. Dosi (1998) 'The Institutional Embeddedness of Economic Change', in B. Johnson and K. Nielsen (eds.), *Institutions and Economic Change: New Perspectives on Markets, Firms and Technology* (Cheltenham: Edward Elgar), 3–32.

Cox, R.W. (1981) 'Social Forces, States and World Orders: Beyond International Relations Theory', *Millennium*, 10:2, 126–55.

Cox, R.W. (1987) *Production, Power, and World Order: Social Forces in the Making of History* (New York: Columbia University Press).

Crouch, C. (2010) 'Complementarity', in G. Morgan, J. Campbell, C. Crouch, O.K. Pedersen and R. Whitley (eds.), *The Oxford Handbook of Comparative Institutional Analysis* (Oxford: Oxford University Press), 117–37.

Crouch, C., W. Streeck, R. Boyer, B. Amable, P. Hall and G. Jackson (2005) 'Dialogue on Institutional Complementarity and Political Economy', *Socio-Economic Review*, 3:2, 359–82.

Deeg, R. and G. Jackson (2007) 'Towards a More Dynamic Theory of Capitalist Variety', *Socio-Economic Review*, 5:1, 149–79.

Esser, H. (2000) *Soziologie: Spezielle Grundlagen. Band 5: Institutionen* (Frankfurt and New York: Campus).

Fleetwood, S. (2008) 'Institutions and Social Structures', *Journal for the Theory of Social Behaviour*, 38:3, 241–65.

Hall, P.A. and D. Soskice (2001) 'An Introduction to Varieties of Capitalism', in P.A. Hall and D. Soskice (eds.), *Varieties of Capitalism: The Institutional Foundations of Comparative Advantage* (Oxford: Oxford University Press), 1–68.

Heires, M. and A. Nölke (2011) 'Das neue Gesicht des Kapitalismus: Finanzkrise in Permanenz?' *Neue Gesellschaft Frankfurter Hefte*, 9:2011, 25–28.

Heires, M. and A. Nölke (ed.) (2014) *Die Politische Ökonomie der Finanzialisierung* (Wiesbaden: Springer VS).

Hodgson, G. (1998) 'Varieties of Capitalism and Varieties of Economic Theory', in B. Johnson and K. Nielsen (eds.), *Institutions and Economic Change: New Perspectives on Markets, Firms and Technology* (Cheltenham: Edward Elgar), 215–42.

Hodgson, G. (2006) 'What Are Institutions?' *Journal of Economic Issues*, 40:1, 1–25.

Höpner, M. (2003) 'Der organisierte Kapitalismus in Deutschland und sein Niedergang', in R. Czada and R. Zintl (eds.), *Politik und Markt* (Wiesbaden: VS), 300–24.

Höpner, A. and A. Schäfer (eds.) (2008) *Die Politische Ökonomie der Euopäischen Integration* (Frankfurt/Main: Campus).

Jackson, G. and R. Deeg (2008) 'From Comparing Capitalisms to the Politics of Institutional Change', *Review of International Political Economy*, 15:4, 680–709.

Kannankulam, J. and F. Georgi (2014) 'Varieties of Capitalism or Varieties of Relationships of Forces? Outlines of a Historical Materialist Policy Analysis', *Capital & Class*, 38:1, 59–71.

Lazonick, W. and M. Mazzucato (2013) 'The Risk-Reward Nexus in the Innovation-Inequality Relationship: Who Takes the Risks? Who Gets the Rewards?' *Industrial and Corporate Change*, 22:4, 1093–128.

Mahoney, J. and K. Thelen (2010) *Explaining Institutional Change: Ambiguity, Agency, and Power* (Cambridge: Cambridge University Press).

Marx, K. (1973) 'Die deutsche Ideologie', in K. Marx and F. Engels (eds.), *Werke* (Band 3) (Berlin: Dietz).

Marx, K. (1974) 'Zur Kritik der politischen Ökonomie', in K. Marx and F. Engels (eds.), *Werke* (Band 13) (Berlin: Dietz).
Marx, K. (1976) *Capital, Volume 1* (London: Penguin).
May, C. (2013) 'Die Dissoziation der BRICs im finanzialisierten Kapitalismus', *Peripherie*, 33:130/131, 264–86.
May, C. and A. Nölke (2013) 'Staatlich durchdrungener Kapitalismus in Indiens metropolitanen Zentren: Die Transformation eines Entwicklungsmodells und seine Schattenseiten', *der moderne staat*, 6:1, 85–104.
May, C., A. Nölke and T. ten Brink (2014) 'Institutionelle Determinanten des Aufstiegs großer Schwellenländer: Eine global-politökonomische Erweiterung der "Varieties of Capitalism"', in C. Jakobeit, F. Müller, E. Sondermann, I. Wehr and A. Ziai (eds.), *Politische Vierteljahresschrift*, 67–94.
Nelson, R. and S. Winter (1982) *An Evolutionary Theory of Economic Change* (Cambridge: Harvard University Press).
Nölke, A. (2008) 'Private Governance in International Affairs and the Erosion of Coordinated Market Economies in the European Union', *Mario Einaudi Center for International Studies Working Paper*, 03–2008 (Ithaca: Cornell University).
Nölke, A. (2009) 'Finanzkrise, Finanzialisierung und vergleichende Kapitalismusforschung', *Zeitschrift für Internationale Beziehungen*, 16:1, 123–39.
Nölke, A. (2011a) 'Transnational Economic Order and National Economic Institutions: Comparative Capitalism Meets International Political Economy', *MPIfG Working Paper*, 11/3 (Cologne: Max-Planck-Institut für Gesellschaftsforschung).
Nölke, A. (2011b) 'Die BRIC-Variante des Kapitalismus und soziale Ungleichheit: Das Beispiel Brasilien', in H.-J. Burchardt and I. Wehr (eds.), *Der verweigerte Sozialvertrag: Politische Partizipation und blockierte soziale Teilhabe in Lateinamerika* (Nomos: Baden-Baden), 137–52.
Nölke, A. (2012) 'The Rise of the B(R)IC Variety of Capitalism' – Towards a New Phase of Organized Capitalism?' in H. Overbeek and B. van Apeldoorn (eds.), *Neoliberalism in Crisis* (Basingstoke: Palgrave Macmillan), 117–37.
Nölke, A. (2013) 'Dampf ablassen! Plädoyer für einen seketiven Rückbau der europäischen Wirtschaftsintegration', *Ipg-Journal*, Dezember.
Nölke, A. (2015) 'Second Image Revisited: The Domestic Sources of China's Foreign Economic Policies (Introduction to the special issue)', *International Politics*, 52, forthcoming.
Nölke, A. and C. May (2013) 'Vergleichende Kapitalismusforschung im Zeitalter der Krise der Finanzialisierung: Vom inter-nationalen zum intertemporalen Studium ökonomischer Institutionen', *Zeitschrift für Außen- und Sicherheitspolitik*, 6:1, 51–70.
Nölke, A. and J. Perry (2007) 'The Power of Transnational Private Governance: Financialization and the IASB', *Business and Politics*, 9:3.
Nölke, A. and A. Vliegenthart (2009) 'Enlarging the Varieties of Capitalism: The Emergence of Dependent Market Economies in East Central Europe', *World Politics*, 61:4, 670–702.
North, D.C. (1990) *Institutions, Institutional Change and Economic Performance* (Cambridge: Cambridge University Press).
O'Hara, P.A. (2006) *Growth and Development in the Global Political Economy: Social Structures of Accumulation and Modes of Regulation* (London: Routledge).
Polanyi, K. (1978) *The Great Transformation: Politische und ökonomische Ursprünge von Gesellschaften und Wirtschaftssystemen* (Frankfurt: Suhrkamp).

Scharpf, F.W. (1997) *Games Real Actors Play. Actor-Centered Institutionalism in Policy Research* (Boulder: Westview).

Schmidt, V.A. (2010) 'Taking Ideas and Discourse Seriously: Explaining Change Through Discursive Institutionalism as the Fourth New Institutionalism', *European Political Science Review*, 2:1, 1–25.

Schütz, A. (1962) *Collected Papers, Vol. I: The Problem of Social Reality* (The Hague, Boston, London: Martinus Nijhoff).

Searle, J. (2005) 'What Is an Institution?' *Journal of Institutional Economics*, 1:1, 1–22.

Soederberg, S., G. Menz and P. Cerny (eds.) (2005) *Internalizing Globalization: The Rise of Neoliberalism and the Decline of National Varieties of Capitalism* (Basingstoke: Palgrave Macmillan).

Streeck, W. (2011) 'Taking Capitalism Seriously: Towards an Institutionalist Approach to Contemporary Political Economy', *Socio-Economic Review*, 9:1, 137–67.

Thelen, K. (2004) *How Institutions Evolve: The Political Economy of Skills in Germany, Britain, the United States and Japan* (Cambridge: Cambridge University Press).

Veblen, T. (1909) 'The Limitations of Marginal Utility', *Journal of Political Economy*, 17:9, 620–36.

Veblen, T. (1998 [1898]) 'Why Is Economics Not an Evolutionary Science?' *Cambridge Journal of Economics*, 22:4, 403–14.

Wigger, A. and A. Nölke (2007) 'Enhanced Roles of Private Actors in EU Business Regulation: The Case of Antitrust Enforcement', *Journal of Common Market Studies*, 45:2, 487–513.

6
Gender Inequalities in the Crisis of Capitalism: Spain and France Compared

Julia Lux and Stefanie Wöhl

In times of crisis, certain characteristics of the capitalist mode of production, social reproduction[1] and the symbolic realm of societal formation become more clearly visible than would otherwise be the case. Capitalism's inherent contradictions come to the fore and constructions of social norms that serve to reproduce the capitalist order may be rearranged or deepened. Additionally, '[o]nce a crisis strikes, inequalities are reinforced as the ability to respond to the shock differs between more powerful and weaker players' (Fukuda-Parr et al., 2013, p. 15). This includes the power asymmetries between capital and labour, as well as inequalities of gender and ethnicity. In the post-2007 world of crisis, it is therefore even more surprising that theoretical approaches in Comparative Capitalisms (CC) research continue to exclude the social construction of gender, ethnicity and gender inequality. Even though gender is sometimes part of the analysis, broader questions of social reproduction, the hegemonic gender order of states and societies and their interplay with firm-centred decisions, are not related to one another.

During times of capitalist crisis, the public–private divide and accompanying unpaid labour in the social reproduction of private households is often reinforced, as one of several dimensions of inequality, in order to secure the capitalist mode of production. A range of well-known feminist economics and political economy scholars have shown this, especially regarding the Asian crisis in the late 1990s and numerous crises in Latin America (Benería, 1992; Elson, 2010; Ferber and Nelson, 2003; Waring and Sumeo, 2010; Young, 2003). Therefore, we argue that a research agenda that encompasses gender and other relations of domination in order to improve our understanding of capitalist economies and societies, and their crises, is needed (see also Tilley, in this volume). The severity of a crisis can only be gauged satisfactorily if we look at what is happening at the core of capitalist societies, namely in social reproduction and gendered labour divisions. This chapter thus seeks to provide a gendered analytical framework, focusing on the effects of crises in Western capitalism. More specifically, it provides a gendered political economy and state-theoretical approach for uncovering the different effects of economic crisis on women and men (see also Lux, 2013; Wöhl, 2014). It thus outlines a perspective which is focused on normative constructions of gender and ethnicity, how these are reproduced in capitalist societies and thereby how they stabilize capitalist (re)production.

In discussing some of the gendered dimensions in contemporary analyses of capitalism and crisis, we argue for the importance of incorporating gender inequalities into critical CC research. Subsequently, we outline a framework for a gendered political economy analysis and then apply it to the cases of France and Spain in order to highlight the gendered effects of European crisis management.

Comparative Capitalisms: A gendered analysis of capitalism and crisis?

CC is a multifaceted research programme. A rough distinction can be made between (new) institutionalist and critical or (neo-)Marxist perspectives (Bruff et al., 2013; see also Coates and Ebenau et al., in this volume). The institutionalist literature is most prominently embodied in the Varieties of Capitalism (VoC) approach (Hall and Soskice, 2001). The general strengths and weaknesses of this approach have already been discussed in greater detail elsewhere (see Coates and Bruff et al., in this volume). What is important here is that one of the key omissions of the VoC approach is to blur the power asymmetries and gender inequalities that constitute the capitalist order as such. Since it misses a conception of the varying gender regimes of different welfare states (Walby, 2004), it also neglects how contradictions of the capitalist mode of production are buffered in the private sphere and reinforced at the same time, thus externalizing those contradictions onto women's unpaid work in social reproduction. Due to the focus on institutions and a rather narrow conception of how institutions are (re)produced over time (Bruff, 2011), the VoC approach is also badly equipped for an understanding of crises (see also Jessop and McDonough, in this volume).

The conception of crisis itself is less of a problem for critical-materialist approaches, as the crisis-prone nature of capitalism is inherent to such analysis. However, most of this research also neglects gender issues. Nevertheless, we argue that for understanding how severe a crisis is, it is particularly useful to look at gender relations. In times of crisis, the question arises whether gender norms are reproduced or change, due to men's losses of or cutbacks in paid employment. This may narrow down the gender employment gap, but often in an unfavourable way for both men and women. In the economic and financial crisis in the European Union (EU), for example, especially men were affected by job losses in a first phase from 2008 onwards, as the crisis hit male-dominated sectors such as finance, manufacturing and construction, but later women working in the public sector were strongly affected (Annesley and Scheele, 2011). This situation questions gendered household relations because many private households, especially in European Mediterranean welfare states, are still organized around a male breadwinner norm. This norm is challenged when men suddenly lose paid employment. Not only job losses, but also the prospect of unemployment and the reduction of paid employment may spread a feeling of insecurity across all household members. This has, for instance, led to more low-educated women in Spain taking up precarious employment to compensate for losses in family income (Gonzáles Gago and Kirzner, 2014). In most cases, women also take over more unpaid care and social reproductive work, as the case of Spain and other countries in crisis show (Waring and Sumeo, 2010). Jointly, these examples indicate that gendered norms and identities ('professional working men/caring women') may be rearranged while at the same time deepened during times of crisis.

Critical CC research therefore needs a gendered understanding of crises in capitalism. It has already been noted that conventional CC perspectives exaggerate differences between different models of capitalism, in contrast to their commonalities: 'there are varieties *of* capitalism, but they are varieties *in* capitalism as well' (Bruff, 2011, p. 482; italics in original). In this vein, we suggest that gender inequalities are to be considered one of the commonalities of different models of capitalism. What differs, in turn, is the form and extent to which gender inequalities and norms are inscribed into societies. Gender relations play an ambiguous role in capitalist accumulation: on the one hand, they have stabilizing effects by externalizing social reproduction and care work to private households, especially in times of crisis, and thus bolster the accumulation process. On the other hand, they have a destabilizing potential as those externalization processes and gender inequalities are questioned and challenged by various individuals and social groups.

The capitalist mode of production is reinforced by different gender regimes and their mode of social reproduction during crises. Therefore, we need to analyse how different welfare regimes rely on women's unpaid work while the economic situation deteriorates and crisis reactions are dominated by cutting back the public sector and public spending (Glassner, 2010). Furthermore, in reaction to higher unemployment in many countries, women are also pushed out of the labour market into unpaid domestic work. Different gender regimes thus lead to varying policy and institutional responses.

Analysing gender inequalities as constitutive of capitalism and the gendered effects of capitalism remains an end in itself for feminist research, especially with regard to transformative social change (cf. Fraser, 2014). Accordingly, in the following we refer to a range of gendered analyses of welfare states, the political economy, labour markets and economic crisis, to unveil the gendered effects of capitalist crises.

Capitalist crises: Towards a gendered analysis

As many feminist scholars have shown, political economies are hierarchically structured along the lines and intersections of race, class, gender and a heterosexual-normative gender order (see, for example, Bedford and Rai, 2010). Therefore, the relations of forces within nation states, their specific gender regime and gendered symbolic order must be considered when seeking to understand which hegemonic actors and institutions play a role in reshaping or modernizing hierarchical heteronormative gender orders on the supranational and nation-state level, in the distribution of labour and in gendered social reproduction. The interplay of international institutions such as the International Monetary Fund (IMF), the World Bank and finance ministries of individual nation states often shape policies in a neoliberal way, as is evidenced, for instance, in the structural adjustment programmes which have been implemented throughout the 'Global South' in the past (Bergeron, 2011). Diane Elson, among others, has warned against long-lasting depletion in social reproduction and conceptualized how the impact of financial crises could be analysed for developing countries (Elson 2010; also see Rai et al., 2014).

Since recent trajectories in developing countries might not be structurally homologous to those within the EU, it is an open question whether these theoretical frameworks could be applied to the latter's different gender regimes. However, one common feature is that private households often adjust in reaction to economic downturns by using unpaid labour 'to replace services that had been purchased in markets before the crisis' (Fukuda-Parr et al., 2013, p. 22). More pressure on individuals, especially women, is thus a widespread aspect of economic crises. Some small-scale studies exist, which have studied the impact of economic crises on social reproduction in households in Mexico City (Benería, 1992), in Indonesia (Knowles et al., 1999) and for informal sector workers in ten cities of the world since 2008 (Horn, 2009). All of these studies show increasing unpaid care work by women and girls, as well as increasing informal paid work of women in the private sector (Elson, 2012). In Indonesia, the Philippines and Thailand, women and children in poor households were affected by health problems because of the need to reduce food expenses and to eat less (Knowles et al., 1999). Women of lower class positions and their children are particularly badly affected by austerity measures in times of crisis. In the case of the EU, women have been hit harder in comparison to men in the years since the emergence of the Eurozone crisis in 2010. This is due to their already-existing lower income and their tendency to be employed in the public sector, which has been cut back severely in member states (such as Greece) receiving financial support from the so-called Troika (European Central Bank, IMF and European Commission) (Antonopoulos, 2009).

The symbolic realm of ideas also plays a vital role as a culturally constructed gendered order, especially during times of crisis. This is because assumptions of competitiveness, risk affinity, liquidity, growth and austerity – to name but a few – are highly gendered masculinized codes and imaginations (de Goede, 2004; Griffin, 2012). Stereotypical gender assumptions and a specific form of neoclassical-oriented economic knowledge underpin the discourse around the implemented austerity policies. This implies that the neoliberal economic rationality which governs the austerity strategies, strongly centred on competitiveness and growth, neglects gender equality policies such as gender budgeting and gender mainstreaming, despite the fact that all member states have committed to implementing these measures at all levels of policymaking (Karamessini and Rubery, 2014). As Shirin Rai and Georgina Waylen (2013, p. 23) remark:

> [I]n times of crisis, the focus on restoring growth continues to displace the debates on gender justice. Feminist work continues to inhabit the margins of mainstream economics, development studies,

and political economy as well as policymaking at the national and international levels.

Women are also disproportionately affected by macroeconomic austerity policies. For example, questions of social reproduction, public health and welfare services are not even considered within the new deficit and debt thresholds inscribed in the EU's new economic governance measures that were formulated in response to the crisis. The negative effects of austerity policies on women, on women's labour market participation and on EU member states' social welfare service quality have been the subject of recent feminist analysis (see, for example, Karamessini and Rubery, 2014). Nevertheless, the changes and strategies in household social reproductive work, and changes occurring in gendered subjectivities and norms therein, need to be analysed further. Such a focus on the micro-level of private households, and how they are affected by macroeconomic and national-level decisions, is necessary so as to capture the possible changes in gendered norms and perceptions of responsibility for social reproductive work. As Bakker and Silvey (2008, p. 5) point out:

> [S]ocial reproduction lends a unique perspective to understandings of the transformation in the global political economy precisely because of its simultaneous focus on caring and provisioning in the everyday and its relationship to policies and decisions made at the national and international levels.

This is why a comparative analysis of capitalist crisis must encompass the unpaid social reproductive work of women (and men), as well as the effects of crisis on labour market participation and the cultural constructions of gendered norms that go along with them.

Another area which needs more analysis is the role of the state in these processes. Feminists have often focused on how '[g]lobal neoliberal restructuring' (Marchand and Runyan, 2011, p. 3) has led to a privatization of public services (education, health, pensions, childcare) in the past decades. However, the state is more than just public services, significant as they may be for our analysis. For instance, neoliberalism has also had a normative influence on democratic institutions themselves, insofar as neoliberal ideas question the liberal tradition that it is the state that governs the economy and not the economy that sets normative standards for the state, democracy and society (Wöhl, 2011). We can see this today in the way that the main democratic institutions within the EU are divested of their powers: member states who signed the Fiscal Compact have agreed to let the European Commission supervise their national budgets and, before their national parliaments are consulted, respond to suggestions made by the Commission for budget consolidation, which often imply austerity measures (Fischer-Lescano and Oberndorfer, 2013).

This highlights the need to discuss the financial and economic crisis, with its effects on gendered social reproduction and labour market participation of women and men, within a gendered state-theoretical framework that takes processes of global and regional governance into account. In the following, we investigate particularly the effects on different gender regimes (Bakker and Gill, 2003; Sauer and Wöhl, 2011). Due to space constraints, we cannot outline this in detail. We will therefore focus on two different gender regimes, those of France and Spain, and their relation to these countries' model of capitalism and the reactions to the crisis in the EU.

Gender implications of EU crisis governance

As we have shown, in times of economic crisis the public–private divide tends to be reinforced, and policies ignore gender concerns even more than before. Rather, the focus is mainly on restoring growth, consolidating state debt in a restrictive manner and regaining competitiveness. A sense of urgency is created, which means that gender equality and other 'optional' concerns (such as the environment) are marginalized. The focus on austerity also inscribes a masculine hegemonic symbolic order into neoliberal crisis management. This has resulted in EU governance measures such as the 'Sixpack' legislation and the 'European Semester', which focus on productive sectors and state budgets at the expense of social welfare and needs, gender equality and gender budgets (for more details, see Wöhl, 2014). In the following case studies, we review the effects of this new supranational economic governance regime, which some authors describe as 'authoritarian neoliberalism' (see, for example, Bruff, 2014).

The case of Spain

The Spanish model of capitalism has traditionally relied on a strong male-breadwinner labour market tradition, although changes towards a dual-earner model have taken place. Nevertheless, the social security system still supports the full-time employment norm as a condition for receiving full benefits (Gonzáles Gago and Kirzner, 2014, p. 229). Even

108 *Critical Perspectives and Debates*

though changes to promote gender equality have been initiated since the end of the Franco dictatorship, for instance through the creation of the *Instituto de la Mujer* in 1982 and the introduction of the right to divorce in 1981, progress towards gender equality was rather slow (even after Spain's accession to the European Community in 1986, after which time directives from the supranational European level supported attempts to introduce gender equality policies). For example, in March 2007 a law to support equality between women and men was passed by the parliament, and a Ministry for Equality that was supposed to support the programme for gender equality between 2008 and 2011 was established. Yet, allegedly due to financial reasons, this ministry was closed again in October 2010 (Castellanos Serrano and Gonzáles Gago, 2013, p. 211).

This highlights the politics around gender equality policies in Spain: they seem to be affordable only in times of economic stability and growth. Moreover, progress was slow even in the 1995–2007 period, when Spain was considered a dynamic economy with relatively high GDP growth rates (which averaged 3.7 per cent per year). Until 2007, Spain was thus seen as an example within the EU, creating one out of three new jobs in the EU, and such increases in employment were especially notable in tourism and construction. Spain also experienced a wave of immigration, leading to a cultural and economic modernization and to more women entering the paid labour market. However, the gendered division of labour and social reproductive work only changed slowly. Men still spent most of their time in paid employment and leisure, while women were more often employed in short-term and part-time occupations and undertook care work. Spain's tradition of a segmented labour market and a high rate of structural unemployment remained largely intact, meaning that cyclical downturns in the national economy could still have severe effects (López and Rodríguez, 2011). This meant that, although the Spanish economy was able to rely on certain industrial sectors before 2008 and on asymmetries within the labour market, the positive panorama changed dramatically after 2008.

Mortgage debt rates in private households soared to very high levels, while Spanish exports suffered a decline of over 20 per cent in 2009. Between 2012 and late 2013, Spain received support from the European Stability Mechanism to counter financial instability (ibid.). Already in 2009, Antonopoulos (2009, p. 23) predicted that 'income poor households will also witness a rise in women's time poverty', since women and girls are more likely to take over care work in private households, caring for elderly and sick family members at home while also trying to compensate for the loss of men's paid work by entering the labour market. In particular, female immigrants, for example from Ecuador, often take over social reproductive work in households that are not their own, meaning that these women and their families are affected by austerity measures due to fewer households being willing or able to pay for such work (Hererra, 2012). But not only immigrant women are affected. Many Spanish, highly educated young women and men now leave the country to find jobs in other EU member states or overseas. After the subprime mortgage crisis in 2008, women were also disproportionately affected by not being able to repay mortgage loans and were consequently evicted from housing together with their families.

In the meantime, Germany and Spain signed a bilateral agreement on youth vocational training, because over 55 per cent of Spanish people between 16 and 24 years are unemployed and have no prospect of finding employment in Spain. Taxes have been raised and, simultaneously, cuts in public spending have been implemented, with the biggest of the latter affecting education and health services (Gonzáles Gago and Kirzner, 2014, p. 242). The one-time payment of €2,500 for the birth of a child, introduced in 2008, was cancelled and the retirement age will be raised successively from 65 to 68 years. The increase in parental leave for fathers from 13 to 28 days was suspended and the minimum wage was not adjusted for inflation. The pension reform increased the years needed before being entitled to these benefits, and loans in the public sector were cut by at least 5 per cent. Partly as a result of these policies, the risk of falling into poverty had risen to 21.8 per cent by 2011, and by the end of 2010 fixed-term employment contracts in Spain were twice as high as the EU average (as a proportion of all jobs).

The increase in poverty and precarious employment was clearly gendered. For example, in 2012 the gender pay gap was estimated at 17.8 per cent (Eurostat, 2012), slightly above the EU average. Moreover, although there was a similar proportion of men and women on fixed-term contracts, with women at 25.9 per cent and men at 23.8 per cent in the last quarter of 2010, the proportion of part-time work stood at 23.4 per cent for women compared to 5.3 per cent for men (Castellanos Serrano and Gonzáles Gago, 2013, p. 208). Compounding this was the aforementioned dissolution of the equality ministry, which meant that no efforts were made to implement gender budgeting in consolidation packages. Since the *Partido Popular* came into government in 2011, even the gender parity within the Spanish government was abolished, with the gender relation in cabinet changing to four women and nine men (Castellanos Serrano and Gonzáles Gago, 2013, p. 212).

All in all, the government's response to the crisis has especially affected women of lower class status, immigrant women and young people. The above-mentioned cuts and policy changes will have further severe effects on the time constraints, working conditions and paid employment for these groups. At the same time, though, alternative forms of economy, such as community kitchens, have been established. The growth of community organizing, for example with the national *Indignados* movement which began on 15 May 2011 and with the *Plataforma de Afectados por la Hipoteca* (PAH, Platform of Those Affected by Mortgage Debt), gained strong momentum and eventually forced the Spanish parliament to reconsider a law on housing evictions (Wöhl, 2013). Effective strategies to prevent housing evictions were also supported by the population and especially those responsible for executing them, such as local firefighters. Resistance against housing evictions and other government decisions concerning austerity has also led to nationwide demonstrations, such as a general strike in November 2012 and assemblies in front of the houses of parliament. This was strongly criticized by the governing conservative *Partido Popular* which passed several laws that, if implemented, could have the effect of undermining the right to free assembly and other basic democratic rights (ibid.). Hence the crisis not merely reproduced gender inequality in new or modified forms, the nature of the austerity measures meant that resistance to such legislation, and the undemocratic attempts to manage them, is also gendered.

The case of France

The French model of capitalism, welfare state and gender regime is difficult to conceptualize since, in many established categorizations, it falls between clusters. As a model of capitalism, France belongs to the continental family, with a tradition of state-organized structures in many parts of the economy (Schmidt, 2003). In the last decades, however, changes have taken place, including a growing degree of financialization and a stronger transnationalization of French firms (Jany-Catrice and Lallement, 2012, p. 104). This model of state-led capitalism is coupled with a strong welfare state that is often classified as 'mixed', combining both Bismarckian and liberal elements (Vail, 2004), as well as a strong natalist element – that is, pro-birth policies. All in all, the resulting gender regime is ambiguous, as we will outline below (Gregory and Milner, 2008, p. 65).

The notion of 'republican universalism', which underpins French political culture and proclaims the equality of all individuals, stands in stark contrast to persisting gender inequalities. It also makes it difficult for differences between individuals or social groups to be pointed out (Lépinard and Mazur, 2009, p. 248). The number of women in politics is low and only slowly increasing, not least because the country's political and economic elite is formed in masculinized circles of the *Grandes Écoles*. While the gap between women's and men's employment rates is small compared to many other countries – 9.1 per cent in 2012, as opposed to an average of 12.9 per cent across the EU (Eurostat, 2012) – inequalities in care responsibilities persist (Gregory and Milner, 2008, p. 66).[2]

This is coupled with the natalist tradition, which implies an acceptance for the state to intervene in family matters through pro-birth policies, especially with strong financial support for the third child and the provision of (full-time) childcare from an early age onwards. School hours also allow for the labour market participation of mothers (Hantrais and Ackers, 2005). Female labour market participation is, however, often characterized by atypical employment, especially part-time work, even though actual differences in working hours between part-time and full-time employment are smaller than in most other European countries. Furthermore, job segregation is a constitutive part of women's labour market participation. At 14.8 per cent (in 2011), the gender pay gap in France is only slightly lower than the 16.2 per cent average in the EU-27 as a whole (Eurostat, 2012). The ambiguity of the French gender regime thus lies in the contrast between, on the one hand, the rhetorical equality of all French citizens, a comparatively high labour market participation of women paired with the highest fertility rate in Europe and a less rigid public–private divide (given that childcare is seen as a collective responsibility), and, on the other hand, low levels of female political representation, unequal pay, job segregation and disadvantaged labour market positions for women, and finally the persistence of traditional roles with regard to unpaid domestic work.

The global economic crisis hit France in a specific way. It was one of the European economies that was affected quite early through the financial market contagion channel, which transferred developments in the United States to Europe and other parts of the world. However, the specificities of the French banking sector meant that the actual economic impact was comparatively modest: in 2008 and 2009, GDP contracted by a combined 3.2 per cent, one of the lowest (negative) scores in Europe. In 2010, the GDP development was positive again (+1.7 per cent). Since then, however, growth has not really picked up (2011: +2 per cent;

2012: ±0 per cent; 2013: +0.2 per cent), and unemployment levels rose from 7.8 to 10.2 per cent between 2008 and 2012 (Eurostat, 2012).

As in Spain, the unfolding of the crisis in France was accompanied by protests and strikes. Incidents of 'bossnapping' received particularly high levels of media coverage. This kind of action was performed by blue-collar workers trying to achieve ameliorations in the social plans concluded at many manufacturing plants in France (Hayes, 2012, p. 188). In these cases, the victims of the crisis that turned to protest against their situation and the management of this situation by factory bosses seemed to be predominantly male, with limited opportunities for women to become visible as either victims of the crisis or actors in protest (Oeser and Tourraille, 2012). Gendered issues related to the crisis were also silenced at government level, due to the absence of a minister for women under the Sarkozy presidency (2007–2012). In contrast, in early 2014 the new women's minister in Ayrault's cabinet (and also in the Valls cabinet that followed in April 2014), Najat Vallaud-Belkacem, succeeded in pushing a new law on the equality of men and women through parliament. This includes, among other things, the introduction of 'Daddy months' to raise the number of men taking paternity leave (and increase the length of this leave), efforts to close the gender pay gap and other measures to reduce professional inequality (Assemblée Nationale, 2014). At the same time, teaching 'gender theory' in school became a hotly debated and contested topic.

Nevertheless, as with Spain, the government's and also the EU's focus is on public budgets and labour market participation. Labour market participation is thereby constructed as the only way out of poverty, social exclusion and economic dependency on another person. This focus, however, hides from view the different forms of labour market participation that often do not prevent poverty (the 'working poor') or economic dependence on others. This is also why a discourse on unemployment levels is too limited in order to grasp the specific impact of the crisis on female labour market participation (Milewski, 2010). As pointed out above, the gendered impact of social cuts needs to be taken into account, yet often it is not. This is particularly important in France, where a complex social security system sometimes makes it difficult to anticipate the effects of certain policies, especially where these are more indirect. For example, because young people are excluded from many social benefits and suffer from a high level of unemployment due to the crisis, they have to rely on their families, which in turn tends to put greater strain on women. As a result, the segmentation of the labour market combined with a high, crisis-induced unemployment rate turned out to be particularly problematic for vulnerable groups such as young people, migrant workers and women (Zemmour, 2010).

While this constitutes a basic similarity with the Spanish case, the French government's response to the crisis has not been as harsh on women as those observed in other countries such as Spain and the United Kingdom (Annesley and Scheele, 2011). This may in part be explained by the normalization of women's labour market participation and by a discourse of equality which promotes a more egalitarian symbolic gender order. Nevertheless, gender stereotypes remain strong in French society: the discourse of universal equality that seemingly knows no gender, race or class often hides from view persisting inequalities, and in doing so it counteracts feminist ambitions. We can conclude that the crisis has not thoroughly challenged the gender relations and gender inequalities characteristic of French capitalism. Therefore, although the crisis has pointed to the potential fragility of France's gender order through its economic and social impacts, underlying inequalities such as the externalization of instabilities into the private sphere have not been politicized.

Conclusions

As we have shown, gender regimes differ across distinct models of capitalism. Due to the fact that Spain was hit harder by the financial crisis, the reactions to the crisis also have a stronger impact, reinforcing gender inequalities in social reproduction and downgrading the quality of work for women, men and especially young people. The situation in France differs, since the crisis has not hit the economy as hard; while the gender regime remains unequal, it has not been reinforced further. Apart from economic factors, we have also shown that it is necessary to look at the power relations in different countries, as well as the norms surrounding their respective gender regimes. In Spain, supranational actors have played a more prominent role in policymaking than in France. Furthermore, the conservative government in Spain has established different political priorities with regard to the promotion of gender equality than its new socialist counterpart in France. In addition, trade unions have been thoroughly weakened in Spain while banks and enterprises have regained their foothold in politics; in France, the situation has been slightly more positive for progressive movements on the left of the political spectrum – although the far right party *Front National* seems to have benefited even more.

When comparing different models of capitalism and the impact of the crisis, it is important to look at power relations rooted in capitalist social and institutional structures, the relation of political forces to one another and how crisis measures are embedded in the hegemonic order of masculine norms. All in all, in Spain and France the crisis has not challenged gender inequalities and neoliberal political hegemony has been restored, even though many observers saw a window of opportunity to abolish neoliberal policies at the beginning of the crisis. In this chapter, we have sought to show that the commonalities in models of capitalism non-coincidentally include gender inequalities, even though different gender regimes imply differences in how such inequalities manifest themselves, for example in the political reactions to economic crises. An analysis that seeks to compare contemporary models of capitalism should be not only aware of these commonalities but also shed light on the differences, including the social effects of government policies. Otherwise, a comprehensive and satisfactory understanding of the (dys)functionalities of different models of capitalism, which critical CC research seeks to provide, will remain difficult to achieve.

Notes

1. In our view, social reproduction comprises affective labour such as caring for dependents and the elderly, cooking, washing, cleaning, time for leisure and replenishment and social reproductive work that includes the wider community. Social reproduction within a neo-Gramscian theoretical framework, moreover, encompasses the reproduction of the human labour force, situating social reproduction within the global political economy and its means of production (Bakker and Gill, 2003).
2. In absolute figures, 68 per cent of men in the age cohort 25–64 years were employed, compared to just under 60 per cent of women in the same cohort.

Bibliography

Annesley, C. and A. Scheele (2011) 'Gender, Capitalism and Economic Crisis: Impact and Responses', *Journal of Contemporary European Studies*, 19:3, 335–47.

Antonopoulos, R. (2009) 'The Current Economic and Financial Crisis: A Gender Perspective', *Levy Economic Institute Working Paper*, no. 562, available at: http://hdl.handle.net/10419/31580 (last accessed 23 April 2013).

Assemblée Nationale (2014) 'Projet de loi adopté par le Sénat pour l'égalité entre les femmes et les hommes'. No. 1380, available at: http://www.assemblee-nationale.fr/14/projets/pl1380.asp (last accessed 30 January 2014).

Bakker, I. and S. Gill (eds.) (2003) *Power, Production and Social Reproduction: Human In/security in the Global Political Economy* (Basingstoke: Palgrave Macmillan).

Bakker, I. and R. Silvey (eds.) (2008) *Beyond States and Markets: The Challenges of Social Reproduction* (New York: Routledge).

Bedford, K. and S.M. Rai (2010) 'Feminists Theorize International Political Economy', *Signs*, 36:1, 1–18.
Benería, L. (1992) 'The Mexican Debt Crisis: Restructuring the Economy and the Household' in L. Benería and S. Feldmann (eds.), *Unequal Burden: Economic Crises, Persistent Poverty and Women's Work* (Boulder: Westview Press), 83–104.
Bergeron, S. (2011) 'Governing Gender in Neoliberal Restructuring: Economics, Performativity, and Social Reproduction', in M.H. Marchand and A.S. Runyan (eds.), *Gender and Global Restructuring: Sightings, Sites, and Resistances* (2nd ed.) (London: Routledge), 66–77.
Bruff, I. (2011) 'What about the Elephant in the Room? Varieties of Capitalism, Varieties in Capitalism', *New Political Economy*, 16:4, 481–500.
Bruff, I. (2014) 'The Rise of Authoritarian Neoliberalism', *Rethinking Marxism*, 26:1, 113–39.
Bruff, I., M. Ebenau, C. May and A. Nölke (eds.) (2013) *Vergleichende Kapitalismusforschung: Stand, Perspektiven, Kritik* (Münster: Westfälisches Dampfboot).
Castellanos Serrano, C. and E. González Gago (2013) 'Wirtschaftskrise, Politik, Protest und Geschlecht in Spanien', in I. Kurz-Scherf and A. Scheele (eds.), *Macht oder ökonomisches Gesetz? Zum Zusammenhang von Krise und Geschlecht* (Münster: Westfälisches Dampfboot), 206–25.
de Goede, M. (2004) 'Repoliticizing Financial Risk', *Economy and Society*, 33:2, 197–217.
Elson, D. (2010) 'Gender and the Global Economic Crisis in Developing Countries: A Framework for Analysis', *Gender & Development*, 18:2, 201–12.
Elson, D. (2012) 'Social Reproduction and the Global Crisis', in P. Utting, R. Varghese Buchholz and S. Razavi (eds.), *Global Crisis and Transformative Social Change* (Basingstoke: Palgrave Macmillan), 63–80.
Eurostat (2012) *Employment in Europe: Recent Trends and Prospects* (Luxembourg: DG Employment and Social Affairs), available at: http://epp.eurostat.ec.europa .eu/portal/page/portal/statistics/search_database (last accessed 13 December 2013).
Ferber, M. and J. Nelson (eds.) (2003) *Feminist Economics Today: Beyond Economic Man* (Chicago: University of Chicago Press).
Fischer-Lescano, A. and L. Oberndorfer (2013) 'Fiskalvertrag und Unionsrecht: Unionsrechtliche Grenzen völkervertraglicher Fiskalregulierung und Organleihe', *Neue Juristische Wochenschrift*, 66:1/2, 9–14.
Fraser, N. (2014) 'Behind Marx's Hidden Abode: For an Expanded Conception of Capitalism', *New Left Review*, 2:86, 55–72.
Fukuda-Parr, S., J. Heintz and S. Seguino (2013) 'Critical Perspectives on Financial and Economic Crises: Heterodox Macroeconomics Meets Feminist Economics', *Feminist Economics*, 19:3, 4–31.
Glassner, V. (2010) 'The Public Sector in Crisis', *European Trade Union Institute Working Paper*, 7/2010 (Brussels: European Trade Union Institute).
González Gago, E. and M.S. Kirzner (2014) 'Women, Gender Equality and the Economic Crisis in Spain', in M. Karamessini and J. Rubery (eds.), *Women and Austerity: The Economic Crisis and the Future for Gender Equality* (London: Routledge), 228–47.
Gregory, A. and S. Milner (2008) 'Fatherhood Regimes and Father Involvement in France and the UK', *Community, Work & Family*, 11:1, 61–84.

Griffin, P. (2012) 'Gendering Global Finance: Crisis, Masculinity, and Responsibility', *Men and Masculinities*, 16:1, 9–34.
Hall, P.A. and D. Soskice (eds.) (2001) *Varieties of Capitalism: The Institutional Foundations of Comparative Advantage* (Oxford: Oxford University Press).
Hantrais, L. and P. Ackers (2005) 'Women's Choices in Europe: Striking the Worklife Balance', *European Journal of Industrial Relations*, 11:2, 197–212.
Hayes, G. (2012) 'Bossnapping: Situating Repertoires of Industrial Action in National and Global Contexts', *Modern & Contemporary France*, 20:2, 185–201.
Hererra, G. (2012) 'Starting Over Again? Crisis, Gender and Social Reproduction Among Ecuadorian Migrants in Spain', *Feminist Economics*, 18:2, 125–48.
Horn, Z.E. (2009) *No Cushion to Fall Back On: The Global Economic Crisis and Informal Workers* (Manchester: WIEGO).
Jany-Catrice, F. and M. Lallement (2012) 'France Confronts the Crisis: Economic Symptoms Exacerbate Social Inequality', in S. Lehndorff (ed.), *A Triumph of Failed Ideas: European Models of Capitalism in Crisis* (Brussels: European Trade Union Institute), 103–20.
Karamessini, M. and J. Rubery (eds.) (2014) *Women and Austerity: The Economic Crisis and the Future for Gender Equality* (Abingdon: Routledge).
Knowles, J., E. Pernia and M. Racelis (1999) 'Social Consequences of the Financial Crisis in Asia', *Economic Staff Paper*, no. 60 (Manila: Asian Development Bank).
Lépinard, E. and A. Mazur (2009) 'Republican Universalism Faces the Feminist Challenge: The Continuing Struggle for Gender Equality', in S. Brouard, A.M. Appleton and A. Mazur (eds.), *The French Fifth Republic at Fifty: Beyond Stereotypes* (Basingstoke: Palgrave Macmillan), 247–66.
López, I. and E. Rodríguez (2011) 'The Spanish Model', *New Left Review*, 2:69, 5–28.
Lux, J. (2013) 'Wie "genderbar" ist der Varieties of Capitalism-Ansatz? Vergleichende Kapitalismusforschung aus einer Geschlechter-Perspektive', in I. Bruff, M. Ebenau, C. May and A. Nölke (eds), *Vergleichende Kapitalismusforschung: Stand, Perspektiven, Kritik* (Münster: Westfälisches Dampfboot), 148–62.
Marchand, M.H. and A.S. Runyan (2011) 'Introduction: Feminist Sightings of Global Restructuring: Old and New Conceptualizations', in M.H. Marchand and A.S. Runyan (eds.), *Gender and Global Restructuring: Sightings, Sites, and Resistances* (2nd ed.) (Abingdon: Routledge), 1–23.
Milewski, F. (2010) 'Chômage et emploi des femmes dans la crise en France (Lettre de l'OFCE)', available at: http://www.ofce.sciences-po.fr/pdf/lettres/318.pdf (last accessed 12 December 2013).
Oeser, A., and F. Tourraille (2012) 'Politics, Work and Family: Gendered Forms of Mobilisation of Working-Class Women in Southern France', *Modern & Contemporary France*, 20:2, 203–19.
Rai, S., C. Hoskyns and D. Thomas (2014) 'Depletion: The Cost of Social Reproduction', *International Feminist Journal of Politics*, 16:1, 86–105.
Sauer, B. and S. Wöhl (2011) 'Feminist Perspectives on the Internationalisation of the State', *Antipode*, 43:1, 108–28.
Schmidt, V.A. (2003) 'French Capitalism Transformed, Yet Still a Third Variety of Capitalism', *Economy and Society*, 32:4, 526–54.
Vail, M.I. (2004) 'The Myth of the Frozen Welfare State and the Dynamics of Contemporary French and German Social-Protection Reform', *French Politics*, 2:2, 151–183.

Walby, S. (2004) 'The European Union and Gender Equality: Emergent Varieties of Gender Regime', *Social Politics*, 11:1, 4–29.
Walby, S. (2009) 'Gender and the Financial Crisis', UNESCO paper, available at: http://www.lancaster.ac.uk/fass/doc_library/sociology/Gender_and _financial_crisis_Sylvia_Walby.pdf (last accessed 11 October 2013).
Waring, M. and K. Sumeo (2010) 'Economic Crisis and Unpaid Care Work in the Pacific', *UNDP Report*, Presented at the Pacific Conference on the Human Face of the Global Economic Crisis, Port Vila, Vanuatu, 10–12 December 2010.
Waylen, G. and S. Rai (eds.) (2013) *New Frontiers in Feminist Political Economy* (Abingdon: Routledge).
Wöhl, S. (2011) 'The Political Rationality of Neoliberalism: A View Following Wendy Brown's Reflections on Democracy', *Österreichische Zeitschrift für Politikwissenschaft*, 40:1, 37–48 (in German).
Wöhl, S. (2013) 'The "Crisis" of Representative Democracy in Europe: Democratic Theory and Policy Field Related Reflections', *Forschungsjournal Soziale Bewegungen*, 26:1, 64–75 (in German).
Wöhl, S. (2014) 'The State and Gender Relations in International Political Economy: A State-Theoretical Approach to Varieties of Capitalism in Crisis', *Capital & Class*, 38:1, 83–95.
Young, B. (2003) 'Financial Crises and Social Reproduction: Asia, Argentina and Brazil', in I. Bakker and S. Gill (eds.), *Power, Production and Social Reproduction: Human In/security in the Global Political Economy* (Basingstoke: Palgrave Macmillan), 103–24.
Zemmour, M. (2010) 'Trois approches du lien entre pauvreté et crise en 2009', *Observatoire National de la Pauvreté et de l'Exclusion Sociale* (Paris: ONPES), available at: http://www.onpes.gouv.fr/IMG/pdf/Zemmour.pdf (last accessed 12 December 2013).

7
Social Structures of Accumulation: A Marxist Comparison of Capitalisms?

Terrence McDonough

This chapter will examine whether a dialogue with the Marxist tradition of historical capitalist stages can serve to address a number of shortcomings in the Comparative Capitalisms (CC) literatures. In order to do so, I will first return to some common criticisms of the standard approaches to capitalist variation, which are particularly relevant for such a dialogue. Subsequently, the *Social Structure of Accumulation* (SSA) framework will be described. Thereby, an argument will be made that the SSA framework develops an institutional approach which avoids the previously identified problems, partially because it emphasizes variation across time as well as variation across space. The strengths of the approach will be illustrated by a brief study of the recent economic development of Ireland before concluding.

Ian Bruff (2011, p. 482) defines the CC literatures as 'a body of knowledge comprised of contributions which take institutions as their starting point when considering the evolution of national political economies'. The broad and varied criticisms of the dominant VoC strand of this literature are reviewed elsewhere in this volume (see Coates and Bruff et al.). At this point, only a number of common themes of this critique, which are particularly relevant for the argument to be developed subsequently, shall be re-emphasized. The first is that the framework is biased towards an assumption of stability rather than change (Deeg and Jackson, 2007, p. 150). Dorothee Bohle and Béla Greskovits (2009, p. 370) sum up this perspective in the following way:

> From the very moment that factor-based and specific asset-based models are imputed into history, they set in motion a 'perpetuum

mobile' of systemic logics, which then allow LMEs and CMEs to survive as clear alternatives world wars, global economic crises and political cataclysms.

A second critique partially follows from the first: the observation of widespread change in institutional structures challenges the coherence of the limited number of typologies. Rather, empirical investigations have uncovered a wider variety of institutional configurations than is usually assumed in conventional CC scholarship (Deeg and Jackson, 2007, p. 157). In addition to these specific criticisms, a more foundational critique has been advanced. This is that the CC literature has become so enamoured with its discovery of the trees that it has started to ignore the wood to its cost. Bohle and Greskovits (2009, p. 382; original emphasis) thus conclude their consideration with the following:

> More fundamentally, the instability of contemporary capitalism in all its variants suggests the need for a return to very old literatures and debates, which had had crucial insights into the system's expansionary nature, specific vulnerabilities, destructive and irrational tendencies, and recurrent crises: that is, features of capitalism *tout court* that got lost in the course of the extensive study of its varieties.

In this regard, Hugo Radice (2000, p. 736) underlines that 'capitalism is historically founded on a separation of workers from ownership and possession of the means of production' and that this means that 'economic and political institutions and practices centre on the core dynamics of competition, accumulation and reproduction, which characterize historical capitalism'. This understanding of capitalism lays the ground for an approach to institutions and their role in the reproduction of the accumulation process, which differs fundamentally from that found in conventional neoinstitutionalist CC approaches (see also Jessop, in this volume).

Such an approach can be found in the Marxian stage-theoretic tradition. As the label suggests, this tradition particularly emphasizes capitalist variation across time, in addition to its emphasis on the problems of the reproduction of capitalism as such. While it by no means denies the possibility of capitalist variation across countries or regions, the Marxian stage-theoretic tradition locates these differences in specific responses to capitalist crises, which demand for their resolution the reorganization of the institutional conditions of the accumulation process. In this way, the emphasis is on the dynamics of capitalism over time, the reproduction of these dynamics over time and the recovery of capitalist social formations from periodic major crises of capitalist reproduction. This contrasts with the mainstream CC emphasis on the survival of capitalist variation over space in the context of global competition. In what follows, the central lineages and key tenets of Marxian stages theory will be outlined.

Marxian stages theory

There is a fundamentally continuous tradition of Marxian stages theory from the beginning of the 20th century until the present day. This history begins with the pioneering work of Rudolf Hilferding (1910) on finance capital, Nicolai Bukharin (1915) on the world economy and V.I. Lenin (1917) on imperialism. All three argued that the capitalist economy had, with the advent of monopoly capitalism, entered into a new and higher stage of capitalism. The second wave of Marxian stage theorizing emerged with the end of the post–World War II expansion. Ernest Mandel's Long Wave Theory (LWT), the SSA framework and the Regulation Approach (RA) analysed the stagflationary crises of most of the advanced capitalist countries as the long wave of growth following World War II came to an end. This long wave of accumulation was underpinned by the emergence of a new stage of post-WWII capitalism, which was analogous to the reorganization brought about by monopoly capital at the turn of the century.[1] This new stage was the resolution of the crisis of the monopoly stage, and it indicated that the stagflationary crisis could potentially be resolved through the construction of a new stage of capitalism, thus opening up the possibility of further stages of capitalism in the future.

At the end of the 1970s, David Gordon (1978, 1980) published two articles linking long cycle theory with the concept of stages of capitalism. In this reading, the advent of monopoly capital at the turn of the century coincides with the completion of the long wave at the end of the 19th century and the inauguration of the long-wave expansion, which ended with the Great Depression of the 1930s. The new question, which the adoption of a long-wave perspective posed to the monopoly stage of capitalism tradition, was whether the post-war expansion was associated with a similar set of multidimensional institutional changes. Gordon (1978) answers this question by pointing to a set of post-war institutions whose establishment, in his view, accounted for the long period of post-war prosperity. These institutions included among others multinational corporate structures, dual labour markets associated with a bread-and-butter industrial unionism, US international economic and military hegemony, easy credit, conservative Keynesian state policy and bureaucratic control of workers. In this way, Gordon established the possibility of articulating a post-war set of institutions, which conditioned the subsequent expansion of the economy in a way similar to the manner in which the set of institutions analysed by Hilferding, Bukharin and Lenin accounted for the turn of the century expansion. Thus, the multi-institutional analysis of monopoly capital is implicitly used by Gordon as a model for explaining the post-war expansion.

The repetitive use of this kind of explanation raised the question as to whether the assembling of such sets of institutions could be generalized as the basis of a comprehensive theory of stages of capitalism. Gordon (1978, 1980) himself responded to this question by proposing that both the institutions comprising monopoly capital and those making up the post-war social order constituted examples of what he called social structures of accumulation (SSAs). The construction of a new SSA thereby provided the basis for a new stage of capitalism. The disintegration of such a set of institutions, in turn, marks the end of each stage.

The SSA approach achieved its definitive form shortly thereafter with the publication of the seminal book *Segmented Work, Divided Workers*, which Gordon co-authored with Richard Edwards and Michael Reich (Gordon et al., 1982). This volume used Gordon's SSA approach to capitalist stages to reformulate the participating authors' earlier analysis of the history of capital–labour relations in the United States. In this version, stage theory occupies an intermediate level of analysis in the sense that it identifies periods intermediate in length between the conjuncture and overall capitalist history. The justification for focusing on this intermediate period of analysis is founded on the observation that while all economies are embedded in the broader array of social institutions, this is especially important in the capitalist era because of the conflictual foundations of capitalism in class division and capitalist competition. Thus, for accumulation to proceed relatively smoothly, these sources of instability must be countered through the construction of a set of stable institutions at not only the economic but also the political and ideological levels.

The construction of such a social structure underpins the profit rate and creates the secure expectations that make long-term investment possible. Nevertheless, as accumulation proceeds, the institutions are undermined by class conflict, capitalist competition and accumulation itself. According to the stage-theoretical view, these forces and the interdependence of the institutions will periodically lead to a breakdown of the relevant set of institutions, a fall in the profit rate and the collapse of accumulation, initiating a period of crisis and stagnation, which is only overcome with the construction of a new set of institutions. Thus, capitalist stages are constituted by the sets of interdependent economic, political and ideological institutions, which underpin relatively successful accumulation separated by intervening periods of crisis.[2]

Marxian stages theory and the Varieties of Capitalism approach

In addition to providing a Marxian tradition of the integration of institutions into the creation of dynamic capitalist variety, the Marxian stage-theoretic tradition and the SSA framework, more specifically, have the potential to move towards a resolution of the problems identified earlier in the conventional CC literatures. The emphasis of the following discussion is specifically on the Varieties of Capitalism (VoC) school, which in recent years has been one of the most prominent parts of CC work, as discussed in the chapters in the first part of this volume. Some contributors to the broader 'post-VoC' CC discussion have tried to address questions of multiple variations and change over time in different varieties or models of capitalism. In the process, however, they have lessened to a greater or lesser extent the commendable 'systematicity' of the framework first proposed by Peter Hall and David Soskice (2001) (see also Drahokoupil and Myant, in this volume). The broader kind of analysis that has resulted from these efforts relies less on a general conceptual framework and more on the collection of concrete case studies and examples. In its dialogue with the core VoC literature (see McDonough et al., 2010, pp. 6–8), the Marxian stage-theoretic position has been concerned with addressing the identified weaknesses of the former position without sacrificing its systematicity.[3]

As stated above, the most fundamental critique is that institutional analysis needs to be rooted in a conception of the basic underlying nature and dynamics of capitalism. This is indeed the starting point of the stage-theoretic tradition and the SSA framework. Similar to Radice's characterization, Gordon, Edwards and Reich define capitalism 'as a wage-labor system of commodity production for profit' (Gordon et al., 1982, p. 18) which, as such, has five principal tendencies (ibid., pp. 19–20):

- First, capitalist accumulation continually attempts to *expand* the boundaries of the capitalist system.

- Second, capitalist accumulation persistently increases the size of large corporations and *concentrates* the control and ownership of capital in proportionately fewer hands.
- Third, the accumulation of capital *spreads wage labour* as the prevalent system of production, draws a larger proportion of the population into wage–labour status, and *replenishes the reserve pool of labour*.
- Fourth, capitalist accumulation continually *changes the labour process*.
- And fifth, in order to defend themselves against the effects of capitalist accumulation, workers respond with their own activities and struggles.

In addition, according to the SSA framework, the realization of these tendencies has institutional preconditions and capitalism contains multiple conflicts, instabilities and crisis tendencies, which need to be moderated and channelled through institutional means. At the same time, capital accumulation tends to erode its own institutional preconditions. This creates a historical dynamic of both the success and failure of capital accumulation, in which periods of growth and crisis alternate.

It is the focus on the probability of capitalist crises that allows the stage-theoretic tradition to escape the first critique of the CC literature, according to which the interrelated character and complementarity of the institutions predicts too much stasis and thus an inability to transit from one institutional regime to another. The SSA framework in a sense predicts precisely the opposite dynamic: capitalist contradictions eventually come to the fore, eroding the institutional conditions of capitalist accumulation and precipitating crisis. The failure of institutional resources as well as conflict in the context of the developing crisis further erodes the institutions. The stagnation will only be overcome eventually through the construction of a new SSA. Contrary to any stability thesis, the new SSA will differ fundamentally from the previous one.

Applying the stage-theoretic vision, Martin Wolfson and David Kotz (2010, pp. 81–9) elaborate a conception of liberal and regulated SSAs. Despite rough parallels, this draws a striking contrast with Hall and Soskice's classical but limited conceptualization of liberal and coordinated market economies (LMEs and CMEs) and their relationship over historical time. According to Wolfson and Kotz, liberal SSAs tend to enter into crisis because capital's ability to dominate labour leads to stagnant wages, inadequate demand and overcapacity. Unregulated economies are often prey to financial crises. These liberal crises are most easily resolved through an increase in the strength of labour, a limited redistribution of income and the regulation of demand and finance – that is, the establishment of a regulated SSA. Regulated SSAs by contrast are prone to 'profit-squeeze' crises, due to rising wages and popular demands for intervention by government in the markets. These crises are most often resolved through the reassertion of capital's dominance over labour and the promotion of deregulation through the creation of a liberal SSA. Thus, the assumed dynamic is directly the opposite of that hypothesized in the classical VoC argument: pre-existing varieties or models of capitalism are not internally reproduced over the medium term, but rather they enter into crisis and succeed one another, sometimes in a repeated leapfrog fashion.

This analysis does not require any purity in the two types of SSA. Indeed, the suggestion of two types runs against the tendency of the rest of the literature. The emphasis is on the concrete historical origins of SSAs in the context of the crisis that precedes them. Further, the inclusion of political institutions, as well as cultural and ideological institutions, means that, at least before advent of the global neoliberal SSA in the 1980s, SSAs were conceived as primarily national in character. Thus, a large variety of institutional regimes can potentially be characterized as SSAs (see, for example, Hamilton, 1994; Jeong, 1997; Mihail, 1995; Melendez, 1994; Harriss-White, 2003; Heintz 2010; Salas, 2010; Pfeifer, 2010). Therefore, the critique of the conventional CC literatures that an insufficient variety of institutional structures are catered for cannot be applied to the SSA framework.

The following table brings out the points of similarity and contrast between the VoC approach and the SSA framework. In both approaches, the role of institutions in economic outcomes is central, and the interdependence of institutions and the potential for the development of complementarities are emphasized. They differ significantly, however, in their view of the stability of institutions. While both regard institutions as stable in the short run and consequently share a degree of systematicity, the stages of capitalism analysis argues that the contradictory dynamics of capitalism produce the instability of capitalist institutions in the long run. In this way, the importance of general capitalist dynamics and specifically the possibility of crisis are at the core of the stages of capitalism approach. Inter- and intra-class conflicts are central to the production of these capitalist dynamics in the stages of capitalism analysis, while these factors are approached more narrowly in the VoC literature, where they are subsumed under the rubric of varying industrial relations. Thus, capitalist structural contradictions and class conflict become fecund sources for analysing change in the stages of capitalism analysis, while such potential sources of change are limited in the VoC approach. Finally, while the VoC approach is not strictly limited to Hall and Soskice's two varieties, the number of varieties is not at all limited in the SSA approach to stages of capitalism.

The 'Celtic Tiger' revisited: An SSA case study of the Irish political economy

The similarities and differences between the VoC and SSA frameworks will now be illustrated through an analysis of a specific country case: that of Ireland, which, for reasons that will be outlined below, constitutes an interesting testing ground for theories intent on analysing the institutional specificities of particular historical models of capitalism and linking these to economic performance.

Within the conventional VoC literature, Ireland is customarily included in the group of exemplary LMEs (see, for example, Soskice, 2007). While we will discuss ways in which Ireland departs from the usual LME description below, this characterization can nevertheless potentially be defended. However, Ireland was for several decades famous as the 'Celtic Tiger', a moniker that emphasized a sharp break in the continuity of its economic performance. Such a sharp break is perhaps difficult to explain if we assume a persisting LME, which should condition a more or less continuing level of performance. It will be argued that the Celtic Tiger experience can be made comprehensible by identifying a break between successive stages of the post-war Irish economy, even if both stages might be characterized at a higher level of abstraction as LMEs.

During the depression and war years, Ireland, like many newly independent states, pursued a policy of import-substituting industrialization. However, the latter 1950s saw a definitive shift in policy with the 1956 Finance Act, the 1958 Whitaker Report and the 1959 establishment of the Shannon Airport free trade zone. Henceforth, Ireland's development strategy would be dependent on coaxing in foreign direct investment, a strategy that has been characterized as one of 'industrialization by invitation' (Andreosso-O'Callaghan, 2005). This policy of economic openness has been consistently pursued since. Landmarks include the Anglo-Irish Free Trade Agreement in 1965 and entry into the European Community in 1973. This consistency has been underpinned by Ireland's political system, which is dominated by two large centrist parties, Fianna Fail and Fine Gael, which are primarily divided by different positions taken during the Irish civil war of the early 1920s rather than by any ongoing ideological divisions. This policy consensus is represented by Ireland's low taxation regime for foreign firms, which began with a 0 per cent profits tax rate on manufactured exports and is currently maintained with a low 12.5 per cent rate on all corporate profits. In addition, it can be argued that all other policy domains – financial, industrial relations, education and social security – have been subordinated to the fundamental priority of attracting foreign investment.

The Industrial Development Authority (IDA) and related state agencies have been tasked with 'hunting and gathering' investment projects by foreign multinationals. Initially indiscriminate, the IDA aided industries that ranged from the labour-intensive clothing sector to highly automated pharmaceutical manufacturing. In the 1980s, information and communication technology was emphasized and financial services were attracted to a purpose-built International Financial Services Centre (IFSC). This emphasis has continued up to the current Fine Gael-Labour coalition's 'Action Plan for Jobs'. This strategy has been supplemented by a policy of 'light touch regulation' in the financial sector and the tolerance of a climate of non-compliance in regard to company rules in general (Grant Thornton, 2010, p. 3). Similarly, despite a series of national wage agreements, industrial relation institutions have relied on voluntary participation by both firms and unions. Most foreign multinationals have conducted a policy of avoiding union representation of their employees. In the area of social security provision, the Irish welfare state has been historically meagre by European standards. During the expansionary Celtic Tiger years, state welfare expenditures did not keep pace with growth in the rest of the economy. Various programmes have been developed on an ad hoc and reactive basis, while increasing social welfare has been seen as potentially harmful for competitiveness. Moreover, education policy has centred on increasing the capacity of the educational system to provide the kind of technical training and skills demanded by multinationals.

Ireland's high level of dependence on foreign firms and a commitment to maintaining 'competitiveness' have established a path dependence, which limits both the opportunity and the capacity of the state to develop a more coordinated, locally embedded approach to national development. Linkages between multinational firms and much of the innovative capacity of these firms is located across borders in their transnational operations. There is limited occasion for the collaborative networks that characterize CMEs. In this way, the economy during the

Table 7.1 Comparing VoC and SSA frameworks

	Varieties of Capitalism	Stages of Capitalism
Role of institutions in economic outcomes	Central	Central
Complementarity and interdependence of institutions	Important	Important
Stability of institutions	Stable in short run and long run	Stable in short-run, not stable in long-run
Importance of general capitalist dynamics	Not central	Central
Possibility of crisis	Limited	Central
Class relations	Approached narrowly as industrial relations	Central to dynamics
Sources of change	Limited	Structural contradictions and class conflict
Number of types of institutional structure	Limited	Unlimited

entire period from around 1957 to the present day in Ireland can be plausibly characterized as being of the LME type. An analysis of this type demonstrates the characteristics of the VoC school listed in Table 7.1. Once established in the 1950s, a particular strategy of economic development and competitiveness has been consistently pursued. A high degree of institutional complementarity has been created with a range of institutional factors such as taxation policy, social security provision, education and corporate regulation subordinated to the basically liberal inward investment strategy. The persistence of this strategy until the present day is certainly consistent with a tendency towards path-dependent reproduction of existing strategies. Similarly, the Irish case, seen in this light, does not challenge the assumption of a limited number of potentially successful strategies. Analyses of crisis, where they exist, tend to focus on the idiosyncratic factors endemic to the Irish case (see, for example, Hardiman, 2010).

In line with the theoretical and analytical fundamentals outlined above, the basic contention of the SSA framework is that theorizing this kind of continuity over time can obscure at least as much as it reveals. Beginning with the first oil crisis in 1973, Ireland entered into a traumatic period, which one analysis identifies as 'Ireland's Great

Depression' (Ahearne et al., 2006). Its authors find that by 1983, GDP per head of working-age population was 15.5 per cent below trend. A local minimum of 23.5 per cent below trend was reached in 1988. Unemployment peaked at 14.6 per cent in 1989, while inflation had already passed 20 per cent early during that decade, in 1981. Ireland certainly participated in the stagflationary crisis of the mid-1970s and remained mired in it longer than most other countries. This crisis marked the end of the post-war SSA or, in RA terminology, the Fordist era. Ireland's subsequent emergence from this crisis is accompanied by a sharp break in the performance of the economy. This break in 1987–1988 marks the beginning of Ireland's famous Celtic Tiger period and is difficult to explain from a perspective that emphasizes continuity.

By contrast with the VoC school, most versions of the SSA framework distinguish between a post-war SSA and its crisis prior to the 1980s and a subsequent period of global neoliberalism (Kotz and McDonough, 2010). If the trajectory of the Irish economy were consistent with the expectations of the SSA framework, the stagflationary downturn would not be startling to analysts who could, in turn, relate the period subsequent to the stagflationary crisis of the 1970s to changed institutional factors likely indicating a changed level of performance. The question is thus whether it is possible to locate a coherent set of institutional transformations at the end of Ireland's crisis period, which would be consistent with the growth of the Celtic Tiger years.

In this regard, the years around 1987 did indeed witness a number of significant institutional innovations. In 1986, a tripartite consultative body, the National Economic and Social Council (NESC), published a report, which among other recommendations presented an emerging consensus advocating the reform of public finances and accepting that moderation in wage increases was needed to enhance competitiveness. This position would form the basis of both the new macroeconomic policy of the incoming minority Fianna Fail government in 1987 and the initiation of an ongoing programme of social partnership negotiations in which the first Programme for National Recovery (PNR) was agreed in 1987 (Hardiman, 2000, p. 290). The new government set about substantially reducing government deficit spending and cutting marginal tax rates at the same time. The leader of the Fine Gael party, Fianna Fail's main electoral rival, announced support for the government's macroeconomic policy in what became known at the 'Tallaght strategy', underlining the consensual nature of the new approach (Fitzgerald and Girvin, 2000, p. 279). The PNR basically traded wage moderation for decreases in income taxes, which in theory increases take-home pay even after the lower wage rises, and this set the pattern for future agreements. Both the government's new economic strategy and the partnership negotiations took place in the context of preparing for the Single European Market and Economic and Monetary Union (EMU). The Single European Act was adopted in the European Union (EU) in 1986. After a court challenge, it was overwhelmingly approved by referendum in 1987. The act outlawed certain restrictive practices in Europe, which greatly increased Ireland's share of incoming foreign investment. EU structural funds began to flow in 1988 in order to prepare the cohesion countries for the impact of the single market, for example, through the construction of essential infrastructure. Structural funds also played an important role in the provision of training essential for the attraction of high-tech foreign investment. The rigorous evaluation procedures, which accompanied the structural funds, set much higher standards for Irish public policymaking (Mac Sharry and White, 2000).

Here, we can examine the IDA more closely, for it was at the centre of a complex of state and semi-state agencies responsible for the industrial development of Ireland. This network came together in the late 1980s and has been identified by the sociologist Seán Ó Riain (2004) as an example of a Developmental Network State, a structure dedicated to economic development and particularly suited to small states in the era of globalization that need to promote better connections between the global and the local levels. The IDA adopted a more targeted strategy aimed at the electronics and computer industries in 1983 and succeeded in attracting a pivotal major investment by Intel in 1989. The experience of the IDA was called upon in a new field with the establishment of the Irish Financial Services Centre in 1987. An urban regeneration project designated a section of the Dublin docks for international investment in financial services, and the overall strategy relied on Ireland's favourable corporate tax rate, financial liberalization and the creation of a light-touch regulatory environment. Substantial economic activity was required, ruling out strictly 'brass plate' operations. Over 10,000 jobs were created (White, 2005, p. 387). In 2001, the IFSC was responsible for 15 per cent of all corporate taxes collected (ibid., p. 393). In the banking system, more broadly, growing access to international finance meant that private sector credit could expand sharply after 1994, tracking growth more generally (Kelly and Everett, 2004, p. 92).

This perspective shares the VoC approach's emphasis on the relationship between supportive institutions and economic performance. The various institutional initiatives were generally consistent with one other. The most important institutional changes, which made the Celtic Tiger expansion possible followed the Irish stagflationary crisis around 1987 and were to a considerable extent responses to this crisis. This pattern is consistent with the one that would be predicted by the SSA framework. In addition to being primarily concerned with the capital accumulation process, the SSA framework, when applied to the Irish case, proves capable of dealing with the principal criticisms levelled at conventional theories of capitalist variation. While the institutions of the Celtic Tiger period could conceivably be subsumed within the LME category, the SSA framework identifies the possibility of substantial variation over both institutions and time within this category. It is also capable of integrating several scales of institutional change by locating the EU single market as essential to the structure of accumulation within Ireland. The Irish structure is also broadly consistent with a conception of global neoliberalism as an outcome of capitalist class struggle operating at the transnational level.

Conclusion

The wide body of academic literature on the importance of institutions in capitalist economies has suffered from traditional divisions of labour within the social sciences. Economics has by and large seen capitalism as a system directed by market interactions, which both are and ought to be disembedded from influences emanating from the rest of society. More sociological traditions do not suffer from an inability to perceive the importance of institutional determination in relation to the economy but have had a tendency to ignore work on the fundamental nature and dynamics of capitalism as a system and as a mode of production. The institutionalist CC literature is, as set out earlier in this contribution and also elsewhere in this volume, a strong case in point. As a way of overcoming this dichotomy, Ian Bruff and Laura Horn (2012, p. 163) have called for a move away from 'institutionalist theories of capitalism' and towards 'capitalist theories of institutions' in treatments of capitalist variation. The Marxian tradition as a whole has developed as a comprehensive theory of capitalist history, thus integrating political, ideological and cultural concerns and consequently holds considerable promise in this regard. Nevertheless, even here, academic divisions of labour have discouraged the full integration of political and ideological institutions into the basic theory of capital accumulation.

The Marxian theory of stages of capitalism, while less prominent in the literature than the Marxian theory (or theories) of capitalism, holds one important key to overcoming this weakness. The modern form of

Marxian stages theory finds expression in continuations of the early Marxian version of the RA and the SSA framework. The SSA framework develops a historically intermediate analysis of capitalist stages, which are particular to specific periods in capitalist history and which differ from one another in the character of the institutions that condition the reproduction of capitalism and the capitalist accumulation process. The framework thus crosses paths with institutionalist theories of capitalist variation. New avenues are opened up at this intersection, which could potentially resolve some of the theoretical impasses in the traditional approaches to capitalist variation.

Notes

1. Within a Marxian framework, accumulation is not simply the accumulation of physical capital but also the extension of capitalist social relations. Nevertheless, the term 'accumulation' is often used synonymously with reinvestment and growth.
2. For useful collections of articles explaining, reviewing and applying the SSA framework, see Kotz et al. (1994) and McDonough et al. (2010).
3. For discussions of these issues from a CC perspective, see Becker (2007, 2009).

Bibliography

Ahearne, A., M. Kydland and M.A. Wynne (2006) 'Ireland's Great Depression', *Economic and Social Review*, 37:2, 215–43.

Andreosso-O'Callaghan, B. (2005) 'The Economic Challenge of Enlargement', in M. Holmes (ed.), *Ireland and the European Union: Nice, Enlargement and the Future of Europe* (Manchester: Manchester University Press), 14–35.

Becker, U. (2007) 'Open Systemness and Contested Reference Frames and Change: A Reformulation of the Varieties of Capitalism Theory', *Socio-Economic Review*, 5:2, 261–86.

Becker, U. (2009) *Open Varieties of Capitalism: Continuity, Change and Performances* (Basingstoke: Palgrave Macmillan).

Bohle, D. and B. Greskovits (2009) 'Varieties of Capitalism and Capitalism Tout Court', *European Journal of Sociology*, 50:3, 355–86.

Bruff, I. (2011) 'What about the Elephant in the Room? Varieties of Capitalism, Varieties in Capitalism', *New Political Economy*, 16:4, 481–500.

Bruff, I. and L. Horn (2012) 'Varieties of Capitalism in Crisis?' *Competition & Change*, 16:3, 161–8.

Bukharin, N. (1973 [1915]) *Imperialism and World Economy* (New York: Monthly Review Press).

Deeg, R. and G. Jackson (2007) 'Towards a More Dynamic Theory of Capitalist Variety', *Socio-Economic Review*, 5:1, 149–79.

Fitzgerald, R. and B. Girvin (2000) 'Political Culture, Growth and the Conditions for Success in the Irish Economy', in B. Nolan, P.J. O'Connell and C.T. Whelan

(eds.), *Bust to Boom? The Irish Experience of Growth and Inequality* (Dublin: IPA).
Gordon, D.M. (1978) 'Up and Down the Long Roller Coaster', in Union for Radical Political Economics (ed.), *US Capitalism in Crisis* (New York: Union for Radical Political Economics), 22–35.
Gordon, D.M. (1980) 'Stages of Accumulation and Long Economic Cycles', in T. Hopkins and I. Wallerstein (eds.), *Processes of the World System* (Beverly Hills: Sage), 9–45.
Gordon, D.M., R.C. Edwards and M. Reich (1982) *Segmented Work, Divided Workers* (Cambridge: Cambridge University Press).
Grant Thornton International (2010) *International Business Report 2010. Focus On: Ireland Regaining Competitiveness*, available at: http://www.grantthornton.ie/db/Attachments/Publications/International_b/Focus_on_Irelan/GTI%20IBR%20Ireland%20focus%2010%20New13%20Full1.pdf. (last accessed 26 November 2014)
Hall, P.A. and D. Soskice (eds.) (2001) *Varieties of Capitalism: The Institutional Foundations of Comparative Advantage* (Oxford: Oxford University Press).
Hamilton, R. (1994) 'Analyzing Real Wages, Prices and Productivity and the Effects of State Intervention in Caribbean-Type Economies', *Social and Economic Studies* 43:1, 1–42.
Hardiman, N. (2000) 'Social Partnership, Wage Bargaining and Growth', in B. Nolan, P.J. O'Connell and C.T. Whelan (eds.), *Bust to Boom? The Irish Experience of Growth and Inequality* (Dublin: IPA), 286–309.
Hardiman, N. (2010) 'Bringing Domestic Institutions Back into an Understanding of Ireland's Economic Crisis', *Irish Studies in International Affairs*, 21, 71–87.
Harriss-White, B. (2003) *India Working: Essays on Society and Economy* (Cambridge: Cambridge University Press).
Heintz, J. (2010) 'The Social Structure of Accumulation in South Africa', in T. McDonough, M. Reich and D.M. Kotz (eds.), *Contemporary Capitalism and Its Crises: Social Structure of Accumulation Theory for the 21st Century* (Cambridge: Cambridge University Press), 267–85.
Hilferding, R. (1980 [1910]) *Finance Capital* (London: Routledge and Kegan Paul).
Jeong, S. (1997) 'The Social Structure of Accumulation in South Korea', *Review of Radical Political Economics*, 29:4, 92–112.
Kelly, J. and M. Everett (2004) 'Financial Liberalisation and Economic Growth in Ireland', *Irish Central Bank Quarterly Bulletin*, Autumn, 91–112.
Kotz, D.M. and T. McDonough (2010) 'Global Neoliberalism and the Contemporary Social Structure of Accumulation', in T. McDonough, M. Reich and D.M. Kotz (eds.), *Contemporary Capitalism and Its Crises: Social Structure of Accumulation Theory for the 21st Century* (Cambridge: Cambridge University Press), 93–120.
Lenin, V.I. (1968 [1917]) *Imperialism, the Highest Stage of Capitalism in Selected Works* (Moscow: Progress Publishers), 169–262.
Mac Sharry, R. and P. White (2000) *The Making of the Celtic Tiger: The Inside Story of Ireland's Boom Economy* (Cork: Mercier Press).
McDonough, T., M. Reich and D.M. Kotz (2010) *Contemporary Capitalism and Its Crises: Social Structure of Accumulation Theory for the 21st Century* (Cambridge: Cambridge University Press).

Melendez, E. (1994) 'Accumulation and Crisis in a Small and Open Economy: The Post-War Social Structure of Accumulation in Puerto Rico', in D.M. Kotz, T. McDonough and M. Reich (eds.), *Social Structures of Accumulation: The Political Economy of Growth and Crisis* (Cambridge: Cambridge University Press), 233–52.

Mihail, D. (1995) 'The Productivity Slowdown in Postwar Greece', *Labour*, 9:2, 189–205.

Ó Riain, S. (2004) *The Politics of High-Tech Growth: Developmental Network States in the Global Economy* (Cambridge: Cambridge University Press).

Pfeifer, K. (2010) 'Social Structure of Accumulation Theory for the Arab World: The Economies of Egypt, Jordan and Kuwait in the Regional System', in T. McDonough, M. Reich and D.M. Kotz (eds.), *Contemporary Capitalism and Its Crises: Social Structure of Accumulation Theory for the 21st Century* (Cambridge: Cambridge University Press), 309–54.

Radice, H. (2000) 'Globalization and National Capitalisms: Theorizing Convergence and Differentiation', *Review of International Political Economy*, 7:4, 719–42.

Salas, C. (2010) 'Social Structures of Accumulation and the Condition of the Working Class in Mexico', in T. McDonough, M. Reich and D.M. Kotz (eds.), *Contemporary Capitalism and Its Crises: Social Structure of Accumulation Theory for the 21st Century* (Cambridge: Cambridge University Press), 286–308.

Soskice, D. (2007) 'Macroeconomics and Varieties of Capitalism', in B. Hancké, M. Rhodes and M. Thatcher (eds.), *Beyond Varieties of Capitalism. Conflict, Contradictions, and Complementarities in the European Economy* (Oxford: Oxford University Press), 89–121.

White, M.C. (2005) 'Assessing the Role of the International Financial Services Centre in Irish Regional Development', *European Planning Studies*, 13:3, 387–405.

Wolfson, M.H. and D.M. Kotz (2010) 'A Reconceptualization of Social Structure of Accumulation Theory', in T. McDonough, M. Reich and D.M. Kotz (eds.), *Contemporary Capitalism and Its Crises: Social Structure of Accumulation Theory for the 21st Century* (Cambridge: Cambridge University Press), 72–90.

8
Entangled Modernity and the Study of Variegated Capitalism: Some Suggestions for a Postcolonial Research Agenda

Ingrid Wehr

Industrial capitalism, right from its beginnings in Southern Lancashire and Northern Cheshire at the end of the 18th century, has been characterized by its expansive and tendentially global character. Yet, apart from a few exceptions, the (post-)Varieties of Capitalism (VoC) and Comparative Capitalisms (CC) literatures have mainly produced a large variety of national case studies, 'typically framed in "horizontal" comparisons with other national models' (Zhang and Peck, 2014, p. 3). Whereas the Triad has ceased to be the only reference point, in particular for a new generation of scholars, this geographical expansion (or 'globalization') of CC research has not overcome some of the central methodological shortcomings. For example, by focusing on supposedly *national* production and regulation regimes, most of the current research turns a blind eye to the conceptual challenge of analysing capitalism as a variegated but interconnected global system, characterized by power asymmetries, conflicts and contradictions (see also Jessop, in this volume). The relational character of capitalism – that is, the fact that national forms of production and social regulation are influenced by international competition, predominant (global) modes of capital accumulation and transnational (inter-)dependencies – remains largely under-theorized. Most importantly, though, comparative research on capitalism suffers from a lack of historical depth and a widespread blindness concerning

---

I would like to thank Christian May and Matthias Ebenau for critical and constructive comments on earlier versions of this chapter.

Ingrid Wehr 135

the colonial and imperialist foundations of capitalist expansion and their repercussions for 'postcolonial' societies (but see Coates, 2014b; see also Tilley, in this volume). Accordingly, this chapter will first embark on a deconstruction of the Eurocentric and modernization–theoretic shortcomings of most strands of post-VoC and CC literatures. It does so by focusing on the recent debate on 'patrimonial capitalism', which can be considered a particularly telling example. In a second step, it will sketch the contours of a research agenda, which builds on insights from both postcolonial studies on entangled modernity and the literature on variegated capitalism (Jessop, 2014; Kößler, 2013; Peck and Theodore, 2007). This new but growing strand of research privileges the relational analysis of an unevenly developing, multiscalar and polymorphic capitalism over the search for institutionally stabilized 'system integrity' at the national scale. In this perspective, the analysis of elements of connectivity and commonality across capitalism(s) stands in a creative tension with the search for geographical divergence and difference.

Beyond the original LME–CME dichotomy: VoC research travels East and South

In the last few years, comparative research on capitalist varieties has increasingly turned its attention to cases outside the so-called Triad of Western Europe, North America and East Asia (see also Ebenau, as well as Drahokoupil and Myant, in this volume). Whereas first studies spent considerable energy on fitting diverse empirical realities into Hall and Soskice's (2001) classical typology, by comparing them with ideal types derived from an analysis of the US and (West-)German cases, a second generation of studies pushed the development of typologies beyond the original binary distinction between liberal and coordinated market economies (LMEs/CMEs). Bruno Amable (2003) was among the pioneers who included non-Triad economies into a typology of varieties of capitalism. With insights from regulation theory and based on an inductive cluster analysis, he developed a broad-based typology. This included a meso-corporatist 'Asian' model characterized by a strong dependence on business strategies of large corporations in collaboration with the state and a centralized financial system, which allows the development of long-term strategies.

According to this analysis, Asian models protect workers' specific investments by de facto employment protection and offer possibilities for retraining and career-making within the corporation. At the same time, deficient social protection and sophisticated financial markets make risk diversification difficult and render the stability provided by large corporations crucial to the persistence of the model (Amable, 2003, pp. 15–16). However, what Amable subsumed under the category of the 'Asian' model was a rather restricted snapshot analysis of Japan and South Korea based on data collected in the late 1990s (for a critique, see Nölke and Claar, 2013). Consequently, a look at the growing literature on Chinese capitalism shows that Amable's classification does not adequately represent the development of this specific capitalist variety, which is characterized by (for instance) the interplay of market forces, competitive private–public partnerships and specific forms of state interventionism and corporatism (see McNally, 2012; ten Brink, 2013). Nor does it do justice to the 'patterned heterogeneity' of the Chinese model of capitalism (Zhang and Peck, 2014, p. 7), which in fact consists of a complex universe of subnational models with different centre–local regulatory relations and transnational economic links (see also Redding and Witt, 2007; Tilley, in this volume).

Other widely discussed non-traditional conceptualizations of capitalist varieties outside the Triad have been proposed by Andreas Nölke and Arjan Vliegenthart and also by Ben Ross Schneider. Based on an analysis of the Visegrád group of countries (Poland, Hungary, the Czech Republic and Slovakia) and on a version of Hall and Soskice's original institutionalist framework, which is infused with some elements of dependency theory, Nölke and Vliegenthart (2009) identify what they call 'dependent market economies' (DMEs) as a distinctive form of capitalist organization. These are characterized by a subordinated insertion into Western European networks of investment and production as industrial assembly platforms (with comparative advantages in sectors such as automobiles and consumer electronics), a relatively promising economic and social performance – at least in comparison with other transition economies – and a system of corporate governance strongly geared towards the corporate hierarchies of Transnational Corporations (TNCs) (for a more detailed exposition and critique, see Ebenau, in this volume; see also Drahokoupil and Myant, 2013).

Schneider, in turn, took the VoC toolkit south, to Latin America, where he sought to describe an ideal type of 'hierarchical market economies' (HMEs) characterizing capitalism throughout the region. In this view, Latin American economies are deeply penetrated by market relations and private property (unlike the post-socialist economies) but characterized by hierarchical relations, which pervade the core relations of capitalist organization (Schneider, 2013; for comprehensive criticisms, see Bizberg, 2011; Ebenau, 2012, 2014; Fernández and Alfaro, 2011). Additionally to DMEs and HMEs, a lively debate is developing on whether certain emerging economies, in particular the BRIC(S) countries, could be classified as state-permeated market economies (SMEs), which are characterized by – varying degrees of – centralization, dominance of public enterprises and public planning and more or less bureaucratic or patrimonial (variously called clan-dominated) relations between business and government officials (Nölke, 2011; Nölke and Claar, 2013, pp. 35–6).

By now, an animated discussion has developed on the problems and blind spots of conceptions such as dependent, hierarchical and state-permeated capitalism and on the problems and blind spots of this new generation of research on global capitalist diversity (see Bruff et al., 2013; Bruff and Ebenau, 2014a; Ebenau, Gaitán and Boschi and Suau Arinci et al., in this volume). This contribution adds to the debate by focusing on one particular methodological shortcoming, which has received less attention so far: the inherent Eurocentrism and Orientalism[1], which find their most explicit expression in the ongoing debate on so-called patrimonial forms of capitalist regulation.

Patrimonial varieties of capitalism as a 'peripheral' phenomenon

Following the growing interest in the so-called BRIC(S) countries and the reasons for their recent economic success, many CC researchers have turned their attention to these large 'emerging' economies as well. Defying expectations derived from conventional economic theory, these countries have managed to obtain high levels of development (usually measured by the traditional economic indicators such as GDP growth, exports, and so on). To an extent, their development surprised mainstream institutionalists as well, since these countries are said to lack institutional coherence and therefore tend to promote crony and patrimonial ties, with negative consequences for economic development.

The late Uwe Becker's (2013) comparative analysis of the BRICs and other emerging economies is a good reference point for summarizing the methodological problems which characterize the resulting debate on 'patrimonial' capitalism. According to Becker, patrimonial capitalism – often conflated with the concept of crony capitalism (see Haber, 2001) – can be described as 'an *allegedly* capitalist economy in which success in business depends on close relationships between businessmen and government officials' (Becker, 2013, p. 35; my emphasis). These 'buddy' relationships might express themselves in the form of favours concerning the distribution of legal permits, public grants, special tax breaks and so forth. According to Becker (ibid., p. 36), 'patrimonialism seems to qualify for a separate ideal-typical variety of capitalism because it involves not only a culture denoting clientelist patterns of interaction among individuals and between the state and individuals but also, unlike societal clientelism, a structural relation between the state and the economy'. Hence, patrimonialism seems to strongly penetrate capitalism in almost all emerging political economies, fostering significant levels of corruption. In consequence, competition and meritocratic principles, and thus the efficacy of the market and of general administrative rules, are undermined (ibid.).

Similar arguments are found elsewhere. For instance, Neil Robinson (2011) attempts to explain Russia's model of capitalism as a synthesis between pre-existing (neo-) patrimonial structures and externally induced market reforms. This leads to a predominance of informal rules, a concentration of economic power in the hands of elites, high transaction costs due to a lack of rule of law and a lack of democratic control of political power. This narrative reproduces an interpretation of patrimonialism, which goes back to Max Weber and which, based on a binary distinction between supposedly traditional and modern political and economic structures, sees it as an intrinsic impediment to economic development. Such patrimonial forms of social organization are detected in other parts of the 'non-Western' world as well. For example, Oliver Schlumberger (2008, p. 633) identifies 'patrimonial capitalism' in Arabic countries as the main cause for a lack of economic development despite two decades of structural reforms. According to Schlumberger, these countries are characterized by competitive economic systems and political systems suffering from crony relationships, excessive political interference into economic issues and a lack of rule of law. Market mechanisms are thus seriously hampered, and the regulating state is mainly oriented towards generating overlapping and contradictory formal laws, which coexist with informal forms of decision-making (Schlumberger, 2008, p. 637). Patrimonial capitalism is thus defined as a clash of formal and informal rules with a predominance of the latter. It lacks the rule of law and the protection of private property, and competition policies are weakly regulated. Reforms follow authoritarian and not economic interests, resulting in considerable transaction costs and a general lack of democratic institutions. Schlumberger concludes that capitalism intrinsically presupposes a liberal political system (Schlumberger, 2008, pp. 633–6).

Some CC authors are clearly aware that the interpretation of patrimonialism as an obstacle to capitalist development clashes with the obvious economic success of many countries dubbed as patrimonial (see, for example, Storz et al., 2013, p. 217). For instance, authors such as Schlumberger (2008) and Robinson (2011) share Weber's scepticism concerning the (economic) development potential of patrimonial forms of rule *and* note the Orientalist bias of his comparative research (for a critique of Weber's orientalism, see Hobson, 2004, p. 14). However, such arguments are largely based on a deductively derived model mixed with some anecdotal evidence (for a detailed criticism of Schlumberger, see Hauck et al., 2013, pp. 259–60), which ultimately reproduces numerous modernization–theoretic shortcomings.

As a result, the Eurocentric bias is responsible for the fact that the geographical opening to varieties outside the Triad has, with very few exceptions, been based on an effort to fit 'empirical pegs into Western theoretical holes' (critically on China, see Saich, 2002, p. 99). Resembling the debate on 'defective' democracy (for a critical discussion, see Krennerich, 2005) and on open and limited access orders within economics (North et al., 2009), varieties of capitalism in the global South are measured against obviously Western standards and, therefore, cannot be more than 'hybrid' or 'not fully capitalist' countries (Becker, 2013, p. 37). As 'hybrids', they supposedly lack institutional coherence and the comparative advantages associated with it. There are some notable examples that develop more differentiated comparisons of state-centred capitalism based on different degrees of bureaucratic and patrimonial incorporation (see Buhr and Frankenberger, 2013). Nevertheless, most CC research on emerging economies reproduces Eurocentric perspectives by making binary distinctions between supposedly bureaucratic or rational forms of capitalist organization in the West and patrimonial – that is, incoherent, irrational and dysfunctional forms of organization – in other parts of the world, thereby turning a blind eye to crony structures in supposedly rational, fully capitalist Western countries (for a detailed critique, see Hauck et al., 2013, pp. 319–22; see also Tilley, in this volume).

Additionally, Eurocentric views are not only reproduced as far as the classification of forms of capitalist organization is concerned, but they are also related to distinguishing capitalist from non-capitalist economies. For instance, Becker (2013, p. 37) argues that a considerable number of countries in the global South, such as India, where large parts of the economy take place at the subsistence level of agricultural village production, are not fully capitalist or not capitalist to the same degree as the United States, France or Germany. This binary distinction between capitalism in the global North and the survival of non-capitalist forms of production in the global South ignores the fact that the dependence on subsistence production and unpaid domestic work is not an exclusive feature of 'peripheral' societies but equally characteristic – not least through the gendered division of labour (see Lux and Wöhl, in this volume) – for supposedly 'fully developed' capitalist countries in the North.

As such, this kind of research may be said to reproduce certain methodological problems, which it had originally set out to overcome. An analogy with classical dependency theory can serve to illustrate this point. Although dependency theory had clearly been designed as a critique of modernization theory, it failed to elaborate an alternative conception of development and thus remained bound to the latter's methodological nationalism and its binary distinctions between 'development' and 'underdevelopment' (for a critique, see Grosfoguel, 2000). In a similar vein, most of the debate on 'patrimonial capitalism' construes binary distinctions between 'rational' forms of capitalist organization co-evolving with formal, democratic institutions in the 'West' and an assemblage of rational and irrational forms of political organization and formal and informal institutions challenging democratic decision-making in the non-Western 'periphery'. Again, this simplistic division between 'patrimonial' and 'rational' forms of capitalism overlooks the fact that patrimonial forms of social and political control are an attribute of capitalist countries in the North as well. For instance, Thomas Piketty (2014, p. 173) has recently described Europe and the United States as the historical forerunners for the 'emergence of a new patrimonial capitalism', which is characterized by the predominance of inheritance and birthright privileges over meritocratic principles. In such a context, the 'entrepreneur inevitably tends to become a rentier, more and more dominant over those who own nothing but their labour' (ibid., p. 571). However, in contrast to Piketty's analysis, the debate on patrimonial capitalism turns a blind eye on patrimonial forms of organization in supposedly 'mature' capitalist societies.

As will be shown in the next section, simplistic binary juxtapositions of patrimonial and non-patrimonial forms of capitalism are not only problematic because they reproduce Orientalist perspectives, but they also largely neglect the entangled co-evolution of global capitalism and colonialism.

Orientalism in CC research and the neglect of the colonial origins of global capitalism

Large parts of the CC literature on non-Triad models of capitalism tend to reproduce Orientalist perspectives in the tradition of analysis, which, like Weber, conceives of the development of modern capitalism as a genuinely Western, internally driven enterprise (for a critique, see Hobson 2004, pp. 12–20; see also Seidman, 2014; Hobson, 2013). In this context, categories such as 'patrimonial capitalism' are frequently based on a rather sloppy empirical measuring of patrimonialism. In a highly problematic way, the construction of typologies often resembles a process of 'othering' rather than a rigorous and systematic comparison based on clear criteria. Furthermore, due to the Eurocentric bias in their institutionalist perspective, some strands of the CC literatures still attribute the achievements of different models of capitalist production and regulation mainly to internal factors such as supposedly better, more coherent, more functional and more rational institutions. Hence, they ignore the fact that models of accumulation and regulation are highly dependent on global structures (for typical examples, see Schlumberger, 2008; Robinson, 2011; Schneider, 2013; for a critique, see May, 2013).

This is not to say that all of the literature is guilty as charged. On the contrary, the debate on HMEs and DMEs, which reintroduced considerations derived from dependency theory into debates on capitalist diversity, emphasizes the interweaving of internal and external causes of the institutional deficiencies, which CC analysis identifies but often does not consider in any depth. In particular, the dependent insertion into world markets as natural resource exporters and/or the predominance of TNCs are significant elements of these discussions (for a summary, see Ebenau et al., 2013; see also Domingues 2012 and Vliegenthart 2010). Also, Tobias ten Brink's (2013) in-depth analysis of the origins, evolution and contradictions of Chinese capitalism is a fine example of a differentiated analysis of the economic success of state-permeated capitalism, as an alternative model to the industrial capitalism of Western Europe and North America. The great challenge, then, is to strengthen the approaches which emphasize global (inter-)dependencies and the ongoing transformation of centre–periphery relations without reproducing the modernization–theoretic bias of the CC literatures and the dependency debate of the 1970s.

As mentioned earlier, some studies question the capitalist nature of 'patrimonial' economies without actually providing a rigorous distinction between capitalist and non-capitalist forms of production, apart from some eclectic references to informal labour markets and subsistence production (see, for example, Becker, 2013, p. 37). This perspective remains characterized by a normative master narrative of modern capitalism based mainly on Western European and North American realities, interpreting varieties of capitalist organization in other parts of the world as idiosyncratic deviations from an ideal historical standard. What such visions tend to overlook is the fact that modern societies around the world are characterized by a fundamental social heterogeneity, something which is based on the simple premise that social reproduction presupposes the combination of wage labour, subsistence production and largely unpaid care and reproductive work. Structural heterogeneity is therefore an inherent characteristic not only of 'peripheral' capitalist formations but also of global capitalism in all of its varieties. In some ways, current debates on 'patrimonial' capitalism thus seem to fall behind the debate on the gender blindness of Marxist theory, as staged by feminist political economists in recent decades. The latter have repeatedly pointed to the fact that capitalism relies on the gendered reproduction of state and society, that is, to a large part on non-wage forms of labour and increasingly also on globalized care chains (see Sauer and Wöhl (2011), Bauhardt and Caglâr (2010); see also Lux and Wöhl, in this volume).

Furthermore, what most current CC research tends to forget is the fact that capitalism from its very beginnings has been a global enterprise, not only in the sense of establishing contacts between geographically distant regions through trade but also by linking diverse geographical spaces and forms of production, consumption and social regulation (Kößler, 2013, pp. 151, 158–62; see also Harvey, 2004). For instance, the breakthrough of industrial capitalism in England cannot be explained without the intimate entanglement of wage and slave labour. Or, in the words of Hobson (2004, p. 244): 'The racist imperial appropriation of Eastern resources constituted a crucial external contribution to British industrialization.' As Inikori (1992) and others (Morgan 2000, Solow 1991, Zahedieh 2010) have shown, English industrial growth in the late 17th and early 18th centuries can be interpreted as a successful process of import substitution. In turn, the enormous expansion of the export sector was based on the production of cotton textiles for the slave trade in Africa and for clothing African slaves on the New World plantations (Inikori, 1992, p. 171). In other words, the breakthrough of capitalist production would not have been successful if it had been based solely on wage labour. Although capitalism is characterized by the commodification of labour, it is not restricted to wage labour and from its beginnings subsumed different forms of production and, therefore, of different labour forms (cf. Taylor, 2014). According to Reinhard Kößler (2013, pp. 151, 160), one of the major theoretical challenges for critical CC research thus lies in developing concepts that include these non-capitalist forms in a general analysis of capitalist modes of production.

Additionally, Latin American postcolonial scholars have pointed to the fact that the colonization of the Americas played a crucial role in the constitution of modern capitalism beyond the so-called primitive accumulation of capital, because the colonies, especially the large sugar cane plantations in Brazil and the Antilles, served as laboratories for modern techniques of social control (Mintz, 1985; Mitchell, 2000, p. 8; see also Bortoluci and Jansen 2013 and Tilley, in this volume). Furthermore, similar to feminist contributions, which point to the co-evolution of capitalist production and a heterosexual-normative gender order and therefore emphasized the intersections between race, class, gender and religion, Latin American decolonial thinkers have criticized the class-based myopia of Euro- and androcentric research on capitalism. The discussion on the 'coloniality of power' (Quijano, 2000) has stressed the central importance of the categories of race and racism in the international and transnational division of labour and thus the constitution of modern capitalism (cf. Grosfoguel, 2010).

Unfortunately, while classical political economy focused on important variations in the world market ranging from primitive accumulation and mercantilism to imperialism and colonialism, recent research on varieties of capitalism is mainly occupied with snapshot analyses of national case studies (for a critique, see Jessop 2014, pp. 45–6, and Kößler 2013). Most comparisons rely on taxonomic classifications or statistical induction using recent data sets, neither of which takes different historical development paths into account. For many CC scholars, the world economy is largely an aggregate of distinct national models competing with each other, rather than an interactive production system characterized by huge power asymmetries and highly uneven integration into world markets which are shaped by (post-)colonial relations (see also Hardy, 2014). The last section will therefore propose a number of suggestions for a postcolonial research agenda on global but variegated capitalism, which merges two relatively disconnected lines of debate: critical political economy discussions of variegated capitalism and the ongoing debate on 'entangled modernity' within development studies.

Some suggestions for a postcolonial research agenda on variegated, entangled capitalism

Recently, the neoinstitutionalist meta-theory underpinning CC approaches, which has long dominated comparative research on capitalist diversity, has met with increasing criticism from critical-materialist perspectives (see Bruff and Ebenau 2014b, Bruff and Hartmann 2014; see also Coates and Bruff et al., in this volume). For example, there is a need to re-emphasize the state and labour as central dimensions of capitalist orders. Moreover, even in supposedly market-dominated economies such as the United States, the state (at its various levels) plays an important role in organizing social reproduction and overall conditions of capitalist production and social regulation (Coates, 2014a). Most importantly, neo-Gramscian, Poulantzian and regulationist perspectives have introduced into the CC debate conceptions of the state as an institutionalized arena of social (class) struggles or as a strategic field of intersecting power networks (Bieling, 2014). This points to the central importance of welfare states in the making of capitalist societies in the West[2] and the inextricably political nature of capitalist systems.

Following the tradition of Marxist theorists such as (the early work of) Claus Offe, I define welfare states as central agents of regulation. Considering the structural inconsistencies of late capitalist societies – that is, the fact that the functional logic of the capitalist economy stands in open contradiction with the legitimating demands of the (democratic) political system – the modern welfare state is assigned the difficult task of simultaneously guaranteeing a 'democratic domestication of capitalism' and a 'capitalist conditioning of democracy' (Borchert and Lessenich, 2004, p. 580). In order to succeed in this and to guarantee that the capitalist economy runs smoothly, capitalist welfare states are selective in two ways: on the one hand, the overall interest of capital has to be protected from the narrow-mindedness of individual capitalist interests; on the other hand, the supposedly democratic political process has to be manipulated in such a way as to filter out anti-capitalist interests and thus contribute to stabilizing the capitalist system (Offe, 2006 [1969], pp. 31; 38). Hence, neo-Gramscian and regulationist approaches certainly have the merit of emphasizing the internally conflictual social structures of capitalist accumulation. Nevertheless, by treating modes of regulation primarily as stabilizers of predominant accumulation regimes, they tend to remain trapped in a functionalist form of methodological nationalism. Efforts to expand and transnationalize regulation theory with the help of neo-Gramscian IPE (such as Bieling, 2014) have thus far – with very few exceptions (see, for example, Boyer, 2014) – largely remained on a theoretical level without empirical anchorage in the global South (although see May and Nölke, in this volume).

This criticism notwithstanding, neo-Gramscian and regulationist approaches have been helpful in preparing the ground for bringing the proverbial 'elephant' back into the room (cf. Bruff, 2011), reactivating the conceptual debate on capitalism as a hegemonic form of production. Apart from strengthening power-centred and conflict–theoretic perspectives, this highlights that mechanisms and institutions of political regulation and different forms of accumulation can be interrelated without the scholar resorting to problematic and reductionist classifications. Furthermore, it emphasizes one crucial point, which has remained clearly under-theorized in CC debates: capitalism, although tendentially global, is a multiscalar and polymorphous interactive system characterized by contradictions, conflicts, hierarchical orderings and centre–periphery relations, rather than a mere aggregation of national models (cf. Peck and Theodore, 2007; Jessop, 2014; Kößler, 2013, p. 167).

The great challenge for future research will be to return to the historical depth of classical political economy without reproducing its Eurocentric and class-centric biases. As Cooper (2005, p. 125) stressed:

> The best historical scholarship on capitalism has emphasized that the story needs to be pulled apart rather than mushed together: it brings out different trajectories of capitalist development; the extent to which different forms of production are articulated with each other, the importance of state protection, regulation of markets and support to particular capitalist classes; the varied trajectories of capitalist economies; the unevenness and segmentation of labour markets; the varied role of gender in the organization of production; and the importance of territorially bounded institutions for containing the contradictions and dangers of capitalism and deterritorialized exchange.

In this sense, a relational analysis of unevenly developed, multiscalar and variegated capitalism might benefit enormously from a closer engagement with the ongoing debate on entangled modernity. Like capitalism, modernity is deliberately used in the singular form to emphasize the fact that both concepts refer to polymorphous but nevertheless global systems. In contrast to the earlier debate on multiple modernities, the concept of entangled modernity rejects the idea of specific models of modernity or processes of modernization occurring in isolated national containers (cf. Conrad and Randeria, 2002; for a detailed discussion, see Wehr, 2014). Instead, it emphasizes the constitutive role of centre–periphery relations in the development of modern institutions and structures. Most importantly, one of the main contributions is the emphasis on colonialism as a constitutive part of European capitalist expansion, a topic largely neglected in narratives on the different phases of capitalist development in the West (Randeria et al., 2004, p. 11). The concept of entanglement neither suggests that relations are characterized by reciprocity or mutually beneficial interdependencies nor does it imply that increasingly dense global networks would lead to convergent institutions or structures. In sharp contrast to arguments from systems or modernization theory, the research programme on entangled modernity emphasizes the contradictions, constructions and transformations of borders, the related processes of inclusion and exclusion and the violence involved in the co-evolution of capitalist and colonial expansion in different spatio-temporal contexts. This perspective is rather different from Shmuel Eisenstadt's conceptualization of 'multiple *modernities*' (emphasis mine) or the debate on Beck's ideas of a 'second modernity'. Although critical of classical modernization theory and recognizing different varieties of modernity outside Europe, Eisenstadt (2006) sticks to the idea of Western society as a 'lead society' (Parsons, 1971). The following quotation from Bhambra neatly summarizes the criticisms of this position:

> Sociological theorists of modernity (and of multiple modernities), put forward ideas of the modern world, emerging out of the twin processes of economic and political revolution located in Europe, thus conflating Europe with modernity, and rendering the process of becoming modern, at least in the first instance, one of endogenous European development. Accordingly, the rest of the world is assumed to be external to this world-historical process and, concretely, colonial connections significant to the processes under discussion are erased or rendered silent.
>
> (Bhambra 2010, 34f.)[3]

Furthermore, the research programme on 'entanglement' should not be confused with the Eurocentric agenda on 'Second Modernity' and the discussion on a much needed cosmopolitan turn in social theory (see Beck and Grande, 2010), which limits entanglements to recent developments in global society, ignoring the fact that mutual (asymmetrical) interdependencies have been a constitutive feature of capitalist modernity more generally and turning a blind eye on 'how colonialism might have been *generative* of cosmopolitanism' (Go, 2013, p. 209, emphasis in the original). CC research would therefore benefit enormously from incorporating insights from global history and the ongoing debate on entangled modernity, both of which draw our attention to the global character of (often violent) capitalist expansion, its inherently polymorphous character and the entangled development of different accumulation regimes and associated forms of political regulation. Although nation states may still retain important functions in shaping regulation regimes – that is, the political and social forms of organizing capitalist production in a wider sense – they are not necessarily the only important categories of analysis and should be complemented by, for example, a discussion of transnational production and care networks. The concept of entanglement thus analyses and theorizes underlying asymmetrical power relations and identifies (colonial) violence as the driving force of capitalist expansion. Hence, it strengthens a classical topic, which has been largely absent in the research agenda on comparing capitalisms.

Within the context of the (re-)emergence of a polyarchic world order (see Wehr, 2014) and of the repercussions of changing capitalist accumulation regimes at the global level that have highly divergent regional and local effects, bringing global history back in might thus help to overcome both methodological nationalism and Orientalist perspectives in CC research.

Notes

1. 'Orientalism' is a term coined by Said (1978) when criticizing a 'Peter Pan' theory of the East, which essentialized differences based on a binary distinction between a dynamic, forward-looking West and an unchanging, backward East.
2. Most of the predominantly Western researchers tend to forget, however, that welfare states, as with capitalism, are not an exclusive accomplishment of Northern industrialized countries. To the contrary, in some countries of the global South, public social policies as a means of maintaining order predated Western experiences (for a discussion of the Eurocentric bias of welfare regime research, see Wehr, 2011).
3. For a detailed discussion on the differences between multiple modernities and entangled modernity, see Wehr (2014).

Bibliography

Amable, B. (2003) *The Diversity of Modern Capitalism* (Oxford: Oxford University Press).

Bauhardt C. and G. Caglâr (eds.) (2010) *Gender and Economics: Feministische Kritik der politischen Ökonomie* (Wiesbaden: VS Verlag).
Beck, U. and E. Grande (2010) 'Varieties of Second Modernity: The Cosmopolitan Turn in Social and Political Theory and Research', *British Journal of Sociology*, 61:3, 409–43.
Becker, U. (2013) 'Institutional Change in the BRICs, Eastern Europe, South Africa and Turkey, 1998–2008', in U. Becker (ed.), *The BRICs and Emerging Economies in Comparative Perspective: Political Economy, Liberalization and Institutional Change* (Abingdon: Routledge), 27–52.
Bhambra, G.K. (2010) 'Sociology After Postcolonialism: Provincialized Cosmopolitanisms and Connected Sociologies', in E. Gutiérrez Rodríguez, M. Boatcă, Manuela and S. Costa (eds.), *Decolonizing European Sociology. Transdisciplinary Approaches* (London: Ashgate) 33–47.
Bieling, H.-J. (2014) 'Comparative Analysis of Capitalism from a Regulationist Perspective Extended by Neo-Gramscian IPE', *Capital & Class*, 38:1, 31–43.
Bizberg, I. (2011) 'The Global Economic Crisis as Disclosure of Different Types of Capitalism in Latin America', *Swiss Journal of Sociology*, 37:2, 321–39.
Borchert, J. and S. Lessenich (2004) ' "Spätkapitalismus" revisited: Claus Offes Theorie und die adaptive Selbsttransformation der Wohlfahrtsstaatsanalyse', *Zeitschrift für Sozialreform*, 60:6, 563–83.
Bortoluci, J.H. and R. Jansen (2013) 'Toward a Postcolonial Sociology: The View from Latin America', in J. Go (ed.), *Postcolonial Sociology, Political Power and Social Theory* Volume 24 (Emerald Group Publishing Limited), 199–229.
Boyer, R. (2005) 'How and Why Capitalisms Differ', *Economy and Society*, 34:4, 509–57.
Boyer, R. (2014) *Is More Equality Possible in Latin America? A Challenge in a World of Contrasted but Interdependent Inequalities* (Berlin: Desigualdades.net), Working Paper No. 67.
Bruff, I. (2011) 'What about the Elephant in the Room? Varieties of Capitalism, Varieties in Capitalism', *New Political Economy*, 16:4, 481–500.
Bruff, I. and M. Ebenau (eds.) (2014a) *Critical Political Economy and Capitalist Diversity*, Special Issue of *Capital & Class*, 38:1, 3–251.
Bruff, I. and M. Ebenau (2014b) 'Critical Political Economy and the Critique of Comparative Capitalisms Scholarship on Capitalist Diversity', *Capital & Class*, 38:1, 3–15.
Bruff, I., M. Ebenau, C. May and A. Nölke (eds.) (2013) *Vergleichende Kapitalismusforschung: Stand, Perspektiven, Kritik* (Münster: Westfälisches Dampfboot).
Bruff, I. and E. Hartmann (2014) 'Neo-Pluralist Political Science, Economic Sociology and the Conceptual Foundations of the Comparative Capitalisms Literatures', *Capital & Class*, 38:1, 73–85.
Buhr, D. and R. Frankenberger (2013) 'Spielarten des inkorporierten Kapitalismus', in A. Nölke, C. May and S. Claar (eds.), *Die großen Schwellenländer. Ursachen und Folgen ihres Aufstiegs in der Weltwirtschaft* (Wiesbaden: Springer), 61–84.
Coates, D. (2014a) 'Studying Comparative Capitalisms by Going Left and by Going Deeper', *Capital & Class*, 38:1, 18–30.
Coates, D. (2014b) 'The UK: Less a Liberal Market Economy, More a post-Imperial One', *Capital & Class*, 38:1, 171–82.

Conrad, S. and S. Randeria (2002) *Jenseits des Eurozentrismus. Postkoloniale Perspektiven in den Geschichts- und Kulturwissenschaften* (Frankfurt/Main: Campus Verlag).
Cooper, F. (2005) *Colonialism in Question: Theory, Knowledge, History* (Berkeley/Los Angeles/London: Cambridge University Press).
Domingues, J.M. (2012) 'Development and Dependency, Developmentalism and Alternatives', in R.R. Boschi and C.H. Santana (eds.), *Development and Semi-Periphery: Post-Neoliberal Trajectories in South America and Central Eastern Europe* (London: Anthem Press), 83–101.
Drahokoupil, J. and M. Myant (2013) 'Institutionalismus jenseits der "Spielarten des Kapitalismus": Transitionsökonomien in der Vergleichenden Kapitalismusforschung', in I. Bruff, M. Ebenau, C. May and A. Nölke (eds.), *Vergleichende Kapitalismusforschung: Stand, Perspektiven, Kritik* (Münster: Westfälisches Dampfboot), 85–102.
Ebenau, M. (2012) 'Varieties of Capitalism or Dependency? A Critique of the VoC Approach for Latin America', *Competition & Change*, 16:3, 206–23.
Ebenau, M. (2014) 'Comparative Capitalisms and Latin American Developmentalism: A Critical Political Economy View', *Capital & Class*, 38:1, 102–14.
Ebenau, M., F. Parés and L. Suau Arinci (2013) 'Zurück in die Zukunft? Dependenzperspektiven in der Analyse der Diversität des Gegenwartskapitalismus', *PERIPHERIE: Zeitschrift für Politik und Ökonomie in der Dritten Welt*, 130/131, 220–42.
Eisenstadt, S.N. (2006) *The Great Revolutions and the Civilizations of Modernity* (Leiden: Brill).
Fernández, V.R. and M.B. Alfaro (2011) 'Ideas y políticas del desarrollo regional bajo variedades del capitalismo: contribuciones desde la periferia', *Revista Paranaense de Desenvolvimento*, 120, 57–99.
Go, J. (2013) 'Fanon's Postcolonial Cosmopolitanism', *European Journal of Social Theory*, 16:2, 208–25.
Grosfoguel, R. (2000) 'Developmentalism, Modernity, and Dependency Theory in Latin America', *Nepantla: Views from the South*, 1:1, 347–74.
Grosfoguel, R. (2010) 'Die Dekolonisation der politischen Ökonomie und der postkolonialen Studien: Transmoderne, Grenzdenken und globale Kolonialität', in M. Boatcă and W. Spohn (eds.), *Globale, multiple und postkoloniale Modernen* (München: Rainer Hampp), 309–38.
Haber, S. (ed.) (2001) *Crony Capitalism and Economic Growth in Latin America: Theory and Evidence* (Stanford: Hoover Institution Press).
Hall, P.A. and D. Soskice (eds.) (2001) *Varieties of Capitalism: The Institutional Foundations of Comparative Advantage* (Oxford: Oxford University Press).
Hardy, J. (2014) 'Transformation and Crisis in Central and Eastern Europe: A Combined and Uneven Development Perspective', *Capital & Class* 38:1, 143–55.
Harvey, D. (2004) 'Notes Towards a Theory of Uneven Geographical Development', in D. Harvey (ed.), *Spaces of Neoliberalization: Towards a Theory of Uneven Geographical Development* (Heidelberg: Franz Steiner Verlag), 53–89.
Hauck, G., R. Kößler, D. Kumitz and I. Wehr (2013) 'Neopatrimonialismus? Vom Sinn und Unsinn eines Diskurses', *PERIPHERIE: Zeitschrift für Politik und Ökonomie in der Dritten Welt*, 130/131, 279–302.

Hobson, J.M. (2004) *The Eastern Origins of Western Civilisation* (Cambridge: Cambridge University Press).
Hobson, J.M. (2013) 'Part 1 – Revealing the Eurocentric Foundations of IPE: A Critical Historiography of the Discipline from the Classical to the Modern Era', *Review of International Political Economy*, 20:5, 1024–54.
Inikori, J.E. (1992) 'Slavery and the Revolution in Cotton Textile Production in England', in J.E. Inikori and S.L. Engerman (eds.), *The Atlantic Slave Trade: Effects on Economies, Societies and Peoples in Africa, the Americas and Europe* (Durham: Duke University Press), 145–81.
Jessop, B. (2014) 'Capitalist Diversity and Variety: Variegation, the World Market, Compossibility and Ecological Dominance', *Capital & Class*, 38:1, 45–58.
Kößler, R. (2013) 'Kapitalismus und Moderne', *PERIPHERIE: Zeitschrift für Politik und Ökonomie in der Dritten Welt*, 130/131, 148–77.
Krennerich, M. (2005) 'Defekte Demokratie', in D. Nohlen and R.-O. Schultze (eds.), *Lexikon der Politikwissenschaft* (München: Beck), 119–21.
May, C. (2013) 'Jenseits von Markt und Staat: die Kultur des Kapitalismus in den BRICs', in A. Nölke, C. May and S. Claar (eds.), *Die großen Schwellenländer: Ursachen und Folgen ihres Aufstiegs in der Weltwirtschaft* (Wiesbaden: Springer), 85–99.
McNally, C. (2012) 'Sino-Capitalism: China's Reemergence and the International Political Economy', *World Politics*, 64:4, 741–76.
Mintz, S.W. (1985) *Sweetness and Power: The Place of Sugar in Modern History* (New York: Viking Press).
Mitchell, T. (2000) 'The Stage of Modernity', in T. Mitchell (ed.), *Questions of Modernity* (Minneapolis: University of Minnesota Press), 1–34.
Morgan, K. (2000) *Slavery, Atlantic Trade and the British Economy, 1660–1800* (Cambridge: Cambridge University Press).
Nölke, A. (2011) 'Die BRIC-Variante des Kapitalismus und soziale Ungleichheit. Das Beispiel Brasilien', in I. Wehr and H.-J. Burchardt (eds.), *Soziale Ungleichheiten in Lateinamerika. Neue Perspektiven auf Wirtschaft, Politik und Umwelt* (Baden-Baden: Nomos), 137–52.
Nölke, A. and S. Claar (2013) 'Varieties of Capitalism in Emerging Economies', *Transformation: Critical Perspectives on Southern Africa*, 81/82, 33–54.
Nölke, A. and A. Vliegenthart (2009) 'Enlarging the Varieties of Capitalism: The Emergence of Dependent Market Economies in East Central Europe', *World Politics*, 61:4, 670–702.
North, D., J. Wallis and B. Weingast (2009) *Violance and Social Orders: A Conceptual Framework for Interpreting Recorded Human History* (Cambridge: Cambridge University Press).
Offe, C. [1969] (2006) *Strukturprobleme des kapitalistischen Staates* (revised edition) (Frankfurt and New York: Campus).
Parsons, T. (1971) *The System of Modern Societies* (Englewood Cliffs, NJ: Prentice-Hall).
Peck, J. and N. Theodore (2007) 'Variegated Capitalism', *Progress in Human Geography*, 31:6, 731–72.
Piketty, T. (2014) *Capital in the Twenty-first Century* (Cambridge and London: The Belknap Press of Harvard University Press).
Quijano, A. (2000) 'Coloniality of Power, Eurocentrism, and Latin America', *Nepantla: Views from the South*, 1:3, 533–80.

Randeria, S., M. Fuchs and A. Linkenbach (2004) 'Konfigurationen der Moderne: Zur Einleitung', in S. Randeria, M. Fuchs and A. Linkenbach (eds.), *Konfigurationen der Moderne: Diskurse zu Indien*, Soziale Welt Sonderband 15 (Baden-Baden: Nomos), 9–34.

Redding, G. and M.A. Witt (2007) *The Future of Chinese Capitalism: Choices and Chances* (Oxford: Oxford University Press).

Robinson, N. (2011) 'Russian Patrimonial Capitalism and the International Financial Crisis', *Journal of Communist Studies and Transition Politics*, 27:3–4, 434–55.

Saich, A. (2002) 'The Blind Man and the Elephant: Analyzing the Local State in China', in L. Tomba (ed.), *On the Roots of Growth and Crisis: Capitalism, State and Society in East Asia* (Milan: Annale Feltinelli), 75–99.

Said, E. (1978) *Orientalism* (New York: Pantheon).

Sauer, B. and S. Wöhl (2011) 'Feminist Perspectives on the Internationalization of the State', *Antipode*, 43:1, 108–28.

Schlumberger, O. (2008) 'Structural Reform, Economic Order, and Development: Patrimonial Capitalism', *Review of International Political Economy*, 15:4, 622–49.

Schneider, B.R. (2013) *Hierarchical Capitalism in Latin America: Business, Labor, and the Challenges of Equitable Development* (Cambridge: Cambridge University Press).

Seidman, S. (2014) 'The Colonial Unconscious of Classical Sociology', in J. Go (ed.), *Postcolonial Sociology, Political Power and Social Theory* Volume 24, 35–54.

Solow, B.L. (ed.) (1991) *Slavery and the Rise of the Atlantic System* (Cambridge: Cambridge University Press).

Storz, C., B. Amable, S. Casper and S. Lechevalier (2013) 'Bringing Asia into the Comparative Capitalism Perspective', *Socio-Economic Review*, 11:2, 217–32.

ten Brink, T. (2013) *Chinas Kapitalismus: Entstehung, Verlauf, Paradoxien* (Frankfurt and New York: Campus).

Taylor, N. (2014) 'Theorising Capitalist Diversity: The Uneven and Combined Development of Labour Forms', *Capital & Class*, 38:1, 129–41.

Vliegenthart, A. (2010) 'Bringing Dependency Back In: The Economic Crisis in Post-Socialist Europe and the Continued Relevance of Dependent Development', *Historical Social Research/Historische Sozialforschung*, 35:2, 242–65.

Wehr, I. (2011) 'Wohlfahrtsregime und soziale Ungleichheit in Lateinamerika', in I. Wehr and H.-J. Burchardt (eds.), *Soziale Ungleichheiten in Lateinamerika. Neue Perspektiven auf Wirtschaft, Politik und Umwelt* (Baden-Baden: Nomos), 257–81.

Wehr, I. (2014) 'Auf dem Weg zur großen Entwicklungstheorie 2.0? Multiple und verwobene Moderne und die Rückkehr der großen Fragestellungen', in A. Ziai (ed.) *Im Westen nichts Neues. Stand und Perspektiven der Entwicklungstheorie* (Baden-Baden: Nomos), 43–69.

Zahedieh, N. (2010) *The Capital and the Colonies: London and the Atlantic Economy, 1660–1700* (Cambridge: Cambridge University Press).

Zhang, J. and J. Peck (2014) 'Variegated Capitalism, Chinese Style: Regional Models, Multi-Scalar Constructions', *Regional Studies*, advance online publication.

Part III
Global Perspectives and Debates

9
Putting Comparative Capitalisms Research in Its Place: Varieties of Capitalism in Transition Economies

Jan Drahokoupil and Martin Myant

This chapter introduces an approach to capitalist variety in transition economies in order to make a renewed case for typological theories of economic performance. We argue that Comparative Capitalisms (CC) research, the Varieties of Capitalism (VoC) approach in particular, was a victim of its success. The debate it triggered has made many of its weak points apparent (see also Bruff et al., in this volume), but the added value of the perspectives were lost in a discussion that often blamed the VoC approach for failing to deliver on agendas that were beyond its original aims. Against this background, we argue that the underlying analytical assumptions of the CC literatures remain useful and appropriate for understanding the diversity of economic and political outcomes. Many of the assumptions of the VoC approach proved problematic, but it remains exemplary in pursuing a clearly delimited explanatory agenda. This aim, unfortunately, was obscured in many contributions – from both institutionalist CC and critical perspectives – that aimed to provide more appropriate and comprehensive frameworks for understanding contemporary political economies. We thus make a case for a more sympathetic reading of the VoC contributions. In particular, we consider developing typological theories – that is, using typologies as explanatory tools (cf. George and Bennett, 2005) – the main added value of CC research.

The debate triggered by the VoC approach has finally led to a degree of consensus in the CC literatures as to its shortcomings (see recent state-of-the-art discussions, including Deeg and Jackson, 2007; Bohle and Greskovits, 2009; see also Coates, in this volume). The consensus includes the need to go beyond static models, which assume a need for coherence and the need to bring politics and power in (Streeck, 2009; Bruff, 2011). However, much of the criticism of the VoC approach is less relevant if considered in the context of its underlying aims. This applies both to what it can explain (the choice of the dependent variable) and how it explains (the causal mechanisms, or the nature of independent variables). The approach is still useful and continues to provide a valuable new direction for CC research, with its focus on the role of institutions in determining economic performance. Our own CC framework introduced in the next section thus reflects a number of substantial reservations about the applicability of the VoC approach, but it considers only those points that are relevant to the aim of explaining economic performance. The section that follows develops our CC approach to capitalist variety in transition economies. It aims to go beyond the pitfalls of the VoC approach while consistently pursuing its aim of producing a typological theory of economic performance. Further sections then apply the approach and briefly outline the basic features of capitalist variation in transition economies.[1]

A CC approach to transition economies

The CC framework developed here follows the Hall and Soskice (2001) approach in linking institutional forms to international competitiveness. A substantial body of literature exists on the use of the VoC framework for transition economies. Some authors have tried to set countries under the headings developed by Hall and Soskice (for example, Feldmann, 2006; Knell and Srholec, 2007; Mykhnenko, 2007; Buchen, 2007), but the specific features chosen miss the important features that differentiate transition economies from both Germany and the United States (see also Gaitán and Boschi on Latin America, in this volume). Moreover, it would be misleading to assume that the presence of similar institutions leads to the same effects in terms of coordination mechanisms, as identified within coordinated and liberal market economies (CMEs and LMEs), respectively (Drahokoupil, 2009). It is also very clear that any apparent similarities in some institutional features are not associated with similar levels of innovative activity: this is relatively low in all transition economies. Another group of authors have indicated the fruitlessness of such efforts, sometimes proposing new forms and labels, such as the 'dependent market economy' referred to by Nölke and Vliegenthart (2009) or acknowledging the emergence of a number of different forms, none of which corresponds precisely to types previously identified (Lane, 2007).

In the analysis that follows, we develop a different typology, which is explicitly limited and partial. Thus, we do not attempt full descriptions of the types of capitalisms in different countries. Instead, we start from the major differences between transition countries in terms of their integration into the world economy. These differences are linked to their preconditions, including both institutional and other factors. Institutions are thus used as an 'independent variable' to explain the existence of different types of coordination and innovation as linked to distinct comparative advantages. Our approach therefore differs from that of authors who have started from established varieties of capitalism and also from that of others who have sought alternative frameworks, starting from consideration of institutional features. Similarly, our approach does not attempt to explain why or how particular social formations arose and what might lead them to change. Instead, we aim to contribute to the debate with a narrower focus on how institutional forms are linked to diverse forms of international integration (for a contrasting approach to the same question, see Hardy 2014). This leads to a demonstration of preconditions for levels and forms of competitiveness rather than precise determinants. Beyond some fairly clear preconditions, we find quite wide ranges of variation in possible institutional forms.

We build on varied sources in the literature, which refer to links between institutions and levels of economic development. Thus, measures of, among others, corruption, governance quality and protection of property can be shown to correlate with per capita GDP (for example, Knack and Keefer, 1995; de Vaal and Ebben, 2011), albeit without certainty as to the direction of causation and with reservations that different formal methods seem able to achieve the same outcome in different societies. A second source is Porter's (1990, pp. 545–56) notion of stages of competitiveness, rather than a continuous scale. Countries export different kinds of products depending on a number of aspects of their economic and political environments. This is further developed, for example, by the World Economic Forum (Schwab, 2013), with a complex array of indicators that determine the environment for businesses as they compete in the international arena. The Hall and Soskice version avoids such quantification but adds a further element with the argument that competing in different kinds of products is made possible by different institutional settings. However, they are dealing only with advanced economies, in which many of the basic problems that are still relevant for other parts of the world have been largely resolved.

Our approach can be characterized by four points. The first is an adaptation of the 'dependent variable' in order to incorporate a focus on broader forms of integration into the world economy. Export competitiveness remains one element within that, but it need not imply anything approaching world leadership. It is supplemented by a variety of other ways in which countries could achieve external balance, ranging from exports of manufactured goods through exports of natural resources and openness to inflows of private finance to dependence on remittances and foreign aid. The second is the recognition that other factors, and not just institutional frameworks, influence the relevant forms of international integration. These include the structure of the inherited industrial bases, natural resource endowments and also geography (cf. Greskovits, 2005). Institutions thus appear as one element that interacts with these other factors, but it is not sufficient alone for explaining economic performance.

The third adaptation is a broader notion of institutional advantage, differentiating between the specific institutional advantages considered by the VoC approach and more generic institutional advantages that dominated the analysis of transition economies. Much of the comparative political economy literature takes for granted the basic themes that often remained unresolved in transition economies, including state capacity, the rule of law, a functioning system of corporate governance, a stable financial system, clarity in ownership of enterprises and a separation between the spheres of business and politics. However, clientelism, the contested nature of property rights and weak rule of law were widely considered to be a key defining feature of capitalist varieties in the post-Soviet Commonwealth of Independent States (King, 2007; Lane and Myant, 2007; Lane, 2007). This fact does not fit comfortably into the VoC framework (cf. Becker, 2009, pp. 59–63; Nölke and Vliegenthart, 2009, pp. 695–6).

Following these issues requires treading on ground unfamiliar in much of mainstream economics and political economy (but see, for example, Alston and Mueller, 2005), where it is typically assumed that rules are followed, that debts are paid, that credits are returned, that depositors can trust a banking system and that government policies, once decided, will be implemented. Institutionalist writings frequently include the recognition that 'informal' rules may be as important as formal rules, but that does not do justice to the extent of the differences between advanced and transition economies. This is recognized in Becker's framework, which suggests the 'patrimonial type' to be strongly present in 'emerging economies' (Becker, 2009). Our framework, however, sees clear implications of the patrimonial type for economic specialization and performance.

Fourthly, we subscribe to a weaker notion of complementarity between elements of a type of capitalism. We emphasize the diversity within individual political economies and the role of contingency and politics. This means that we can set out specific preconditions for a particular form of international integration, but that does not encompass all institutional features within a political economy. Different forms and different combinations may be compatible with the same form of international integration.

Varieties of capitalism in transition economies

The above discussion provides a starting point for applying a CC approach to transition economies. The separation into types of capitalism is linked to classification of types of international integration. We distinguish four forms of integration through production networks, based not only on what they produce (product complexity), but also how they do it (type of production network). The four forms include (i) export-oriented foreign direct investment (FDI) in complex sectors; (ii) export-oriented complex sectors without FDI; (iii) simple manufacturing through subcontracting and (iv) commodities and semi-manufactures. There are also two forms of integration through finance: dependence on remittances and aid and integration through financial inflows. The latter form, associated with financialized development, is not appropriate for use here as a basis for a specific type of capitalism, partly because it is a phenomenon that varied greatly over short time periods, rising up to the crisis of 2008 and then falling dramatically. It also takes different forms that can be compatible with different types of capitalism and very varied levels of economic development. It is therefore not used here as a defining feature (see Myant and Drahokoupil, 2012). The remaining five forms of integration can be set against their preconditions in terms of state capacity (rule of law and the separation of business and politics), state activity (state policy), business development and the financial system.[2]

In this sense, the forms of integration and their preconditions can be linked to five types of capitalism that explain the nature of economic integration characterizing a given country: FDI-based market economies, peripheral market economies, order states, oligarchic (clientelistic) capitalism and remittance/aid-based economies (see Table 9.1). The institutional and policy preconditions for forms of international

Table 9.1 Varieties of capitalism and forms of integration

Type of capitalism	FDI based	Peripheral market economies	Order states	Oligarchic or clientelistic	Remittance- and aid-based
Form of integration	Complex manuf. with FDI	Subcontracted manufacturing	Complex manuf. without FDI	Commodity including semi-manufacturing	Remittances
State capacity					
– rule of law	Requires **stable** environment **for all business**	Requires **stable** environment **for all business**	Requires protection only **for key enterprises**	Requires protection only **for key enterprises**	No requirements
– separation of business and politics	**Separation** of business from direct dependence on politics	**Separation** of business from direct dependence on politics	**Close linking** of key business and political power	**Does not require independence** of business from political power	No requirements
State activity	Creates infrastructure for economy and support for FDI	Basic economic infrastructure	Can protect and help particular activities, **substituting for rule of law**	Basic economic infrastructure	No requirements
Business development	Only limitation is that it does not require development of new, innovative businesses	Requires independent businesses	No requirements	No requirements	No requirements
Financial system	Complex financial systems and capital markets are not important for FDI	Likely to require some **independent** sources of finance	State can **direct finance**	Big business can seek state help and/or external finance	No requirements
Other factors	Inherited (complex) industrial base	Cheap labour		Resource endowments favourable	
Embeddedness	Industrial relations, labour markets and welfare systems are not important preconditions. Their development reflects internal social conditions and political forces.				

Jan Drahokoupil and Martin Myant 161

integration can be set in an approximate hierarchy, in that the institutional preconditions appear less demanding from the first to the last. The simplest business transactions, requiring only barter, can coexist with a very simple institutional environment. Production for trade requires a degree of guaranteed relationships and some security for private property. A more complex economy develops with the growth of a financial system such that savings can be mobilized for investment. That requires sophisticated rules, regulatory systems and a reasonable certainty that rules will be applied. Requirements of an economy that is a source of leading innovations are still more demanding, including established research and education systems, incentives to innovate within firms and a financial system that can provide venture capital.

The framework suggests flexibility in industrial relations, labour markets and welfare systems. These aspects – that could be summarized under the term 'social embeddedness' – are not among the important preconditions for any of the forms of integration. Rather, their development reflects internal social conditions and political forces. On the other hand, the political–economic context can limit opportunities for welfare strategies: for instance, complex manufacturing seems to be most favourable to higher welfare spending. Empirically, therefore, it is associated with a variety of welfare-state outcomes. In practice, every country combined more than one form of international integration. However, there are enormous variations in the relative importance of different forms of integration. Thus, several country groups where one or the other of the forms of integration became predominant can be identified. Therefore, by combining forms of integration with internal economic, political and institutional forms, an approximate classification into five types can be made. In some cases, though, there is overlap between them, and none is fixed. All countries are, to varying extents, in a process of change. In time, they could move from being close to one individual type to approximating another.

Table 9.2 provides indicators of the diversity of the forms of integration for selected countries that represent individual ideal types. It refers to the pre-crisis period in order to capture the importance of financial inflows,[3] though it should be noted that export structures did not change dramatically after 2008. Central and Eastern European Countries (CEECs) were characterized by a high share of exports by modern manufacturing industries.[4] Indeed, using a definition of complex products that includes machinery and identifiable high-tech products, these constituted over 60 per cent of Hungarian exports in that year. For Russia,

Table 9.2 Indicators for principal forms of international integration: Countries representative of ideal types (2007, percentage of GDP)

	Complex products	Light industry	Commodities		Financial account-FDI	Remittances*
			without fuels and unclassified	fuels		
FDI-based (second-rank) market economies						
Czech Republic	39.5	6.3	21.8	1.8	−1.5	0.8
Slovakia	37.9	5.6	21.9	3.2	0.2	1.8
Peripheral market economies						
Bulgaria	8.5	7.6	24.8	6	18.3	4.3
Latvia	5.8	2.7	17.9	1	17.7	1.9
Order states						
Belarus	11.8	2.9	20.2	18.8	7.6	0.8
Uzbekistan	3.9	0.3	20	4.3		17.0*
Oligarchic/clientelistic capitalism						
Azerbaijan	0.5	0	2.9	14.9	−5.6	3.9
Kazakhstan	0.9	0	14.5	30.1	0.3	0.2
Russia	1.1	0.1	9.2	16.7	6.7	0.4
Ukraine	6	1.1	25.6	1.8	4.1	3.2
Remittance- and aid-based economies						
Armenia	0.8	0.7	10.5	0.1	3.3	9.2
Tajikistan	0.1	0.4	28	0	12.1	45.5

*The figures for remittances are from the World Bank and show recorded transfers reported by central banks. An alternative measure (calculated from the International Fund for Agricultural Development, 2007), based on survey data, showed similar levels in most countries but notably higher levels in Armenia (18.5 per cent of GDP) and Belarus (6.3 per cent of GDP). For Uzbekistan, only survey data were available.
Notes: The categories are adaptations from Standard International Trade Classification (see Myant and Drahokoupil, 2011).
Source: Calculated by authors from International Monetary Fund (IMF) Financial Statistics, COMTRADE database of the United Nations, and World Development Indicators.

they amounted to barely 10 per cent, while in Belarus they varied between 20 and 30 per cent in the years up to 2008. The sectoral allocation of FDI varied, but foreign investment was particularly important for modern manufacturing industry. Thus, the stock of FDI in 2007 was equivalent to 143.2 per cent in Hungary and 80.3 per cent of GDP in Estonia, but only 7.4 per cent in Belarus.

There were similarly striking variations in exports of simpler products. Semi-manufactures were of declining importance in CEECs but continued to be important in almost all other countries, including the Baltic Republics and Southeast European Countries (SEECs).[5] For Ukraine, they contributed over 50 per cent of exports and about 20 per cent for Russia.

Raw materials were also more important for CIS countries than for CEECs: for example, fuels accounted for up to 90 per cent of Azerbaijan's exports and over 60 per cent for Russia. In the latter case, other raw materials were also important. Light industries, such as garments and footwear, rose and fell in importance in the CEECs. They had never been important for lower-income CIS countries but still accounted for over 20 per cent of Bulgarian exports in 2007, falling from 40 per cent a few years earlier.

Remittances were extremely important for some of the lowest-income countries, approaching the equivalent of 40 per cent of GDP in Tajikistan and Moldova, but only 0.8 per cent in Hungary. This link to income levels is less clear for financial inflows, measured by financial account surpluses relative to GDP. High figures were recorded in 2007 for Bulgaria (18.2 per cent), Latvia (17.9 per cent) and Tajikistan (12.2 per cent), albeit with a much lower per capita GDP level in the last country. FDI has been excluded from these data as it can contribute to technological advancements and better export performance. It was therefore often a factor for stabilizing economies, in the sense that it increased resilience to the effects of the crisis, while inflows of bank credit were to prove a major source of instability after they dried up, or were reversed, in 2008.

The individual types of capitalism and how the degree of membership of individual cases developed are discussed in the next section.

Types of capitalism in transition economies

FDI-based (second-rank) market economies are distinguished by democratic political systems, integration into the European Union (EU) and export structures increasingly built around manufactured goods produced by foreign-owned multinational corporations (MNCs). This type characterizes the CEECs. These economies have developed complex export structures, but they have only a second-rank position in international production networks. There is, nevertheless, a considerable potential for upgrading and development, making this variety more promising than other outcomes of transition. There is also flexibility on other features, which range from quite substantial labour protection and welfare provision to a more neoliberal approach. Although these countries lack the infrastructure for high-level innovations – including established and experienced businesses, strong higher education and research bases and access to venture capital – they do have sound environments for domestic business development that uses innovations developed elsewhere.

The export of high-value products into Western Europe, manufactured in branches of large MNCs, is the most secure form of international integration, offering the highest incomes. The internal preconditions for this form of international integration vary, depending on the nature of the investment and the sector concerned. A leading force in CEECs has been the automotive industry, with the creation of large-scale assembly and accompanying component manufacture (cf. Pavlínek et al., 2009). Preconditions for the companies concerned include a transport and communications infrastructure, a system for stable relations with large concentrations of employees, a government and administrative system that operates effectively and legal preconditions for stable relations between firms. However, they neither need a strong base for developing innovations nor do they need to raise finance within those countries. These institutional preconditions have been broadly achieved in the CEECs, the Baltic Republics and to a growing extent throughout Southeast Europe, although geography and past histories are, as indicated below, much more favourable in CEECs so that they alone have developed this form of integration to a significant scale. However, none of these countries have the full environment for business found in advanced market economies, including access to large-scale finance for their own firms and to a research base appropriate for systematic innovation activity.

MNCs have been attracted to these countries by more than just institutional factors. They came to CEECs as countries with which they had been in contact in the past, which had heritages of a reasonably modern industry, good physical infrastructures and links to Western Europe. Political stability has also been important to companies undertaking long-term investment and the likelihood of EU accession – as was the case for CEECs from early in the 1990s – served as a useful stamp of approval. The MNCs need a secure legal and business environment, giving confidence that contracts would be honoured. Policies could also influence the 'structural advantages' to the extent that the maintenance of pre-existing industrial bases has attracted investors seeking to acquire companies operating in similar activities to their own (cf. Greskovits, 2005, pp. 117–19; Kurth, 1979, pp. 3–4; Drahokoupil, 2008).

Characterizing these countries as 'dependent' is not ideal. There is dependence on technology from outside, but there is potential for substantial economic development and for development of the relationship between countries and MNCs by the upgrading of activities, and indeed some MNCs have brought and maintained research and development (R&D) activities. It is also an economic structure that led to reasonable resilience to the effects of the economic crisis (Myant and Drahokoupil, 2012; Myant et al., 2013). MNCs did not reduce their presence in CEECs after 2008. The relationship contains elements of mutual advantage as much as one-sided dependency. Nor does foreign ownership of banks, which has reached very high levels in CEECs, imply dependence on external finance. In a number of countries, notably the Czech Republic and Slovakia, credits have been based on domestic savings. Inflows of finance up to 2008 were characteristic of countries with lower deposit bases that also had nothing to do with bank ownership (Myant and Drahokoupil, 2011b). Thus, again, use of the term 'dependent' can give a deceptive impression.

Peripheral market economies have reasonably democratic political systems and basic legal and institutional conditions for business, but they rely on less stable manufactured goods and raw material exports. This form of integration was important in CEECs in the early 1990s but became less important as export structures shifted towards motor vehicles and other products of modern manufacturing. That transformation brought with it higher wage levels, which made it more difficult to compete with Asian countries in the production of simpler manufactured goods, such as garments and footwear. However, exports of such products continue to be more important in SEECs and raw materials continue to be important in the Baltic Republics' exports. These are therefore grouped together under this heading.

A number of these countries were also highly dependent on inflows of finance in the pre-2008 period. The Baltic Republics were an extreme example (see Kattel and Raudla, 2013). Indeed, in view of their weak export potential in sophisticated manufacturing products, due to past history and to geography, alongside wage levels considerably above those of CEECs, this was an essential mechanism for ensuring overall external balance. Dependence on external finance followed from a failure of internal savings to match demand for credits. Financial inflows were attracted by the highly liberalized market conditions, which gave them good reputations in international financial circles, thus belying their economic weaknesses. Such reputations were not harmed by low levels of welfare provision.

The export of garments, footwear and simpler components depend on subcontracting from MNCs, typically with very precise specifications as to what is required, and in some cases direct investment. There also has to be an adequate transport and communications infrastructure, but required skill levels are low – all product development can take place in a richer country – so that low labour costs are a key factor in deciding the location of production. The industrial structure inherited from the past is also important, as it typically provides the productive capacity and labour force that can quickly be adapted to satisfy new orders. Issues of corporate governance or privatization policies are of little significance to foreign companies, but MNCs do need a secure enough legal framework to give confidence that contracts with local firms will be honoured. Their limited involvement in local production structures means that they are not a significant force for economic upgrading. That depends on domestic firms or on the arrival of MNCs with completely different kinds of activities.

The *order states* type applies to those countries of the CIS that underwent the most limited reforms, notably Belarus and Uzbekistan (cf. Iwasaki, 2004). As such, their very classification as capitalist can be questioned. Even though substantial state ownership remained, they clearly did undergo substantial transformations after 1989, as indicated by their degrees of integration into the global economy, their use of a price mechanism and price levels at least close to the world level, and the scope for private enterprise. They are characterized by authoritarian political systems that also dominate the main economic decisions. International integration depends on activities inherited from the past and on state support for export either of manufactured goods or of commodities. The environment for business from outside the state sector is poor. The authoritarian and arbitrary states and the low levels of financial development make growth of new businesses difficult. Welfare provision reflects continuity with the past, leading to relatively high levels of public spending (see Myant and Drahokoupil, 2011b, Chapter 10). This distinguishes them from many other CIS countries, in which welfare provision was drastically reduced in the turmoil of the early 1990s. High spending in order states helps secure the necessary popular backing for the political survival of the authoritarian regimes.

Belarus benefits from its relationship with Russia, exporting processed petrochemical products. It is also reasonably successful in exporting vehicles, from enterprises developed in the Soviet period, on the basis of an 'order state' (Iwasaki, 2004). The state owns the key enterprises and directs banks' lending policies. These provide some financial resources and a greater level of managerial stability than in countries where similar enterprises were privatized and often faced immense difficulties or where they were allowed to disappear in total, as in the Baltic Republics. The Belarussian firms benefit from some international cooperation to gain access to modern technology, but there is also substantial autonomous product development. However, these products are able to compete only in less demanding markets, which are not dominated by established MNCs, and it remains to be seen whether this model will prove to be more than transient.

There has been an attempt to use the order state framework to promote development of complex sectors from scratch (cf. Myant and Drahokoupil, 2011a). The Uzbek government sought to develop a motor vehicle industry, starting production in 1996 with a joint venture with the South Korean manufacturer Daewoo, which was taken over the General Motors in 2002. This started as a precarious assembly operation, but in later years the government set out to promote development of a full range of component manufacturers. The results of this strategy remain to be seen. The country lacks a past history of modern manufacturing, reliable transport contacts with other component suppliers and a secure legal and institutional environment for business.

The *oligarchic* or *clientelistic capitalism* category applies to much of the CIS and indicates a type of capitalism with some distinctive features, particularly in relation to links between 'business' and 'political power'. Neither of the two terms is ideal; one seems more appropriate for some countries and the other for other countries. Thus, in Russia, the source of the term 'oligarch', powerful business groups were either created by or benefited from privatization policies in the 1990s. However, this private property is not as secure as in more established capitalist systems. Expropriation by those with political power remains an ever-present threat. In return, business groups have had considerable influence over politics, financing election campaigns and using the media they control to favour particular candidates. The two terms used for characterizing this group imply different balances of power between the political and business groups, a feature that is both difficult to determine and subject to quite rapid change.

These countries are all characterized by relatively authoritarian political systems, albeit with differences over the extent to which formally democratic practices play a role. This type of capitalism is compatible with lower levels of state capacity and with institutional environments that do not provide a basis for secure links between enterprises, still less for the development of innovative, newer firms. The themes of employment relations, links between firms and the development of a finance sector are therefore not important to this form of international integration. Exporting firms could prosper in the absence of a stable legal and business environment as long as they are favoured by those with political power. Politics has proved crucial to changing the form of international integration. In Ukraine, significant FDI came into the country only after its reputation improved in Western eyes (it remains to be seen what the impact of the 2013 crisis will be in this respect). The key economic change was the sale of steel capacity, which was followed by the international integration of production and modernization of technology. Social and employment protection and an environment for dynamic new businesses are generally very weakly developed, not because they would harm the forms of international integration that dominate but because they are irrelevant to those forms and to the interests of those with political power.

There are differences between oil and gas exporters and other commodity exporters, owing to the exceptionally high revenues and low employment needs of the former. That makes oil and gas exporting even more compatible with a weak environment for the rest of the economy. Exporters can create their own physical infrastructure, raise capital from their own profits or from abroad and need only very limited contacts to local businesses. This has no direct implications for labour relations, welfare provision and the environment for business overall. It has long been argued that oil and gas exporting limits the scope for export-oriented manufacturing by raising the exchange rate. This has been described as the 'Dutch disease', following the decline of manufacturing in the Netherlands after the discovery and exploitation of natural gas from the 1960s. It is indeed clear that exports of simple manufacturing products from the fuel-exporting countries – notably Azerbaijan, Turkmenistan, Kazakhstan and also Russia – have remained extremely low. However, this may not be due to exchange rate effects alone: it may also be influenced by institutional factors. The preconditions for fuel exporting are compatible with an authoritarian regime that need not listen to voices from society or promote other forms of economic development. Thus, oil and gas wealth can be a force for economic and social inertia, trapping countries within a particular economic structure. This is consistent with Russia's experience, in which other sectors remain geared to the domestic economy with little ability to compete internationally.

Finally, the category of *remittance- and aid-based economies* applies to a number of low-income countries in the CIS – notably Armenia and Kyrgyzstan, Tajikistan and Uzbekistan in Central Asia – and to Albania, Moldova and Bosnia-Herzegovina on the low-income peripheries of Eastern Europe. It is a consequence of a low economic level and the limited scope for other activities to develop. The continual migration of part of the labour force- and in practical terms it is often the most qualified people who take jobs in a more prosperous country- itself limits the scope for internal development. The institutional preconditions for a remittance-based economy are minimal, but there are differences in the prospects for further economic development depending on how the remittances are used. In some cases, notably Armenia, they can support domestic economic development, particularly housing construction. In others, notably in Central Asia, even the institutional basis for a low level of market-based development is very limited and remittances support spending on imports for consumption with no further positive impact on the domestic economy. Without an adequate environment for business and often also a favourable geographical location, much domestic business activity remains at the level of small-scale trading.

Conclusion

The typology introduced above is linked to the single aim of explaining economic performance in transition economies, expressed in the nature of economic integration into the world economy, by linking it to internal conditions. This does not provide a comprehensive framework for understanding the nature of those societies as a whole, still less for identifying forces that might lead them to develop and change. It is clear that a variety of institutional forms can be associated with the same outcomes in terms of economic performance. Nor are institutions the only factor important in determining economic performance. Nevertheless, the concern with institutional performance, howsoever specified, should be one of the central directions in the CC agenda. The VoC approach proposed a typological theory with such a purpose. The debate in the CC literatures that started with a reflection on the weak points of the VoC approach led CC research away from explaining the economic and other effects of institutions. At the same time, the debate was extremely useful in identifying problems with existing explanations of institutional performance. This includes the need to go beyond the national level and analyse the complementarities and, more broadly, the constitution of comparative advantages also on the sectoral and firm levels. In addition, the notion of institutions as continuously evolving forms, the wider understanding of complementarities, and the non-institutional constitution of comparative advantage, also need to be considered (see also May and Nölke, in this volume). The lessons learned should help CC research in formulating better typological theories.

Notes

1. More details, with supporting evidence, can be found in separate contributions (Myant and Drahokoupil, 2011b, 2012).

2. We focus here only on the institutional factors, leaving aside issues of geography and inherited economic structures that are referred to later in relation to particular countries.
3. These and other data on individual countries come from Myant and Drahokoupil (2011b, 2012).
4. CEECs include the Czech Republic, Hungary, Poland, Slovakia and Slovenia.
5. SEECs comprise Bulgaria and Romania. The Baltic Republics include Estonia, Latvia and Lithuania.

Bibliography

Alston, L.J. and B. Mueller (2005) 'Property Rights and the State', in C. Ménard and M.M. Shirley (eds.), *Handbook of New Institutional Economics* (Berlin: Springer), 573–90.
Becker, U. (2009) *Open Varieties of Capitalism: Continuity, Change and Performances* (Basingstoke: Palgrave Macmillan).
Bohle, D. and B. Greskovits (2009) 'Varieties of Capitalism and Capitalism Tout Court', *European Journal of Sociology*, 50:3, 355–86.
Bruff, I. (2011) 'What about the Elephant in the Room? Varieties of Capitalism, Varieties in Capitalism', *New Political Economy*, 16:4, 481–500.
Buchen, C. (2007) 'Estonia and Slovenia as Antipodes', in D. Lane and M. Myant (eds.), *Varieties of Capitalism in Post-Communist Countries* (Basingstoke: Palgrave Macmillan), 65–89.
de Vaal, A. and W. Ebben (2011) 'Institutions and the Relation between Corruption and Economic Growth', *Review of Development Economics*, 15:1, 108–23.
Deeg, R. and G. Jackson (2007) 'Towards a More Dynamic Theory of Capitalist Variety', *Socio-Economic Review*, 5:1, 149–79.
Drahokoupil, J. (2008) *Globalization and the State in Central and Eastern Europe: The Politics of Foreign Direct Investment* (London: Routledge).
Drahokoupil, J. (2009) 'After Transition: Varieties of Political-Economic Development in Eastern Europe and the Former Soviet Union', *Comparative European Politics*, 7:2, 279–98.
Feldmann, M. (2006) 'Emerging Varieties of Capitalism in Transition Countries: Industrial Relations and Wage Bargaining in Estonia and Slovenia', *Comparative Political Studies*, 39:7, 829–54.
George, A.L. and A. Bennett (2005) *Case Studies and Theory Development in the Social Sciences* (Cambridge, MA: MIT Press).
Greskovits, B. (2005) 'Leading Sectors and the Variety of Capitalism in Eastern Europe', *Actes du GERPISA*, 39, 113–28.
Hall, P.A. and D. Soskice (eds.) (2001) *Varieties of Capitalism: the Institutional Foundations of Comparative Advantage* (Oxford: Oxford University Press).
Hardy, J. (2014) 'Transformation and Crisis in Central and Eastern Europe: A Combined and Uneven Development Perspective', *Capital & Class*, 38:1, 143–55.
Iwasaki, I. (2004) 'Evolution of the Government-Business Relationship and Economic Performance in the Former Soviet States: Order State, Rescue State, and Punish State', *Economics of Planning*, 36:3, 223–57.

Kattel, R. and R. Raudla (2013) 'The Baltic Republics and the Crisis of 2008–2011', *Europe-Asia Studies*, 65:3, 426–49.
King, L.P. (2007) 'Central European Capitalism in Comparative Perspective', in B. Hancké, M. Rhodes and M. Thatcher (eds.), *Beyond Varieties of Capitalism: Conflict, Contradictions, and Complementarities in the European Economy* (Oxford: Oxford University Press), 307–27.
Knack, S. and P. Keefer (1995) 'Institutions and Economic Performance: Cross-Country Tests Using Alternative Institutional Measures', *Economics & Politics*, 7:3, 207–27.
Knell, M. and M. Srholec (2007) 'Diverging Pathways in Central and Eastern Europe', in D. Lane and M. Myant (eds.), *Varieties of Capitalism in Post-Communist Countries* (Basingstoke: Palgrave Macmillan), 40–62.
Kurth, J.R. (1979) 'The Political Consequences of the Product Cycle: Industrial History and Political Outcomes', *International Organization*, 33:1, 1–34.
Lane, D. (ed.). (2007) *The Transformation of State Socialism: System Change, Capitalism or Something Else?* (Basingstoke: Palgrave Macmillan).
Lane, D. and M. Myant (eds.) (2007) *Varieties of Capitalism in Post-Communist Countries* (Basingstoke: Palgrave Macmillan).
Myant, M. and J. Drahokoupil (2011a) 'Central Asian Republics: Forms of International Integration and the Impact of the Crisis of 2008', in J. Ahrens and H.W. Hoen (eds.), *Institutional Reform in Central Asia: Politico-Economic Challenges* (London: Routledge), 257–74.
Myant, M. and J. Drahokoupil (2011b) *Transition Economies: Political Economy in Russia, Eastern Europe, and Central Asia* (Hoboken, NJ: Wiley-Blackwell).
Myant, M. and J. Drahokoupil (2012) 'International Integration, Varieties of Capitalism, and Resilience to Crisis in Transition Economies', *Europe-Asia Studies*, 64:1, 1–33.
Myant, M., J. Drahokoupil and I. Lesay (2013) 'Political Economy of Crisis Management in East-Central European Countries', *Europe-Asia Studies*, 65:3, 383–410.
Mykhnenko, V. (2007) 'Poland and Ukraine: Institutional Structures and Economic Performance', in D. Lane and M. Myant (eds.), *Varieties of Capitalism in Post-Communist Countries* (Basingstoke: Palgrave Macmillan), 124–48.
Nölke, A. and A. Vliegenthart (2009) 'Enlarging the Varieties of Capitalism: The Emergence of Dependent Market Economies in East Central Europe', *World Politics*, 61:4, 670–702.
Pavlínek, P., B. Domański and R. Guzik (2009) 'Industrial Upgrading Through Foreign Direct Investment in Central European Automotive Manufacturing', *European Urban and Regional Studies*, 16:1, 43–63.
Porter, M.E. (1990) *The Competitive Advantage of Nations* (London: Macmillan).
Schwab, K. (ed.). (2013) *The Global Competitiveness Report, 2013–2014* (Geneva: World Economic Forum).
Streeck, W. (2009) *Re-Forming Capitalism: Institutional Change in the German Political Economy* (Oxford: Oxford University Press).

# 10
State–Business–Labour Relations and Patterns of Development in Latin America

Flavio Gaitán and Renato Boschi

Following the broader trend towards a 'globalization' of the Comparative Capitalisms (CC) field (see also Bruff et al. and Ebenau, in this volume), this chapter introduces Latin America into the examination of different types of capitalism. In particular, we propose to analyse the institutional settings of the political economies of Latin America in terms of their relevance for the definition and implementation of different development strategies. We argue that now, more than ever, it is necessary to question the ubiquitous neoliberal convergence discourse and to reassert the national and regional dimensions of analysing contemporary capitalism. In this vein, the global capitalist crisis and the recuperation of the state as a key economic player jointly constitute a window of opportunity for reconsidering capitalist diversity and the associated diversity of development trajectories.

This chapter is divided into three sections. The first outlines the core elements of our approach, followed by a second section presenting a rough analysis of the diversity of Latin American political economies. Thereby, instead of creating yet another typology, we are interested in studying concrete differences and processes of divergence between national political economies.[1] This chapter thus reiterates the difficulties inevitably encountered when attempting to frame particular empirical cases in ideal-typical terms as well as the need to emphasize both endogenous and exogenous transformative factors when explaining institutional change. The third section presents a number of tentative conclusions from our analysis.

The state and development in (semi-)peripheral varieties of capitalism

In this section, we briefly present the theoretical framework underlying our approach to institutions and particularly the recuperation of the state as a promoter of development. We therefore suggest that national political economies should be compared on the basis of an assessment of their contemporary development dynamics (see also Drahokoupil and Myant, in this volume). Such an analysis involves recognizing that policies developed in response to the challenges of globalization and increasing global interdependence differ between countries and regions. Development, thus understood, is an endogenous process, shaped over time through trajectories that are continuously redefined according to specific political conjunctures (Amable, 2003; Boyer, 2009; Bresser-Pereira, 2007, 2008; Boschi and Gaitán, 2013). In our view, an analysis of contemporary capitalist formations is impossible without reference to the state. Of course, in post-market reform scenarios with open economies, the conditions for competitiveness and growth are closely related to the consolidation of a dynamic domestic business sector. Nevertheless, in the case of Latin America – and (semi-)peripheral world regions more generally – the role of the state is crucial for potentially reversing vicious cycles and negative complementarities, which stem from the structural and social inequalities within and between countries in the region (Boschi and Gaitán, 2009). In particular, the state plays a key role in creating the conditions for innovation (Mazzucatto, 2013) and competitiveness (ECLAC, 2012).

The role of government and of political institutions more generally needs to be examined in relation to this broader significance of the state. This is concomitant to the recognition in development studies that 'institutions matter' (Rodrik, 2007; Chang, 2005; Evans, 1995). Historically, the characteristics of different productive systems were shaped by the institutionalization of capital–labour relations and, later on, the role of labour in the institutionalization of democratic competition. Furthermore, the effects of the more recent market reforms are important: the question in this regard is whether previously established developmental institutions were preserved, complemented or destroyed (Boschi, 2013). Taken together, these dimensions generate trajectory effects (or dependencies), which are central to characterizing different varieties of capitalism. In the words of Marino Regini (2006, p. 611), 'institutional orderings governing a national economic system are always the product of past conflicts, and as such, should be acknowledged or renegotiated periodically.' Analysing different models of capitalist development therefore requires broadening the analytical toolkit to include elements such as social coalitions and the distribution of power (Coates, 2005; Sánchez-Ancochea, 2006). Politics and, more specifically, the role of strategic elites are central to understanding the trajectories of capitalist models. Any development project aiming to become hegemonic must be adopted by and diffused through relevant epistemic communities; it must furthermore be transformed into laws, regulations and other forms of public policy at the national level (Diniz, 2008).

Some scholars have emphasized the difficulties for Latin American and other (semi-)peripheral countries to achieve a more virtuous insertion into the global economy (see, for example, Ebenau, 2012, 2014). We agree with these and similar positions insofar as we assume that the global context may generate constraints and opportunities for national development trajectories. Thus, we also concur with the basic argument advanced by dependency theorists that the development of particular models of capitalism can only be understood in the context of global capitalist development (see also Wehr and Suau Arinci et al., in this volume). Changes in the capitalist mode of production on a global scale will lead to constant re-accommodations of the limits for interventions by public authorities in specific countries. Nevertheless, globalization does not necessarily reduce the power of the state: it also increases its fundamental strategic significance for supporting firms in order to enable them to compete successfully in the international arena (Bresser-Pereira, 2010). We thus reiterate our principal point: the recognition of the hierarchical character of the capitalist system and its effects on (semi-)peripheral economies do not force us to deny the ability of nation states to reverse the entrenched dynamics of the reproduction of underdevelopment.

National states are no passive hostages of external dynamics but develop – with varying degrees of success – strategies of confronting them, even though financial globalization and value chain fragmentation tend to increase the weight of the international system over national strategies. Still, asymmetries between countries are to be explained mainly by reference to endogenous factors and development has to be understood as a primarily endogenous process. This is particularly significant at certain historical junctures, when capitalism is open to fundamental changes, including processes of economic catch-up (Pipitone, 2006; Chang, 2002). For seizing such opportunities, the formulation and implementation of national development strategies are key (Boschi and Gaitán, 2009, 2011, 2013). Central to the success of such strategies is the carving out of national spaces in open systems and maintaining them in constant adaptation processes, even against exogenous pressures arising from the characteristics of the globalized international system. The notion of dependency can thus only describe historically specific balances of power, which influence, but do not prevent, structural transformations. More rigid interpretations of the dependency tradition ignore the reality of change in the global capitalist system. Here, we refer not only to the well-known East Asian success stories (see, for example, Chang, 2002) but also to a complex of contemporary changes in the international system in which (semi-)peripheral countries play a central part. This includes, among other things, the growth in the importance of firms and governments from non-core economies in innovation, production and finance and the gradual transition from a Triad-dominated world order towards a multipolar one in which emerging countries play a more prominent role (WTO, 2013a, 2013b). These processes make wider margins for state action possible.

Capitalist development trajectories in Latin America

Generally speaking, it is possible to broadly identify similar historical trajectories which different varieties of capitalism in Latin America have undergone. Under neoliberal influence, all countries have been transformed from protected to more open economies (Williamson, 1990). In contrast, in recent years a shift towards a new developmental model premised on greater state involvement is taking place in most countries in the region. These commonalities notwithstanding, however, differences persist regarding the relative importance of the state and the specific orientation of intervention, the underlying modes of productive development and the role of labour and social policies. In what follows, we present a tentative analysis of three key elements of different economies in Latin America: the type of external integration, the type of state intervention and the labour and social protection regime (for a contrasting approach to Latin America, see Suau Arinci et al., in this volume; see also Drahokoupil and Myant, in this volume for their approach to transition economies). As stated earlier, we do not intend to establish a typology, but we do believe that different countries can be analysed along common features and stable patterns of behaviour, which vary according to the variable being studied.

Integration into the world economy

One factor influencing the configuration of production systems is the historically developed connection between particular economies and the global system. The plurality of national strategies for dealing with the changing international system gives rise to a great diversity of particular situations. These can be disaggregated along three axes: the sectoral or product focus of foreign trade, the general trade openness and the concentration/diversification of trading partners.

Within the group of Andean-Pacific countries, not only a number of fundamental similarities but also some distinctions can be identified: Chilean and Peruvian exports are dominated by metal and mining products (61.6 per cent in Chile, 63 per cent in Peru) and, to a lesser degree, foodstuffs, even though manufactures also play a certain role in Chile (13.3 per cent).[2] In the South American context, Chile is exceptionally open (with a ratio of 78.4 per cent of trade to GDP). It is also the country that has followed most strongly a course of radical and strategic trade liberalization, having signed a total of 23 free trade agreements with 65 countries. Colombia shares the emphasis on non-renewable resources (65.7 per cent of all exports are petrol based), but the significance of industrial goods is higher (16.3 per cent) and external openness is lower (40.9 per cent). Recently, there have been initiatives for increasing the strategic integration among the countries of the so-called *Alianza del Pacífico* (Chile, Mexico, Peru and Colombia).

Ecuador, Venezuela and Bolivia are often defined as petro-states. In all three countries, primary products dominate foreign trade. Oil and gas account for more than half of all sales in Ecuador (52.1 per cent) and Bolivia (50.5 per cent; 77 per cent when mining is included) and even more in Venezuela (82.1 per cent). However, in the latter case, a growing participation of manufactures (from 3.1 per cent in 1995 to 14.4 per cent in 2012) reflects efforts to reform the productive structure. Argentina, Uruguay and Paraguay are mainly food exporters (accounting for around 60 to 65 per cent in all three of them). The manufacturing industry constitutes an important subsidiary sector in Argentina and Uruguay (at around 20 per cent in both cases). The second important export complex in resource-dependent Paraguay is petrol-based products (23.2 per cent). In Brazil, the historically high export participation of manufacturing products has fallen strikingly (from more than 50 to 33.8 per cent) in recent years, matched by a concomitant rise in the sales of metals, oil and food. However, the significance of this trend should not be overestimated, since such shifts constitute a common characteristic of post-industrial capitalist economies (WTO, 2013a; UNCTAD, 2013). Also, Brazil is the least open of all Latin American economies (34.2 per cent trade-GDP ratio). Over the last decade, the Partido dos Trabalhadores (PT) governments have pursued a strategy of foreign trade diversification, related to broader initiatives aimed at forming new

South-South alliances (IBSA, BRICS and so on) (Boschi and Gaitán, 2009, 2011).

In Mexico and some Central American countries, manufacturing – based on *maquila* production – occupies a strategic role in exports. The participation of manufacturing goods is traditionally high in Mexico (75 per cent). It has grown considerably in Costa Rica (from 35 per cent in 1995 to 71 per cent in 2012), El Salvador (52.3 to 69.9 per cent), Panama (61.7 to 77.6 per cent) and, on a lower level, Honduras (42.7 to just over 50 per cent). However, in all cases but Costa Rica, the considerable weight of imports indicates a lack of ability to create local value chains (Aguilera, 2013; Sánchez-Ancochea, 2006). Some Central American economies are among the most open in the region (Costa Rica, 91.1 per cent; El Salvador, 72.2 per cent). Mexico and most Central American economies are strongly integrated with the United States, with limited ability to expand value chains due to the prevailing subcontracting mode of production (Bizberg, 2012; Palma, 2005).

From the discussion of these stylized facts, we can infer that there are three basic patterns of insertion into the international system for Latin American countries (Ocampo, 2001): first, the integration into vertical trade flows of manufactured goods peculiar to internationally integrated production systems, centred particularly on the United States; second, the integration into horizontal production and trade networks focused on raw materials and resource-based commodities and characterized by stronger intra-regional ties and less market concentration; and third, the integration based on services exports, particularly tourism but also finance, transport and energy. And there are at least three ways of how states manage their insertion into the global economy: the strategic promotion of open economy models (mainly through Free Trade Agreements), the maintenance of or return to more protected economies (using tariff and non-tariff protective measures) and the outright subjection to relations of dependency. Differences not only stem from the size of the respective economies but also from their governments' different abilities to promote the formation of local linkages. For instance, Costa Rica constitutes an example of a small and very open economy where the state has successfully promoted the establishment of a local-high tech industry (Sánchez-Ancochea, 2006), Chile is a country where elites pursue an open economy approach, whereas Argentina and Brazil have returned to policies aiming to protect internal markets.

This way, our brief survey shows that, although all countries in question share the (semi-)peripheral position, there is no single mode of insertion into the international system. Far from thinking of a single model of integration, we observe national differences that result from the way the state is led by political elites, based on their different perspectives on development. This underpins our argument that conceptualizing the state as a strategic player in the differentiated development of (semi-)peripheral capitalist economies is crucial. States such as Argentina and Brazil, where some protective capacities have been preserved and where greater importance is attributed to the domestic market, are generally less exposed to periodic crises of the capitalist mode of production and possess greater degrees of freedom to deploy industrial policies. In turn, other states have favoured international opening and in some cases – Chile is the most successful example here – could take advantage of changes in world trade (particularly the shift towards Pacific Asia). At the same time, however, they exhibit a greater dependency on the sales of primary products and a generally weaker development of the national manufacturing industry.

Relations between state and business

The ability to regulate and control the private sector is a key element in the state's role in development (Amsden, 2001). Hence, the state's economic role can be analysed, among other things, with a view on state capacities, its role in financing production, social policies, the permeability to particular interests or the ability to generate broad agreements between relevant actors (mainly business and labour). Here, the relative autonomy of the state is crucial to understand its capacity to deploy development strategies.[3] Moreover, differences in the degree and orientation of government intervention constitute a historically evolving feature of specific national models of capitalism. Thus, *pace* the tendency in parts of the literature to assume static types, the interventionist nature of a state (or its absence) at a given moment in time is based on multiple institutional (re-)configurations and ideological (re-)orientations at different historical junctures. Of course, the ability of governments to adopt specific strategies is limited by state capacities, including their ability to extract tax resources from different social sectors and their infrastructural capacity, particularly with regard to production and the social system.

Despite the long-standing prevalence of liberalism, Chile has preserved a state which regulates economic activity with a degree of autonomy and plays a significant role in the promotion of certain productive sectors such as wine, fruit and vegetables, timber and fishing. The state has also preserved direct ownership of the strategic copper sector and purposefully regulates speculative capital flows (Silva,

2007; Kurtz, 2001). Public spending levels are nevertheless only modest (23.2 per cent of GDP), relative to Chilean income levels. This reflects the state's largely subsidiary role in other fields of action, especially in welfare provision. In contrast, the Venezuelan, Ecuadorian and Bolivian states have historically been highly dependent on oil and gas revenues. Although this remains the case, the last decade saw left-wing governments adopting more strongly statist strategies that attempt to recover degrees of freedom for economic intervention, promote the diversification of exports and expand social policies. Public expenditure levels in all three countries are high by regional and income-level standards (Venezuela: 40.1 per cent; Ecuador: 44 per cent; Bolivia: 35.4 per cent). These countries also maintain important degrees of state ownership in the extractive sectors and have implemented re-nationalizations of strategic companies.

Argentina and Brazil can both be considered interventionist states, but their governments possess different abilities to discipline capital. Argentina's historical trajectory has been highly unstable, and the dominant development models have therefore shifted repeatedly: currently, a neodevelopmentalist political coalition is attempting to reverse the cycle of economic liberalization and deindustrialization (see also Suau Arinci et al., in this volume for more on the recent debates and struggles). Public expenditure has thereby risen from low levels to 40.9 per cent of GDP. Heterodox instruments such as import restrictions, selective capital controls and the establishment of barriers to corporate profit remittances are being applied. Moreover, the state's role in production has been strengthened significantly, both through the recuperation of the previously privatized energy firm *Yacimientos Petrolíferos Fiscales* (YPF) and through the re-nationalization of the pension administration *Administradoras de Fondos de Jubilaciones y Pensiones* (AFJP), which permits the state to act as a shareholder in a considerable number of private companies. Nevertheless, the continuing processes of economic concentration and transnationalization, as well as the government's lack of success at fostering the creation of local production networks (Azpiazu and Schorr, 2010), show that the current paradigm of interventionism is of limited effectiveness.

Brazil has a state which historically possessed greater relative autonomy (Boschi, 2013). More recently, it has come to represent an example of an effective neodevelopmentalist project, owing to its fortuitous combination of political will and public capacity. At 39.1 per cent of GDP, public expenditure levels are high, and heterodox policies akin to those pursued in Argentina have been implemented. The state also retains direct ownership of a number of important companies, among them the energy giant Petrobras. However, one particular strength of the Brazilian state is related to its role in financing productive investment, not least through the public development bank BNDES (Banco Nacional do Desenvolvimento), which acts alongside other, smaller institutions, as well as publicly owned pension funds (Santana, 2011). Together, these have been crucial for stabilizing macroeconomic variables throughout repeated domestic and international crises and for promoting the capacities of Brazilian firms to innovate and compete in global markets. Moreover, they have provided a basis for the establishment of a space in which different business interests can be intermediated and guided towards the formation of new productive coalitions.

Like Chile, present-day Mexico possesses a liberal state that plays a largely residual economic role. From the 1980s onwards, large-scale privatization and state retrenchment policies were implemented, which implied the abandonment of the previous interventionist paradigm. Even though the state retains a presence in the extractive sector, this process has been more radical than in the Chilean case, reflected in the relatively low public expenditure levels (26.6 per cent of GDP). Elsewhere in Central America, we generally find states with lower levels of intervention due to economic and social problems, limited capacity to tax the private sector, higher degrees of dependence on multinationals, the importance of remittances for the national economies and problems in enforcing the law. Therefore, most states in the subregion (with the exception of Costa Rica and Panama) have to be defined as weak states (Brocate et al., 2013). Expectedly, expenditure levels in these countries are extremely low (for example, 14.6 per cent in Guatemala).

In sum, some countries have in recent years advanced towards greater state control of economic activity, broadening its sphere of action from simple regulation to more specific interventions and the proactive use of public ownership. As a result, at present we find in the Latin American region different kinds of state intervention: at one extreme there are those states that assume a merely subsidiary role (Chile, Mexico, Peru, Colombia); at the other, there are those seeking to recover a broad-based interventionist strategy (Argentina and Brazil and, in a different sense, Bolivia, Ecuador and Venezuela). However, static labels – 'liberal', 'statist' and the like – fail to give account of the particularities of the manifold different forms of public intervention. In some countries, such as Chile, where the 'liberal path' has been adopted, the state is still using effective interventionist measures – and the capitalist crisis after 2008 has seen many more supposedly liberal states using them (ECLAC, 2012). On the other hand, attempts to create a new 'developmental state' ought not lead us to conclude that we can put private capital to one side. In fact, differences between effective forms of emerging developmental states concern the way in which the public–private relationship is established or, in other words, the way in which the motto of 'governing the market' is implemented: by appealing to collaboration, as in the Brazilian case, or through more coercive ways, as in Venezuela.

Labour and social protection regimes

Welfare regimes and industrial relations are important factors for issues of capitalist diversity (Théret, 2002; Esping-Andersen, 1990). This influence is transmitted through various mechanisms, such as wage policies, the role of trade unions and the coverage of social protection. Industrial relations and social protection regimes are influenced by the way they were historically deployed and, particularly, their efficiency in facing the 1990s' liberalization processes. Central variables for understanding these dimensions are, among others, employment (including the issue of informality), trade union strength and the reach of collective negotiations, as well as social investment and protection policies. Generally speaking, some broad macro-trends, such as a reduction of unemployment due to a combination of growth and rising external demand, have characterized national experiences throughout Latin America. A further similarity is the fact that, with some limited exceptions, the countries of the region have established forms of formal employment-based social protection. Yet, due to the prevalence of high levels of informality and non-participation in the labour market, protection systems are quite fragmented (Barrientos, 2009). Nevertheless, recent years have seen important divergences as well.

The predominance of liberalism in Chilean policymaking circles is clearly reflected in this country's industrial relations and social protection regimes. Even though unemployment has gone down in recent years and informal employment is less important here than elsewhere in Latin America, union density is low (12 per cent of all employees) and the reach of collective bargaining is limited. In contrast to what has been happening in other countries, the flexibilized labour relations model adopted in the 1980s has even been reinforced in recent years. The statutory minimum wage has increased by just over 30 per cent since 2000, considerably less than in other South American countries (Lanzara, 2013). Furthermore, the social protection model is largely residualist, reflected in institutions such as the pay-as-you-go pensions system and generally low levels of social protection spending

(15.3 per cent of GDP). Even the centre-left *Concertación* governments have not broken with this general pattern (Bizberg, 2012; Bensusán, 2008; Lanzara, 2013).

In many respects, Argentina can be considered a sharply contrasting case. Both union membership (37 per cent) and collective bargaining coverage (60 per cent of all employees) are high and have been reinforced by the labour policies adopted over the last decade (Etchemendy and Collier, 2007; Palomino and Trajtemberg, 2006). For example, the real minimum wage stood a full 3.6 times higher in 2012 than in 2000 and social protection spending has gone up considerably to 24.2 per cent of GDP, which is quite high by regional standards. Similarly, in Brazil there has been a certain resurgence of trade unionism and a strengthening of social protection policies, even though the latter were never as drastically cut back as in Argentina. Union membership (18 per cent) and especially collective bargaining coverage (60 per cent) are comparatively high. In addition, significant progress has been made in reducing the size of the traditionally large informal sector (ECLAC, 2013a), the minimum wage almost doubled between 2000 and 2012 and social protection spending amounts to 26.2 per cent of GDP. However, what most sets the Brazilian case apart from other countries in the region, including Argentina, is the emergence of what might be called a model of 'societal corporatism' (Boschi, 2010, 2013). In particular, this means that worker organizations are integrated into high-level political decision-making processes, for instance through their incorporation into the *Conselho de Desenvolvimento Econômico y Social*.

The left-leaning governments of the poorer Andean countries, including Bolivia, Ecuador and Venezuela, have pursued policies that could be described as strategies of social reparation. Social spending in these countries is not high per se but has grown considerably in recent years (for example, to 13.4 per cent in Venezuela). Nevertheless, apart from Bolivia, trade union membership and collective bargaining coverage rates remain low in all of these countries. Real minimum wages have grown by about 80 per cent since 2000. In most regards, Mexico and the Central American countries represent even more extreme variants of the liberal, residual and minimalist labour and welfare regimes. Social protection expenditure is low (for example, 12.5 per cent in Mexico, even lower in most Central American countries with the exception of Costa Rica), as are trade union affiliation (between 7 and 13 per cent) and collective bargaining coverage rates. Generally speaking, minimum wage growth between 2000 and 2012 has been very modest or, in the case of Mexico, even negative. The processes of liberalization and flexibilization of labour laws initiated during the neoliberal era are being continued in most of these countries.

An important conclusion to be drawn from this presentation is that there are several fundamentally different ways of approaching social protection issues in present-day Latin American capitalism. At one extreme, there are those countries where minimalist and residualist policies prevail (Chile, Mexico, most Central American countries). Other countries where this has previously been the case are now, under left-leaning governments, pursuing strategies of social reparation (Bolivia, Ecuador and Venezuela, among others). Finally, there are the countries (Argentina, Brazil and others) where social policies are functional to the very strategy of economic development and growth. In these countries, social policies serve to sustain consumption alongside increases in the minimum wage, which play a key role in linking employment to models of social development and protection.

Again, although it is common in comparative research on Latin American capitalism to lump the countries of the region together into one supposed type of economy with atomistic models of labour relations and social policies disconnected from production patterns (for example, Schneider, 2013), there exist differences arising from legacies and the ways in which the state and other actors intervene. The past is important, but it does not determine a particular trajectory. As can be seen in the cases of Chile, Mexico and Argentina (countries with a history of workforce protection and the existence of a welfare state), change can take different forms. If Chile and Mexico have evolved to a liberal form of social and labour policies, typical of subsidiary schemes, Argentina shows that change is possible in both directions (from a protective scheme to a liberal one and back). These ruptures result from the ways in which elites and the state institutionalized pressures stemming from the capitalist mode of production. At least in Argentina, Brazil and Uruguay, unions have also been a constitutive part of the ways in which the labour and social protection regimes have been institutionalized. In more liberal economies, weak unions and residual models are concurrent and mutually reinforcing. In weak states, poor tax collection capacities prevent breaking with the historically constructed legacy of poverty and inequality.

Conclusions

In this chapter, we have first presented a theoretical framework for studying capitalist diversity in the (semi-)periphery, which links development to state intervention. We thereby consider the state as the fundamental institution in any capitalist economy. As Uwe Becker (2009) has pointed out, all capitalist economies are to be considered liberal to a certain degree, since otherwise they would not be capitalist. However, at the same time, all economies are influenced by the degree and kind of state regulation and the degree of institutionally mediated interventions. We thereby particularly refer to those institutions that are associated with the systems of production (for example, productive finance, state ownership) and distribution (for example, welfare regimes, labour policies).

The main point of divergence between the approaches, which, like ours, emphasize the potentialities of state action for overcoming backwardness and those that emphasize the dependent character of the (semi-)peripheral economies is, precisely, their understanding of the degrees of freedom of underdeveloped economies under a globally concentrated and hierarchically organized mode of production. In our view, nothing suggests that structural impediments for deploying development strategies prevail. In fact, recent history shows a number of cases where states have been successful in consolidating strategies of economic development. Of course, the ability of (semi-)peripheral states to do so is not equally distributed. But overemphasizing the dependent character of (semi-)peripheral economies means losing sight of the structural changes in global capitalism, which have been unfolding since the 1970s. The fragmentation of value chains and increased financial interdependence redefine the character of centre and periphery. This manifests itself in the emergence of a limited group of countries contesting positions of power in world geopolitics (Aheon, 2011) and with more open windows of opportunity for rethinking national development strategies. State action is key, as is the ability of elites to form stable development coalitions.

Secondly, we have presented a cursory survey of different capitalist configurations to be observed in several countries in the Latin American region. This examination has referred to three dimensions, which we consider key for productive regimes settings: the type of external integration, the capacity for state intervention and the labour relations and social policy model. This has permitted us to conclude that Latin American countries, despite having some common features on these dimensions, adopt different policy strategies that, in turn, give rise to markedly distinctive forms of (semi-)peripheral capitalism. The different paths, which these countries' models of capitalism follow, are continually reconfigured according to the ways in which challenges, crises and external determinants are faced. In this sense, the roads they follow are historically constructed, but they do not imply stasis. Regime configurations are not necessarily stable but undergo constant and sometimes far-reaching institutional change. Pre-established paths have consequences for the formation and re-formation of any particular variety of capitalism, but agency at certain critical junctures can and will lead to fundamental rearrangements. This can be seen when examining cases such as Argentina with its multiple profound regime changes, or the consequential transformations from protected to liberal models in Chile and Mexico.

Regarding the kind of external insertion, all countries examined in more detail have opened their economies over recent decades. With the exception of Mexico with its *maquila industry*, their trading patterns show a strong specialization in primary products. Nevertheless, in the medium-term, this panorama may change since some of the countries considered are exhibiting an increased ability to deploy strategies aimed at diversifying export patterns and/or protecting their respective domestic markets. With regard to the kind and degree of state intervention, we observe marked differences concerning both the strategic orientation and the state capacities. Finally, our analysis of labour relations and social protection regimes showed, beyond some similarities, a broad variety of situations, associated with the strength and importance of the union movement, the significance of social policies and, crucially, the interaction between the latter and the broader development and growth strategies.

The reconfiguration of a particular kind of capitalism towards a model of state-guided development does not guarantee short-term results in the sense of a passage from underdevelopment to development. Rather, the reconfiguration of the type and extent of state intervention will bear fruit only in the long term and thus should be analysed and evaluated with this qualification in mind. If, as we have argued here, differences regarding the role of the state in the development process will over time generate institutional advantages for those countries, such as Brazil, that seek to deploy a broad-based, proactive strategy, this may become visible only over time, when such initiatives finally mature.

Notes

1. Typological discussions of capitalism in Latin America are attempted by, among others, Bizberg (2012), Bogliacini and Filgueira (2011) and Schneider (2009, 2013).

2. All economic data used in this paper are taken from ECLAC (2013b).
3. There is a broad literature on the relative autonomy of the state in capitalist economies. We define it as the capacity that the state (understood as an actor with economic and institutional resources) has to interfere with social processes, independently from other social actors (Sanchez León, 2009). It is related to the state's capacity, defined by Theda Skocpol (1985, 9) as the means to 'implement official goals, especially over the actual or potential opposition of powerful social groups or in the face of recalcitrant socio-economic circumstances.'

Bibliography

Aguilera M. (2013) 'Costa Rica 'una maquila republic exitosa?', *Economía Internacional*, 2, 1–19.
Aheon, R. (2011) 'Rising Economic Powers and the Global Economy: Trends and Issues for Congress', *CRS Report for Congress*, Washington DC.
Amable, B. (2003) *The Diversity of Modern Capitalism* (Oxford: Oxford University Press).
Amsden, A. (2001) *Asia's Next Giant* (New York: Oxford University Press).
Azpiazu, D. and M. Schorr (2010) *Hecho en Argentina, Industria y Economía, 1976–2007* (Buenos Aires: Siglo XXI Editores).
Barrientos, A. (2009) 'Labour Markets and the (Hyphenated) Welfare Regime in Latin America', *Economy and Society*, 38:1, 87–108.
Becker, U. (2009) *Open Varieties of Capitalism: Continuity, Change and Performances* (Basingstoke: Palgrave Macmillan).
Bensusán, G. (2008) *Regulaciones laborales, calidad de los empleos, modelos de inspección: México en el contexto latinoamericano* (Santiago de Chile: CEPAL).
Bizberg, I. (2012) 'Types of Capitalism in Latin America', *Interventions économiques*, 47, 1–26.
Bogliaccini, J.A. and F. Filgueira (2011) 'Capitalismo en el Cono Sur de América Latina luego del final del Consenso de Washington: ¿notas sin partitura?' *Revista del CLAD Reforma y Democracia*, 51, 1–23.
Boschi, R. (2010) 'Corporativismo societal: A democratização do estado e as bases social-democratas do capitalismo brasileiro', *Insight/Inteligência*, 48:12, 86–103.
Boschi, R. (2013) 'Politics and Trajectory in Brazilian Capitalist Development', in U. Becker (ed.), *The BRICS and Emerging Economies in Comparative Perspective: Political Economy, Liberalisation and Institutional Change* (Abingdon: Routledge), 123–43.
Boschi, R. and F. Gaitán (2009) 'Politics and Development: Lessons from Latin America', *Brasilian Political Science Review*, 3:2, 11–29.
Boschi, R. and F. Gaitán (2011) 'Empresas, Capacidades estatales y estrategias de desarrollo en Argentina, Brasil y Chile'. Available at: http://neic.iuperj.br/textos/renato-wkshpniteroi.pdf.
Boschi, R. and F. Gaitán (2013) 'Novo-Desenvolvimentismo', in A. Brito Leal Ivo (ed.), *Dicionário Desenvolvimento e Questão Social* (São Paulo: Annablume).
Boyer, R. (2009) 'Are There Laws of Motion of Capitalism?' *Socio-Economic Review*, 9:1, 59–81.
Bresser-Pereira, L.C. (2007) 'Estado y Mercado en el Nuevo Desarrollismo', *Nueva Sociedad*, 210, 110–25.

Bresser Pereira, L.C. (2008) 'Globalization, Nation-State and Catching Up', *Brazilian Journal of Political Economy*, 28:4, 557–77.
Bresser-Pereira, L.C. (2010) *Globalization and Competition: Why Some Emergent Countries Succeed While Others Fall Behind* (Cambridge: Cambridge University Press).
Brocate, R., B. Tugrul and J. Ríos Sierra (2013) 'América Central: un nuevo concepto de Estado débil', *Documento Marco*, no. 20 (Madrid: Instituto Español de Estudios Estratégicos).
Chang, H.-J. (2002) *Kicking Away the Ladder: Development Strategy in Historical Perspective* (London: Anthem).
Chang, H.-J. (2005) 'Understanding the Relationship Between Institutions and Economic Development: Some Key Theoretical Issues', presented at WIDER Jubilee Conference, Helsinki, Finland, 17–18 June.
Coates, D. (ed.) (2005) *Varieties of Capitalism, Varieties of Approaches* (Basingstoke: Palgrave Macmillan).
Diniz, E. (2008) 'Depois do neoliberalismo. Rediscutindo a articulação estado e desenvolvimento no novo milênio', *Ponto de Vista*, 2008:2. Available at: http://neic.iuperj.br/pontodevista.
Ebenau, M. (2012) 'Varieties of Capitalism or Dependency? A Critique of the VoC Approach for Latin America', *Competition & Change*, 16:3, 206–23.
Ebenau, M. (2014) 'Comparative Capitalisms and Latin American Neodevelopmentalism: A Critical Political Economy View', *Capital & Class*, 38:1, 102–14.
Ebenau, M. and V. Liberatore (2013) 'Neodevelopmentalist State Capitalism in Brazil and Argentina: Chances, Limits and Contradictions', *Der moderne Staat*, 6:1, 105–25.
ECLAC (2012) *La reacción de los gobiernos de América Latina y el Caribe frente a la crisis internacional*. Available at: http://www.eclac.org/cgi-bin/getProd.asp?xml=/prensa/noticias/comunicados/0/35180/P35180.xml&xsl=/prensa/tpl/p6f.xsl&base=/tpl/top-bottom.xslt.
ECLAC (2013a) *Panorama Social de América Latina* (Santiago de Chile: UN Publications).
ECLAC (2013b) *Panorama de la Inserción Internacional de América Latina* (Santiago de Chile: UN Publications).
Etchemendy, S. and R.B. Collier (2007) 'Down But Not Out: Union Resurgence and Segmented Neocorporatism in Argentina (2003–2007)', *Politics & Society*, 35:3, 363–401.
Esping-Andersen, G. (1990) *The Three Worlds of Welfare Capitalism* (Princeton: Princeton University Press).
Evans, P. (1995) *Embedded Autonomy: States & Industrial Transformation* (Princeton: Princeton University Press).
Kurtz, M. (2001) 'State Developmentalism Without a Developmentalist State: The Public Foundations of the "Free-Market Miracle" in Chile', *Latin American Politics and Society*, 43:2, 1–25.
Lanzara, A.P. (2013) 'As Transformações do Estado Social no Brasil e no Chile: privatismo na seguridade e universalização excludente?' in F. Gaitán and A. del Rio (eds.), *Instituições, Política e Desenvolvimento: America Latina frente ao século XXI* (Curitiba: CRV Editora), 235–66.
Mazzucatto, M. (2013) *The Entrepreneurial State: Debunking Public vs Private Sector Myth* (London: Anthem Press).

Ocampo, J.A. (2001) 'Raúl Prebisch y la agenda del Desarrollo en los albores del Siglo XXI', *Revista de la CEPAL*, 75, 25–40.
Palma, G. (2005) 'The Seven Main "Stylized Facts" of the Mexican Economy since Trade Liberalization and NAFTA', *Industrial and Corporate Change*, 14:6, 941–91.
Palomino, H. and D. Trajtemberg (2006) 'Una nueva dinámica de las relaciones laborales y la negociación colectiva en la Argentina', *Revista de Trabajo*, 3:2, 47–68.
Pipitone, U. (2006) 'Salir del Atraso en América Latina', *Pensamiento Iberoamericano*, 0, 25–39.
Regini, M. (2006) 'Del Neocorporativismo a las variedades de Capitalismo', *Desarrollo Económico*, 45:180, 609–12.
Rodrik, D. (2007) *One Economics, Many Recipes: Globalization, Institutions, and Economic Growth* (Princeton: Princeton University Press).
Sánchez Ancochea, D. (2006) 'The Models of Capitalism Approach and Economic Development: An Application to Small Countries in Latin America', *presented at the Annual Meeting of the Latin American Studies Association*, San Juan, Puerto Rico, 16–18 March.
Sánchez León, P. (2009) 'Autonomía del Estado', in *Diccionario Crítico de Ciencias Sociales* (Madrid: Plaza y Valdés Editores), available at: http://pendientedemigracion.ucm.es/info/eurotheo/diccionario/A/autonomiaestado.htm.
Santana, C.H.V. (2011) 'Conjuntura crítica, legados institucionais e comunidades epistêmicas. Limites e possibilidades de uma agenda de desenvolvimento no Brasil', in R. Boschi (ed.), *Variedades de Capitalismo: Política e desenvolvimento na América Latina* (Belo Horizonte: Editora UFMG), 121–63.
Schneider, B.R. (2013) *Hierarchical Capitalism in Latin America: Business, Labour, and the Challenges of Equitable Development* (Cambridge: Cambridge University Press).
Schneider, B.R. and D. Soskice (2009) 'Inequality in Developed Countries and Latin America: Coordinated, Liberal and Hierarchical Systems', *Economy and Society*, 38:1, 17–52.
Silva, E. (2007) 'The Import Substitution Model: Chile in Comparative Perspective', *Latin American Perspectives*, 34:3, 67–90.
Skocpol, T. (1985) 'Bringing the State Back In: Strategies of Analysis in Current Research', in P. Evans, D. Rueschemeyer and T. Skocpol (eds.), *Bringing the State Back In* (Cambridge: Cambridge University Press), 3–37.
Théret, B. (2002) *Protection Sociale et Fédéralisme. L'Europe dans le miroir de l'Amérique du Nord* (Montréal: Presse de l'Université de Montréal).
UNCTAD (2013) *World Investment Report 2013: Toward a New Generation of Investment Policies* (Geneva: United Nations).
Williamson, J. (1990) 'What Washington Means by Policy Reforms', in J. Williamson (ed.), *Latin American Readjustment: How Much Has Happened* (Washington: Institute for International Economics), 7–20.
WTO (2013a) *International Trade Statistics 2013* (Geneva: WTO).
WTO (2013b) *World Trade Report 2013: Factors Shaping the Future of World Trade* (Geneva: WTO).

11
All Varieties Are Equal... Contributions from Dependency Approaches to Critical Comparative Capitalisms Research

Lucía Suau Arinci, Nadia Pessina and Matthias Ebenau

In-depth analyses of the realities of capitalism in different parts of the world presuppose interrogating the multiplicity of factors that affect the economic, social and political development trajectories, which unfold in different, relatively distinct space economies. In this regard, the Comparative Capitalisms (CC) literatures currently constitute one of the most dynamic scholarly fields with respect to both theoretical debate and the systematization of empirical knowledge. Over recent years, Latin America, among other non-core world regions, has increasingly come to the attention of comparativists; conversely, many scholars established in the region have begun to draw on theoretical approaches from the CC field. This chapter inscribes itself into this development, but where others have been primarily concerned with importing and/or adapting theoretical perspectives originated in other contexts, we make a case for reconsidering the virtues of a fundamentally Latin American line of politico-economic thought: the radical dependency tradition founded in the 1960s. Re-interpreting CC's trademark enterprise of analysing locally distinctive configurations of capitalism through dependency lenses can, we maintain, provide an essential corrective to a number of shortcomings identified for the neoinstitutionalist approaches which currently predominate in the field.

To substantiate this claim, we develop an analytical framework, which permits us simultaneously to contextualize and deepen our understanding of the multiple configurations of capitalism in Latin America and beyond. In particular, we seek to provide a critical perspective on the state and its associated institutions and their interrelations with business and labour, as broadly conceived. Within this framework, we attempt to translate some of the principal theoretical concerns associated with the dependency school into a set of heuristic variables, which are meaningful for understanding both the characteristics and the consequences of specific forms of capitalism (for a contrasting approach to Latin America, see also Gaitán and Boschi, in this volume).

We illustrate our analytical proposal by presenting some elements of a broader investigation into the recent development of the agrarian and agro-industrial sectors in Argentina. This will reveal how the relations of dominance and dependency, which cut through this specific space economy, project themselves onto more localized dynamics and contribute to shaping a specific relation of forces between the state, business and labour. In this vein, we seek to understand the positions of different productive economic actors, the constraints to which the state is subject and the political, social and ecological consequences which result from the characteristics and the performance of the sector. This way, in the present chapter, we especially probe into the abilities of our approach to guide investigations on the micro-level, in specific, geographically and sectorally localized processes of contestation surrounding particular capitalist development trajectories. We consider the capacity to make sense of what takes place 'on the ground' to be an essential prerequisite for engaging in other, higher-level forms of systematization and theorization, but our approach is potentially useful for these purposes as well. We seek to substantiate this latter point throughout the empirical section by providing indications as to how the Argentine case is to be situated comparatively alongside that of the recent trajectory of capitalism in Brazil.

Understanding capitalist variegation through *dependentista* lenses

Even though the emergence of a CC literature on capitalism in Latin America is a quite recent development, by now we can already identify at least three distinctive approaches to Latin American capitalism within the broader neoinstitutionalist camp (see also Ebenau, in this volume): the extended Varieties of Capitalism (VoC) framework developed by the American business historian Ben Ross Schneider and colleagues (Schneider and Karcher, 2010; Schneider and Soskice, 2009; Schneider, 2009, 2013); the statist perspective, which is advanced by Renato Boschi and others and which is politically associated with Latin American neodevelopmentalism (Boschi and Gaitán, 2009; Boschi, 2011, 2013; Diniz and Boschi, 2013; see also Gaitán and Boschi, in this volume); and – the latest and thus less developed addition to the literature – the institutionalist–regulationist approach formulated by Ilán Bizberg and others in Mexico (Bizberg and Théret, 2012; Bizberg, 2011, 2012).

The respective strengths and weaknesses of these perspectives have been amply discussed elsewhere, and there is no need to repeat these debates here (Aguirre and Lo Vuolo, 2013; Ebenau and Suau Arinci, 2012; Ebenau, 2012, 2014; Fernández and Alfaro, 2011; Fishwick, 2014; Friel, 2011; Sánchez-Ancochea, 2009; Schrank, 2009). It is sufficient to say that, from a critical political economy vantage point, they all reproduce to a greater or lesser extent a number of shortcomings shared across the broader neoinstitutionalist CC literatures (see also Bruff et al., and Ebenau, in this volume). In the present context, two of these problems should be highlighted. The first is that even where these approaches explicitly consider the global insertion of different space economies, they do so in a largely 'monadic' fashion, which does not recognize the constitutive interplay between factors that appear as 'internal' and others that appear as 'external' in shaping the specific economic, social and political configurations. The second problem, in turn, is that these perspectives tend to interpret conflicts between collective actors and repeated crises as mere residual results of ill-conceived policies and dysfunctional institutions, a view which unduly neglects the inherently conflictual and crisis-prone nature of capitalist accumulation processes.

We suggest that the protagonists of the Latin American dependency school – the *dependentistas* – have provided us with theoretical insights, which permit us to overcome these problems while also retaining the analytically powerful focus on the institutionalization of specific localized forms of capitalism (see also May and Nölke, in this volume). Dependency perspectives first emerged in Latin America as an offspring of structuralist economics, in particular those studies that were concerned with the lack of success of most import substitution models that had been pursued throughout the region (early key texts include Cardoso and Faletto, 1983 [1969]; Marini, 1981 [1973]; Frank, 1966; an excellent review and discussion is offered in Kay, 1989). According to the early *dependentistas*, this failure was primarily due to the predominance of relations of dependency, which had developed between central and peripheral capitalist economies. Along with many classical developmentalists, the *dependentistas* regarded the state as the key actor in bringing about the desired economic and social improvements, but they added to this narrative the precondition of qualitatively transforming the relations with other space economies (cf. Thwaites Rey and Castillo, 2008).

Proposals to recover, adapt and update insights generated by the dependency school until its politically induced demise in the 1980s for the comparative study of contemporary capitalism have already been made by a number of scholars, both in and outside of Latin America (see, for example, Bluhm, 2010; Bruszt and Greskovits, 2009; Fernández and Alfaro, 2011; Nölke and Vliegenthart, 2009). Along with most of these authors, we believe that it is promising to reconsider particularly those parts of the dependency literature that have been concerned with generating the conceptual and methodological toolkit for analysing specific situations of dependency (Cardoso, 1971; Cardoso and Faletto, 1983). Thus, rather than formulating an abstract–general theory of dependency, we wish to contribute to understanding how the distinct modes of insertion of particular, relatively bounded space economies into the 'ecology' of global capitalism imply multiple and changing modes of interrelation among actors and institutions located inside and outside of the territories in question. This implies that our focus is principally on institutionalized relations among actors (or groups of actors) and on higher levels of abstraction, ensembles of such relations insofar as they present themselves in particular space economies whose political, economic and social trajectories they in turn overdetermine.

At the same time, and in contrast to some of those cited above, we argue that it is analytically fruitful to retain the fundamental distinction between the two principles according to which such interrelations can be articulated, namely dominance and dependency. According to Theotonio Dos Santos (1970, p. 231), the concepts of dependency and domination may be used to describe:

> situation[s] in which the economy of certain countries is conditioned by the development and expansion of another economy to which the former is subjected. The relation of interdependence between two or more economies, and between these and world trade, assumes the form of dependence when some countries (the dominant ones) can expand and can be self-sustaining, while others (the dependent ones) can do this only as a reflection of that expansion, which can have either a positive or a negative effect on their immediate development.

The twin notions of dependency and domination thus call attention to a persistent inequality among different space economies and the fact that the trajectories of some will be overdetermined – and can even be actively conditioned – by powerful political and economic actors rooted in others. Of course, when thinking in terms of different territories, either principle will seldom express itself in a 'pure' form. Nevertheless, in concrete empirical cases, one or the other principle will often take precedence over the other, so that many situations can meaningfully be characterized as marked by dominance or, conversely, dependency (Marini, 1981; Frank, 1966).

Significantly, in this conception, relations of dominance and dependence do not just operate from the outside of a particular space economy but simultaneously, and often more importantly, inscribe themselves into the relations among actors and institutions rooted in the territory in question.[1] Thus, in the words of Jõaõ Quartim de Moraes:

> it is necessary to conceive dependence as a dialectical unity of the general determinants of the capitalist mode of production and the specific determinants of each of the dependent societies and, therefore, as the synthesis of the 'external factors' and the 'internal factors'.
>
> (cited in Kay, 1989, p. 160)

Thus, on the one hand, structures and processes internal to the space economy in question are circumscribed by external parameters, and actors are forced to adapt their conduct to these restrictions. One example for this would be the tendency towards 'super-exploitation' identified by Marini (1981, pp. 24–38), according to which capitals rooted in dependent spaces seek to compensate their disadvantages due to the prevailing pattern of 'unequal exchange' in the global market by remunerating labour below its value. Such a vision provides an important corrective to mainstream CC scholarship's theoretical nationalism.

However, if we are to take seriously the external–internal dialectic, we cannot simply subsume the emergence and change of localized institutions under the general dynamics of global capitalism. Rather, we have to take seriously the diversity of ways in which the concrete situation can be processed, negotiated, contested and, potentially, transformed on the local level. For instance, far from being passive objects of external forces, some actors rooted in dependent territories may themselves develop into protagonists in the (re-)production of the prevalent pattern of relations of dominance and dependency, while others may engage in advancing counter-hegemonic projects.

In order to facilitate a fuller understanding of these dialectical processes and their results, the strategic-relational approach to institutions and the state developed by Bob Jessop and others constitutes a valuable complement to the notions of dependency and domination. This approach is presented in more detail elsewhere (see Jessop, in this volume). At this stage, it is therefore sufficient to recall that in this perspective the state is conceived as an ensemble of institutions, which normally possesses some form of autonomy from social forces, but an autonomy that is 'relational' in character in the sense that it derives from and remains conditioned by the specific spatio-temporal class dynamics. For our present debate, this means, for instance, that those actors that defend a situation marked by the prevalence of relations of dependency will seek to align local institutions in accordance with this pattern, which will in turn obstruct transformative projects.

In sum, from our perspective it is important to be attentive to external constraints and (over-)determinations resulting from a particular situation of dependency when studying specific localized institutional configurations, but it is equally important to take seriously the processes of negotiation and contestation that surround this situation. We therefore suggest that a dependency-inspired critical CC research agenda is often best pursued through analyses of situations of dependency and domination 'from the inside out' – by moving from local institutions and actors to the structures of global capitalism, rather than the other way round.

Table 11.1 summarizes the rough outlines of an analytical framework, which we believe to be capable of guiding such fine-grained analyses of the 'how', 'where' and 'when' of dependency. It specifies seven dimensions of analysis, derived from the preceding theoretical considerations, and describes in an ideal-typical fashion some key characteristics, which relations on these dimensions might assume in hypothetical situations where either dominance or dependency prevail. Of course, the disaggregation serves merely analytical purposes and when studying concrete empirical cases manifold interrelations across these dimensions will emerge, as will also be apparent in the following section from our illustrative analysis of the Argentine agricultural and agro-industrial sectors.

To conclude this presentation, let us just briefly state how a hypothetical situation of full-blown dependency might express itself on each of the seven dimensions comprehended in the table. In such a case, we would observe a disorganized and fragmented local business sector, whose most dynamic elements are strongly oriented towards the world market. Conversely, external economic actors would occupy key positions, for instance in advanced manufacturing and the most

Table 11.1 Capitalist variegation between dominance and dependency

Analytical dimension	Dominance	Dependency
1) Local productive structure and composition of business sector	Dense and consolidated local productive structure, business sector strongly integrated into local economic circuits and counting with capacities for strategic trans-localization; abundance of investment capital from internal sources.	Fragmentary and disarticulated productive structure, fragile and/or weakly integrated business sector without trans-local reach; scarcity of investment capital from internal sources.
2) Integration of external economic actors	Strategically mediated integration of external capitals; abundance of investment capital from external sources.	Predominance of external capitals in strategic positions of the economy, despite relative scarcity of investment capital from external sources; lack of effective mediation of their integration; high vulnerability to external processes.
3) Insertion into trans-local production and trade networks	Insertion into high value-added tiers, strong connections between export sector and rest of local economy; dynamic, multiple and diversified competitive advantages.	Insertion into low value-added tiers, weak connections between export sector and rest of local economy, prevalence of rent-seeking behaviour; few competitive advantages, based on static factor endowments.
4) Insertion into trans-local political-regulatory regimes	Proactive stance regarding creation and development of trans-local regulatory regimes; capacity to influence norms in consonance with own political objectives.	Reactive stance regarding creation and development of trans-local regulatory regimes; external imposition of norms, no possibility of realizing own political objectives.
5) State regulatory capacities	Capacity to articulate activities of local and extra-local firms with political objectives and to appropriate large proportions of produced surplus.	Impossibility to articulate activities of local and extra-local firms with political goals, low ability to appropriate parts of produced surplus.
6) Forms and conditions of use and appropriation of human labour power	Capacity to retain highly qualified labour force, possibilities of recourse to extra-local labour; articulation between distinct territories' labour relations and generation/appropriation of social rents.	Impossibility to develop and/or retain highly qualified labour force; lack of social and labour protection, recourse to intensive exploitation of workers partly as a form of adaptation to external exigencies.
7) Forms and conditions of use and appropriation of natural resources and distribution of ecological costs	Capacity to appropriate and develop, at low cost, natural resources from other spaces and to derive benefits; ability to displace ecological costs of production and consumption to other territories.	Impossibility to develop, use and retain resources and derivable benefits in the territory; recourse to intensive exploitation of the environment partly as a form of adaptation to external exigencies; necessity of absorbing ecological costs produced externally.

Source: own elaboration, jointly with Facundo Parés.

internationally competitive activities. In line with the former, firms from dependent space economies would be inserted through the lowest tiers into trans-local networks of production and trade while their links with the rest of the productive structure would be scarcely developed, if at all. State actors would be unable to influence trans-local norms, such as trade and investment regulation, and their capacities to politically integrate or discipline economic actors would be weak. As a result of the above set of factors, firms rooted in dependent territories would routinely recur to highly intensive forms of exploitation of labour and the environment in order to position themselves vis-à-vis external competition and thus reach some degree of competitiveness in global markets.

Actors, institutions and conflicts in the Argentine agricultural and agro-industrial sectors: An illustrative case study

As expressed previously, in this section we apply the framework just presented in order to illustrate how global and regional relations of dominance and dependency inscribe themselves, mediated through specific processes of negotiation and contestation, into the locally institutionalized politico-economic relations, which constitute a particular configuration of capitalism. We choose as empirical reference point for our analysis the Argentine agrarian and agro-industrial sector, which is extremely relevant for any discussion about the development of capitalism in this country since it comprises the most globally competitive activities and is thus the main contributor of foreign exchange.[2] Such a high strategic significance of primary activities is a feature of many non-Triad economies, even where they have reached a considerable degree of productive diversification (see also Drahokoupil and Myant, Gaitán and Boschi, and Tilley in this volume). It is thus worthwhile to broaden the often heavily manufacturing-centred CC frameworks in this sense.

The government of Néstor Kirchner (2003–2007), who was elected president of Argentina in the aftermath of the terminal crisis of neoliberalism in 2001–2002, and later those of his wife and successor Cristina Fernández (2007–2015), led a shift towards a neodevelopmentalist-inspired strategy, mirroring similar political processes in other South American countries including neighbouring Brazil (see also Gaitán & Boschi, in this volume). This had at least two important consequences for Argentine agro-based production: export duties were introduced as a means to collect resources to finance renewed import substitution efforts and to keep domestic prices in check; and somewhat later the government began to attempt incentivizing producers to increase value-added and thus advance industrial development. An official from the National Ministry of Agriculture explained the rationale behind these policies thus:

> [T]here is a recognition from all sectors and the national government of the importance which the sector holds for the country's development, and of the importance of 'de-primarising' it, thus connecting it more to processing and adding value at origin.[3]

Despite this appeal to a putative national development consensus, the neodevelopmentalist project has been subject to repeated, heavy political attacks by Argentine agro-business and its supporters. A member of a regional executive of *Confederaciones Rurales Argentinas* (CRA), one of the organizations representing larger rural producers, succinctly described the underlying motivation, criticizing the tax regime and also dismissing the very neodevelopmentalist aspirations for the sector's development:

> [T]hese days, the national government's perspective on the sector is purely financial, one of extracting tax revenue to finance activities so they can stay in power...We don't need them to lend us a hand, we need them to withdraw the two hands with which they are restraining us.[4]

These structural tensions repeatedly erupted into open, large-scale confrontations and crystallized into a general polarization of the political scenario, leading neoinstitutionalist observers to question in particular the quality of implementation and the supporting institutional infrastructure of Argentine neodevelopmentalism, especially in comparison with its Brazilian cousin (cf. Ebenau and Liberatore, 2013). Defeated in a major conflict in 2008 (see Basualdo and Arceo, 2009), the government turned to the neodevelopmentalist and neoinstitutionalist recommendations, derived not least from their interpretation of the Partido dos Trabalhadores (PT) governments' experience, of striving for an institutionally mediated synergy between public and private interests, thus partly responding to such criticisms. In the context of these efforts, it also sought to improve relations with the rural producers' organizations through negotiating a participatory sectorial development plan, the *Plan Estratégico Agroalimentario y Agroindustrial* (PEA), which was launched in 2011 (Ebenau and Suau Arinci, 2012).

Nevertheless, from our interviews conducted between 2012 and 2013, it emerges that the majority of rural producers and the leadership of their representative organizations do not see the PEA as having any effect in terms of improving relations with the government and its allies. To representatives of Argentine agro-business, the plan is, in the pithy formulation of an executive, 'wishful thinking, painted cardboard'.[5] Rather than the emergence of a public–private synergy, the beginning of 2014 has therefore seen new, heavy political confrontations, as a result of which the government was forced to allow a massive devaluation of the Argentine peso, partly because big exporters refused to liquidate their accumulated stocks. That this formed part of a larger conflict over the general direction of the development of Argentine capitalism becomes clear, for instance, from a communiqué issued by the *Mesa de Enlace*, a forum of joint articulation of the four main producer organizations, which argued:

> It is evident that the government is searching, as it always did, for culprits for its own mistakes, rather than implementing an integral plan for fighting inflation, reducing public spending, improving real competiveness of the economy, and incentivising production, genuine employment and development.[6]

In what follows, we show how the dependency-inspired analytical framework presented above can help to understand and explain the permanence of this bitter conflict better than neoinstitutionalist theories. In contrast to the former, it is capable of elucidating the fundamental pattern of trans-local class relations, which transcend any particular attempt at institutional mediation, such as the PEA, and which condition Argentine neodevelopmentalism in specific ways. We will discuss each of the seven dimensions in turn, even though some will be touched upon only fleetingly due to space constraints.

During the 1990s and 2000s, two intertwined processes rapidly transformed the productive structure of the agricultural sector: the progressive concentration of land ownership in the hands of an agrarian bourgeoisie, which comprises both the old rural oligarchy and new capitalist producers[7] and the development of an ever-stronger predominance of cereal and oilseeds – especially soy – production. These processes were driven by commercial liberalization policies, as well as the introduction of genetically modified varieties and new production techniques during the 1990s. By now, Argentina's main agricultural zones (especially the extended Pampa region) are considered to have one of the most modern agricultural production regimes globally (Bisang and Pontelli, 2012). Smaller producers with fewer resources to adapt had to sell their land or turn to renting out to bigger units; other activities such as cattle production were gradually displaced to other zones less attractive for agriculture (Basualdo et al., 2009). In association with these changes, production volumes of the food industry expanded as well, but the degree of qualitative change, for instance in the sense of an increase in vertical integration, remained limited. As for the integration of external economic actors, while agricultural production proper is dominated by national capitals, foreign transnationals – such as Cargill and Monsanto – occupy some of the most lucrative and strategic positions in the production and commercialization networks, for example in the provision of technology and inputs (seeds, fertilizers, machinery and so on), the processing of primary products and, crucially, exports (López and Ramos, 2009). As a result of these combined processes, Argentina's present-day agro-based production is dominated by a strongly concentrated and primary production-centred bourgeoisie whose very high economic and political power sets Argentina apart from other national experiences, including that of neighbouring Brazil with its more heterogeneous capitalist class.

The composition of the business sector and the productive structure are closely related to the transnational commercial insertion of Argentina's agriculture and agro-industry. Fundamentally speaking, both sectors are heavily transnationalized: taken together, primary agricultural goods and manufactures of agrarian origin accounted for almost 60 per cent of all Argentine exports between 2011 and 2013, around ten times their combined contribution to GDP; the so-called oilseeds complex alone accounted for more than 26 per cent of all exports in 2011.[8] Moreover, agricultural products and foodstuffs constitute the only principal branches where local producers possess broad-scale comparative advantages.[9] Over the past decade and a half, world market prices for the main agrarian and agro-industrial export goods have surged, which has fortified the Argentine agrarian bourgeoisie's power and self-confidence and provided the motivation for destining even more of the production for export rather than for the domestic market (Porta et al., 2009). Destinations for agro-based exports are multiple and diversified and include traditional buyers such as the United States and European countries as well as emerging Asian economies, with China becoming a key destination for Argentine soy (Reboratti, 2010). Beyond the general World Trade Organization (WTO) framework, Argentine intercontinental trade in agricultural and agro-industrial goods is not codified. Thus, (dis-)incentives are largely market generated, and political steering is difficult because it often has to go against the directions indicated by the world market. Even though the Kirchner and Fernández governments have not encountered interlocutors for a constructive dialogue in Argentine agrobusiness, the neodevelopmentalist project they pursue is nevertheless highly dependent on agriculture and the agro-industry. Not only has the debt default implemented in 2002, at the height of the crisis, largely cut off the national economy from global financial markets, but the central state is also lacking major alternative sources of foreign exchange. Again, this sets Argentine neodevelopmentalism apart from its Brazilian counterpart (as well as, say, Chile and Mexico), where government is heavily involved in extractive activities and exports. Vis-à-vis the agricultural and agro-industrial sectors, Argentine state actors therefore have to rely to an important degree on rather heavy-handed policy instruments, such as export taxes, quota regimes and price controls. Their capacities to regulate and/or discipline business rest on an increasingly fragile basis, however. Like the default, the export duty regime as the main instrument of extracting financial resources from agriculture was first re-introduced through emergency decree. When continued beyond the immediate post-crisis stabilization period, it was supported by the considerable political legitimacy, which the Kirchner and later the Fernández governments enjoyed, based on their ability to orchestrate a process of rapid recuperation from the crisis. However, when the upward economic and social trajectories lost their momentum as a combined result of problems in the economic strategy and the increasingly troubled global context, public support for the government, especially from unions and the left, began to wane (Ebenau and Liberatore, 2013). So far, Cristina Fernández's government has managed a balancing act between the actors, which calls for more and faster social progress and an increasingly assertive opposition, but the most recent events, including those discussed above, have shown that this is becoming ever more precarious.

Beyond the inherently conflictual nature and the associated vulnerability of the neodevelopmentalist project, this configuration of the Argentine agrarian and agro-industrial sectors has problematic implications for labour and the environment, which the dependency framework helps to highlight as well. Generally speaking, labour relations in agriculture are extremely segmented: on the one hand, there are the modern production networks located in the traditional agricultural regions, centred on the most internationally competitive products, where pay and other working conditions are generally good but jobs are scarce due to the high degree of technification. In the words of officials of the *Unión Argentina de Trabajadores Rurales y Estibadores* (UATRE) union, which organizes rural workers, speaking about the emblematic case of soy production:

> Paradoxically, in the zone where most production is concentrated, the lowest number of workers is employed. [S]oy has a high economic yield, but very little impact in terms of job generation.[10]

On the other hand, there are other less privileged segments and localities where poorly remunerated and largely unprotected forms of labour prevail. What is more, due to the expansion of large-scale capitalist agriculture, recent years have seen a continuous process of displacement of small farmers and their families, leading to a situation which increasingly approximates what has been called an 'agriculture without agriculturalists' (Tapella, 2004). In this regard, a representative of Asociación de Productores Noroeste de Córdoba (APENOC, an association of small producers from the northwest of Córdoba province) expressed:

> This agro-business model also affects, on the one hand, the use of the soil and, on the other, the possibility to produce, since it does not consider small farmers as productive subjects. Among its effects are depopulation, displacement of workers... and the lack of investment... in small-scale agriculture. We are not part of what the government defines as the countryside. The countryside of which they speak is another; it is that of the agro-export business.[11]

As for the use of natural resources, the expansion of large-scale, technology-intensive and often mono-cultural production is already having measurable effects in terms of soil depletion, reduction of biodiversity, frequency of forest fires, climatic change and so on (Carrasco et al., 2012; Reboratti, 2010).

Considering not only the continuous oppositional stance of the agrarian bourgeoisie but also this problematic social and ecological balance of the current agricultural productive model, it appears even more ironic that the Kirchner and Fernández administrations have continued to support its deepening and expansion. Nevertheless, our analytical framework can be instrumental for unravelling such apparent paradoxes by showing how they form part of a wider context of conflictual trans-local class relations, which reaches deeper than particular attempts at institutional mitigation. This conditions the manoeuvring space for political actors, particularly where they seek to transform these relations' fundamental character in the sense, say, of transcending the dominance of extra-local firms and a fraction of the bourgeoisie whose interests are primarily associated with global markets, rather than locally formulated policy objectives.

Concluding remarks

Some decades ago, the protagonists of the dependency school formulated their key theoretical propositions and, on this basis, presented novel empirical insights regarding the fundamental importance of relations of dominance and dependency in shaping the variegated character of global capitalism. With this chapter, we have sought to advance towards a more systematic integration of these insights into critical CC research. We believe that the dependency tradition has much to offer such a project since it can provide us with the conceptual and analytical means for tackling the most deeply rooted shortcomings of neoinstitutionalist approaches, including their theoretical nationalism and their superficial grasp of conflicts and crises in capitalist societies. In this sense, we suggest that it is complementary to alternative, critical visions of capitalist diversity, which conceive of the multiple institutionally differentiated local instantiations of capitalism as constitutively interconnected parts of a hierarchically structured whole, rather than as apparently self-constituted varieties of capitalism. A key case in point is, as already alluded to above, the 'variegated capitalism' perspective (see also Jessop and Wehr, in this volume).

As we have sought to document, through both our discussion of key notions from the dependency tradition and the subsequent elaboration and illustrative application of a concomitant analytical framework, thinking in terms of dominance and dependence can add both theoretical depth and conceptual precision to such perspectives. The challenges associated with further substantiating this intuition will be to connect more systematically the rich theoretical debates that surrounded the dependency school to those currently conducted in critical CC research and to put the insights and conceptual frameworks thus derived to the test in empirical investigations on multiple levels.

Notes

1. This proposition goes against the grain of much of the well-rehearsed Anglophone critique of the dependency school, which wrongly accuses its proponents of arguing for a simple external (over-)determination of the development of dependent capitalism (Kay, 1989, pp. 174–7).

2. Apart from the cited secondary sources and primary quantitative data, the following builds on a series of around 40 in-depth qualitative interviews which we have conducted with producers, authorities of business associations, representatives of labour and other civil society organizations and relevant public officials.
3. Interview with official of the *Instituto de Planificación Estratégica Agroalimentaria y Agroindustrial*, a dependency of the National Ministry of Agriculture (Ministerio de Agricultura, Ganadería y Pesca, MAGyP), conducted in Ciudad Autónoma de Buenos Aires, 6 August 2012.
4. Interview with member of the executive of Confederación de Asociaciones Rurales de la Tercera Zona (CARTEZ, constitutive part of CRA) conducted in Córdoba Capital, 13 July 2012.
5. Interview with executive director of diversified agricultural producer from the interior of Córdoba province, conducted in Córdoba Capital, 3 August 2012.
6. Cited from article 'Pliego de condiciones desde las silobolsas' by Sebastián Premici, published on 1 February 2014 in *Página 12* newspaper, available online at http://www.pagina12.com.ar/diario/economia/2-238973-2014-02-01.html.
7. Already in 2002, when the last agricultural census was conducted, the smallest 60 per cent of productive units did not even account for 5 per cent of cultivated surface, while conversely the biggest 10 per cent covered 78 per cent of the land (...). (Bidaseca et al., 2013).
8. Data from Argentina's *Instituto Nacional de Estadística y Censos* (INDEC).
9. Revealed comparative advantages – a measure of a country's relative export strength – for these two activities are 6.0 and 7.1, respectively. Automotive products count with an RCA of 1.7, the only major industrial branch where Argentine producers hold a significant comparative advantage (own calculations, based on WTO data).
10. Interview with officials of UATRE, Ciudad Autónoma de Buenos Aires, 7 August 2012.
11. Interview with representatives of APENOC, Casas Viejas, departamento de Cruz del Eje, Córdoba, 2 July 2012.

Bibliography

Aguirre, J. and R. Lo Vuolo (2013) 'Variedades de Capitalismo: Una aproximación al estudio comparado del capitalismo y sus aplicaciones para América', *Documentos de Trabajo CIEPP*, 85 (Buenos Aires: Centro Interdisciplinario para el Estudio de Políticas Públicas).
Basualdo, E.M. and N. Arceo (2009) 'Características estructurales y alianzas sociales en el conflicto por las retenciones móviles', in *La crisis mundial y el conflicto del agro* (Buenos Aires: Editorial La Página), 51–83.
Basualdo, E., N. Arceo, M. González and N. Mendizábal (2009) 'Transformaciones estructurales en el agro pampeano: La consolidación del bloque agrario en la Argentina', *CIFRA Documentos de Trabajo*, 1 (Buenos Aires: CIFRA-CTA).
Bidaseca, K., A. Gigena, F. Gómez, A.M. Weinstock, E. Oyharzábal and D. Otal (2013) *Relevamiento y sistematización de problemas de tierra de los agricultores,*

Proyecto de Desarrollo de Pequeños Productores Agropecuarios (Buenos Aires: PROINDER).
Bisang, R. and C. Pontelli (2012) 'Agroalimentos: Trayectoria reciente y cambios estructurales', in PNUD (ed.), *La Argentina del largo plazo: crecimiento, fluctuaciones y cambio estructural* (Buenos Aires: Programa de las Naciones Unidas para el Desarrollo), 125–65.
Bizberg, I. (2011) 'The Global Economic Crisis as Disclosure of Different Types of Capitalism in Latin America', *Swiss Journal of Sociology*, 37:2, 321–39.
Bizberg, I. (2012) 'Types of Capitalism in Latin America', *Interventions Économiques*, 47, 1–26.
Bizberg, I. and B. Théret (2012) 'La diversidad de los capitalismos latinoamericanos: los casos de Argentina, Brasil y México', *Noticias de La Regulación*, 61, 1–22.
Bluhm, K. (2010) 'Theories of Capitalism Put to the Test: Introduction to a Debate on Central and Eastern Europe', *Historical Social Research/Historische Sozialforschung*, 35:2, 197–217.
Boschi, R.R. (ed.). (2011) *Variedades de capitalismo, política e desenvolvimento na América Latina* (Belo Horizonte: Editora UFMG).
Boschi, R.R. (2013) 'Politics and Trajectory in Brazilian Capitalist Development', in U. Becker (ed.), *The BRICS and Emerging Economies in Comparative Perspective: Political Economy, Liberalisation and Institutional Change* (Abingdon: Routledge), 123–43.
Boschi, R.R. and F. Gaitán (2009) 'Politics and Development: Lessons from Latin America', *Brazilian Political Science Review*, 3:2, 11–29.
Bruszt, L. and B. Greskovits (2009) 'Transnationalization, Social Integration, and Capitalist Diversity in the East and the South', *Studies in Comparative International Development*, 44:4, 411–34.
Cardoso, F.H. (1971) ' "Teoria da dependência" ou análises concretas de situações de dependência?' *Estudos CEBRAP*, 1:1, 25–47.
Cardoso, F.H. and E. Faletto (1983) *Dependencia y desarrollo en América Latina: ensayo de interpretación sociológica* (18th ed.) (México D.F. et al.: Siglo Veintiuno Editores).
Carrasco, A.E., N.E. Sánchez and L.E. Tamagno (2012) *Modelo agrícola e impacto socio-ambiental en la Argentina: monocultivo y agronegocios* (La Plata: AUGM/UNLP).
Diniz, E. and R.R. Boschi (2013) 'Uma nova estratégia de desenvolvimento?' in L.C. Bresser-Pereira (ed.), *O que esperar do Brasil* (Rio de Janeiro: Editora FGV), pre-print version available at http://cemacro.fgv.br/sites/cemacro.fgv.br/files/Eli%20Diniz%20e%20Renato%20Boschi%20-%20Uma%20nova%20estrat%C3%A9gia%20de%20desenvolvimento_0.pdf.
Dos Santos, T. (1970) 'The Structure of Dependence', *The American Economic Review*, 60:2, 231–6.
Ebenau, M. (2012) 'Varieties of Capitalism or Dependency? A Critique of the VoC Approach for Latin America', *Competition & Change*, 16:3, 206–23.
Ebenau, M. (2014) 'Comparative Capitalisms and Latin American Neodevelopmentalism: A Critical Political Economy View', *Capital & Class*, 38:1, 102–14.
Ebenau, M. and V. Liberatore (2013) 'Neodevelopmentalist State Capitalism in Brazil and Argentina: Chances, Limits and Contradictions', *Der Moderne Staat*,

6:1, 105–25.
Ebenau, M. and L. Suau Arinci (2012) 'La heterodoxia permitida: Una crítica al enfoque de las variedades del capitalismo y al paradigma neo-institucionalista', *Anales de las V Jornadas de Economía Crítica* (Buenos Aires: JEC), 1–12.
Fernández, V.R. and M.B. Alfaro (2011) 'Ideas y políticas del desarrollo regional bajo variedades del capitalismo: Contribuciones desde la periferia', *Revista Paranaense de Desenvolvimento*, 120, 57–99.
Fishwick, A. (2014) 'Beyond and Beneath the Hierarchical Market Economy: Global Production and Working Class Conflict in Argentina's Automobile Industry', *Capital & Class*, 38:1, 115–27.
Frank, A.G. (1966) 'The Development of Underdevelopment', *Monthly Review*, 18:4, 17–31.
Friel, D. (2011) 'Forging a Comparative Institutional Advantage in Argentina: Implications for Theory and Praxis', *Human Relations*, 64:4, 553–72.
Kay, C. (1989) *Latin American Theories of Development and Underdevelopment* (London: Routledge).
López, A. and D. Ramos (2009) 'Inversión extranjera directa y cadenas de valor en la industria y servicios', in B. Kosacoff and R. Mercado (eds.), *La Argentina ante la nueva internacionalización de la producción. Crisis y oportunidades* (Buenos Aires: CEPAL-PNUD), 142–215.
Marini, R.M. (1981) *Dialéctica de la dependencia* (5th ed.) (México D.F.: Ediciones Era).
Nölke, A. and A. Vliegenthart (2009) 'Enlarging the Varieties of Capitalism: The Emergence of Dependent Market Economies in East Central Europe', *World Politics*, 61:4, 670–702.
Porta, F., C. Fernández Bugna and P. Moldovan (2009) 'Comercio e inserción internacional', in B. Kosacoff and R. Mercado (eds.), *La Argentina ante la nueva internacionalización de la producción. Crisis y oportunidades* (Buenos Aires: CEPAL-PNUD), 68–139.
Reboratti, C. (2010) 'Un mar de soja: la nueva agricultura en Argentina y sus consecuencias', *Revista de Geografía Norte Grande*, 45, 63–76.
Sánchez-Ancochea, D. (2009) 'State, Firms and the Process of Industrial Upgrading: Latin America's Variety of Capitalism and the Costa Rican Experience', *Economy and Society*, 38:1, 62–86.
Schneider, B.R. (2009) 'Hierarchical Market Economies and Varieties of Capitalism in Latin America', *Journal of Latin American Studies*, 41:3, 553–75.
Schneider, B.R. (2013) *Hierarchical Capitalism in Latin America: Business, Labor, and the Challenges of Equitable Development* (Cambridge: Cambridge University Press).
Schneider, B.R. and S. Karcher (2010) 'Complementarities and Continuities in the Political Economy of Labour Markets in Latin America', *Socio-Economic Review*, 8:4, 623–51.
Schneider, B.R. and D. Soskice (2009) 'Inequality in Developed Countries and Latin America: Coordinated, Liberal and Hierarchical Systems', *Economy and Society*, 38:1, 17–52.
Schrank, A. (2009) 'Understanding Latin American Political Economy: Varieties of Capitalism or Fiscal Sociology?' *Economy and Society*, 38:1, 53–61.

Tapella, E. (2004) 'Reformas estructurales en Argentina y su impacto sobre la pequeña agricultura. Nuevas ruralidades, nuevas políticas?' *Estudios Sociológicos*, 22:3, 669–700.

Thwaites Rey, M. and J. Castillo (2008) 'Desarrollo, dependencia y Estado en el debate latinoamericano', *Araucaria. Revista Iberoamericana de Filosofía, Política Y Humanidades*, 10:19, 24–45.

12
Decolonizing the Study of Capitalist Diversity: Epistemic Disruption and the Varied Geographies of Coloniality

Lisa Tilley

The nation-as-method approach of Comparative Capitalisms (CC) scholarship has generally taken differential economic growth outcomes between national settings as a core *explanandum*. The widening of this scholarship beyond its original concern for the Triad nations of Western Europe, North America and Japan draws in countries from across a much greater disparity in economic performance (see also Ebenau, in this volume). This 'globalizing' CC work therefore more intently confronts the problematic of how the material conditions of people have improved more rapidly and inclusively in some countries than in others, and it is here that CC scholarship begins to more closely resemble strands of development studies. It is also at this juncture that more statist CC scholars have imported the idea of the developmental state, as the literature surrounding this concept shares the interest of the capitalist diversity field in examining relations between degrees of state-strategic coordination and economic performance (see Storz et al., 2013, p. 219; Gaitán and Boschi, in this volume). But in the pursuit of an institutional formula for wealth creation, this CC work and cognate scholarship on the developmental state overlook the prospect that poverty creation (on which see Blaney and Inayatullah, 2010, p. 2) might actually be constitutive of such a process.

This chapter is guided more broadly by postcolonial thought and in particular by the related political project of decolonial scholars (notably Quijano, 1997; Mignolo, 2000). It builds on the decolonial concept of 'coloniality' to draw attention to a metropolitan–rural relation of exploitation, which may act both within and across national borders. As such, it shows how a focus on national capitalism masks such a relation of coloniality, in which the rural province is the site of dispossession and the metropolis the site of accumulation. It also heeds the decolonial concern for epistemic coloniality – understood broadly as the dominance in scholarship of Western concepts and voices – by suggesting that the developmental state concept should be revised from the perspective of Japanese agency rather than told through the standard narrative of an idea developed from Friedrich List through to Chalmers Johnson.

As such, a brief decolonial critique of Varieties of Capitalism (VoC) and CC scholarship more broadly is first advanced. The rest of the chapter is organized around the following three recommendations for those seeking new directions for the study of capitalist diversity beyond its Triad core: firstly, decolonize the study of the developmental state; secondly, disaggregate the nation state along its metropolitan–rural fault lines of internal coloniality; and finally, disrupt the ontological status of the nation by considering how the logics of capitalism produce territorial space itself. These three suggestions are elaborated with reference to existing scholarship, especially that within the 'Asian capitalisms' mode, but also research concerned with Latin America and Africa. Closer reference to Indonesia will be made as a nation very much in production, with exploited rural zones and developmental structures which have not produced the broader prosperity found in Northeast Asian rapid developers.

A decolonial critique of the VoC and CC approaches

Many points of critique of the VoC approach are by now well rehearsed, but it is worth engaging some of the core postcolonial concerns around Eurocentrism and teleological thinking, as their application can reinforce existing criticisms of the still-influential Hall and Soskice (2001) framework (see also Wehr, in this volume). To begin with, the liberal/coordinated market economy (LME/CME) ideal types comprise the dual *teloi* towards which other market economies are assumed to be travelling. These construct Western-situated ideals from highly selective institutional features in which either market coordination (for the LME) or non-market coordination (for the CME) is emphasized. Missing from the absent-state liberal type, for instance, are the persistent state interventions in the supposedly emblematic LME, the United States, evident for example in the guise of infant industry promotion, especially in the

Lisa Tilley 209

area of technological innovation (see Weiss, 2012). Also missing are not only the remarkable state interventions in the economy following the 2008 financial crisis but also the 'state-finance constellation' in place well before this event (Thompson, 2012, p. 399). This construction of partly fictional Western-centric ideal types conforms to narratives of teleological progress, which reproduce selected Western examples as the 'now' and the rest as the 'not yet' (Chakrabarty, 2000, p. 8). Postcolonial scholars have sought the deconstruction of Enlightenment historicism and teleological thinking, which, in classical political economy variants from Smith to Marx, constructed stadial chronologies of historical time, which ordered peoples or nations temporally into stages from primitive to modern. This is important because it still pervades our thinking today and allows us to construct repeatedly the 'colonial difference'. This colonial difference refers to the temporal displacement of people and knowledges perceived as inferior, or 'backward', in historical time and serves to constitute the 'condition of possibility' for the coloniality of power (Mignolo, 2000, p. 16).

Within core VoC scholarship, if a country fails to approximate the imagined Western ideal types, then it is a hybrid, lacking institutional coherence and its associated comparative advantages. Hence, it remains admissible for scholars of capitalist diversity focusing on Asia to begin with 'the puzzle' of how China achieves economic growth despite its 'lack of institutional coherence' (Storz et al., 2013, p. 217). It is also acceptable for those concerned with Latin America to begin from the premise of the continent's inherent deficiencies. Schneider (2009, p. 556) in particular widens the VoC perspective by identifying a 'hierarchical market economy' (HME), which he argues defines and distinguishes economic organization across Latin America whereby 'the institutional components may not fit together as smoothly as those in LMEs and CMEs, and may in some instances be dysfunctional'. Across the wider CC field, countries are referred to as 'developing', 'emerging' (for example, Reslinger, 2013) and so on and as such are temporally displaced into the contemporaneous past. Most importantly, perhaps, such temporal thinking allows us to seal *poverty itself* in the past, thereby separating it in time from wealth and denying that the two might in fact be both coeval and co-constitutive.

Overall, the VoC approach sought to challenge the idea of a shared *telos* in neoliberal convergence, but instead it simply performed a bifurcation of time into two poles of judgement against which to measure the temporally displaced hybrid economies. And although in the past decade or so studies of Asian economies within the broader field have done much to diversify from the original CC inspirations, these still suffer from their foundational links with the VoC literature and, moreover, from their kinship with developmental state scholarship (see Storz et al. 2013 for a summary). Jessop (2014, p. 46) identifies four main fronts of CC scholarship, beginning with the typological form within which the VoC situates itself, the taxonomical approaches identifying more numerous capitalist classifications, other approaches using statistical induction methods to identify clusters and finally the logical–historical approaches preferred by Marxian CC scholars. The first three at least profess to analyse capitalism within nations as isolated containers, without emphasis on its wider interconnections and relations of domination.

To go beyond critiques articulated elsewhere, further concerns for broadening CC scholarship should briefly be raised in relation to the representation and narration of the economic histories and institutional present of countries beyond the West. Attempts have been made to elaborate typologies on the basis of features of non-Triad countries; however, these are again imagined as movable towards the Western liberal type (as in Becker, 2013). Moreover, the identification of types of capitalism 'elsewhere' can become an opportunity to attach pejorative labels such as 'patrimonial capitalism' or 'crony capitalism' (Kang, 2002). Becker (2013, p. 512) notes that patrimonialism is 'strongly present in non-Western economies'. Yet, in no meaningful way is a comparative lens turned back on Western countries to examine forms of corruption – such as sophisticated means of tax avoidance and questionable financial practices – which conveniently evade the indicators of corruption research organizations such as Transparency International (see also Wehr, in this volume).

More pointedly, the common postcolonial condition of almost all countries we label as 'developing' is also overlooked. Furthermore, although it tends towards identifying regional 'styles' – Asian capitalism (see Zhang and Whitley, 2013) and Latin American capitalism (see Schneider, 2009) for instance – the newly broadened CC field has yet to contemplate differential regional and national colonial histories and the longer-term impact of these on national institutions of capitalism. Ultimately, decolonial thinkers would also criticize the hesitation of CC scholarship to bring in past and present thinkers from outside of the Western episteme to tell the histories, travails and the present condition of their own national development endeavours. With this in mind, the legacy of reducing a development experience to the interpretations of Western scholars will be touched upon below in relation to the genealogy of the developmental state concept. Also extended below is a consideration of rural processes of poverty creation alongside metropolitan accumulation, which are not considered even within regionally situated scholarship expressly concerned with inclusive development and poverty reduction (for instance, Boschi and Gaitán, 2013).

Decolonizing capitalist diversity: Three suggestions

Scholars of capitalist diversity in Asia still play an important role in exposing the myth that all countries are converging on an imagined Western liberal-type economy. Persistent evidence of a coordinating state in 'emerging' Asian countries provides counter-evidence for those who insist that a purely market-led route to development is possible (Zhang and Whitley, 2013; Reslinger, 2013; Gaitán and Boschi, in this volume). Yet, this scholarship continues to reproduce some problematic concepts and in the process create its own myths, and as such three suggestions for reforming capitalist diversity scholarship on Asian countries are set out below, with particular attention to the case of Indonesia. However, the suggestions have wider implications for the broadening focus of capitalist diversity scholarship, much of which considers the applicability of reductive 'Asian models' in Latin America and Africa.

Suggestion one: Decolonize the idea of the developmental state

The developmental state has become a key conceptual import within the newly 'globalizing' capitalist diversity literature, its appeal stemming from its association with the high-growth phases of those more recently industrialized countries that would now be recognized as 'developed', such as Japan, Taiwan and South Korea. The concept has also represented the embodiment of state-strategic coordination in Japan as an example of a close approximation of the VoC's CME type. As such, considerable scholarship has emerged seeking to explore its applicability beyond its points of conception in Northeast Asia to Southeast Asian, African or Latin American contexts (see, for example, Edigheji, 2010; Gaitán and Boschi, in this volume; and critically Ebenau, 2014). The note of caution advanced here centres on the reduction of the Japanese economic transition to the agency of the state alone, without consideration of how development was rooted in a wider societal endeavour. In relation to this, the developmental state is considered here to be a discursive construct serving the normative projects of successive Western scholars. From a decolonial position, Eastern agency is downplayed in scholarship on the developmental state, which is framed as a Listian idea (Breslin, 2011; Chang, 2003) conceived in the West and reassembled in Japan to be epitomized in the scholarship of Chalmers Johnson (1982).

Johnson himself was keenly aware of the denial of Japanese agency in the representations of Japan's growth story: noting that the rapid increase in industrial output between the years 1931 and 1934 was portrayed as a 'miracle' that scholars such as Charles Kindleberger came to describe as ' "the riddle" of how Japan "produced Keynesian policies as early as 1932 without a Keynes" ' (Johnson, 1982, p. 6). Yet, Johnson sought to demonstrate that the state was the key to making capitalism function and survive in the face of the communist alternative in a Cold War context (Fine, 2010, p. 170). His own subject position was no doubt an influence when he decided what to include and omit within his representation of Japan's political economy during its high-growth phases. As such, he attributed this growth story to the presence of an economic development-oriented bureaucratic elite operating through a 'pilot agency', itself partly insulated from other branches of government and exercising a 'market-conforming' industrial policy (Johnson, 1982, pp. 314–9). The roles of labour and society, more broadly, while not left out altogether, were given epiphenomenal status. Likewise, more recent scholarship from neostatist authors such as Chang (2003) and Wade (1990) has been steered by their compulsion to contest Washington Consensus-era ideas about the possibilities of pursuing a neoliberal route to development through privatization and deregulation. As such, these authors have persistently neglected to examine the negative impacts of accelerated periods of state-led development, especially on rural populations in such forms as land dispossessions, impoverishment and conflict (cf. Sargeson, 2013; Petras and Veltmeyer, 2007).

The consequence of the reduction of development by these authors to state direction alone at the expense of the societal role is that those marginalized and dispossessed by the development process are either absent from the analysis or implicitly celebrated for creating a low-cost supply of labour. For example, today's Asian capitalism scholarship can foreground the 'great influence of the Asian developmental state' across a sample of Asian political economies, alongside an emphasis on the '[w]ide availability of a malleable workforce', with many countries studied noted to have 'informal human resources systems' in which '[b]asic labour standards are not attained' (Reslinger, 2013, pp. 381–5). This approach thus portrays the expendable condition of low-paid workers as a regrettable strength rather than a structural weakness and neglects to problematize the disparity in workers' rights between the systems labelled equally as 'developmental states'.

Large-scale expendable and exploited labour, however, is symptomatic of a much broader fundamental difference between those Northeast Asian developmental states that became recognizably developed countries and the Southeast Asian 'developmental states' as labelled by the CC literatures. In the former, including Japan, Taiwan and South Korea, developmental structures and policies were instigated following land reforms, which had served to diminish societal inequalities. In contrast, those formerly colonized Southeast Asian states emerged from the formal colonial era with a particular form of extractive institutional configuration still intact. The resource and labour-abundant territories of Southeast Asia had not been organized as settler colonies as such – their European inhabitants only ever reached a fraction of a percentage of the total population – but instead these were administered through 'purely extractive' institutional forms (see Kim, 2009, p. 391). The legacy of these extractive institutional configurations is visible in Indonesia, where national development is steered (at the expense of persistently marginalized floating labour populations) by the politico-business elites who inherited privileged positions from the colonial era. The 'developmental state' in this context begins from a base of profound inequality in contrast to Japan's far from perfect, but nonetheless present, post-war commitment to egalitarianism.

Since independence, Indonesian elites have been persistently oriented towards capitalist economic development and pursued a series of long-term development plans under the presidencies of Sukarno and Suharto. And although it played developmental roles earlier, Indonesia has been observed to have had a recognizable developmental state structure since the 1960s and 1970s (Vu, 2007, p. 31). However, in keeping with dislocated ideas about developmentalism and with a recurring focus on an isolated developmental state, the New Order state under Suharto adopted as its steering theory 'the (internationally-promoted) ideology of Development, with its emphasis on economic growth, a powerful elite and the oppression of the *rakyat jelata*, or ordinary people' (Ford, 2000, p. 62). Industrial relations during the New Order era from 1967 to 1998 reflected a belief that a 'pliable workforce' was essential for development (ibid., p. 64), and continuity in this perception has persisted into Indonesia's post-Asian crisis *reformasi* era.

Furthermore, poverty in Indonesia remains pervasive, with the World Bank (2014) claiming that around 'half of all households remain clustered around the national poverty line set at 200,262 rupiah per month ($22).' That the decades-long developmentalism project in Indonesia has not led to the levels of shared prosperity associated with the 'developed world', as it did in parts of Northeast Asia, leads us to demand a rethink of how the developmental state functions in relation to wider society in different contexts and with differing colonial institutional legacies. Overall, then, the developmental state needs decolonizing, first through a complete *de*construction of its Eurocentric abstractions linked to the geopolitical sympathies of Western commentators and second through a *re*construction, which pays closer attention to local agency and consideration of broader societal aims and inputs, plus to the relations of exploitation which underpinned this.

Suggestion two: Disaggregate the nation state into its metropolitan and rural components

Recent critical scholarship on capitalist diversity has pointed to the importance of being attentive to intersections of domination in the capitalist nation, along gender lines, for instance (Wöhl, 2014), or over informal, reproductive and migrant labour (Taylor, 2014). But here a further heuristic division between the metropolis and the rural province is suggested for 'globalizing' CC scholarship and for two main reasons. First, rural poverty continues to provide the conditions for producing internal populations of floating migrant labour (with respect to China, see Zhang and Peck, 2014, p. 13; and on gendered rural–urban labour migration in Indonesia, see Silvey and Elmhirst, 2003). Second, the wealth accumulated through rural activities, mainly nature-based accumulation, becomes 'national' (or most accurately, metropolitan) wealth and in many cases brings increased dispossession and poverty to rural areas (see Petras and Veltmeyer, 2007; Thorp et al., 2012).

This relation of rural value creation/impoverishment and metropolitan accumulation indicates the importance of paying attention to metropolitan–rural interaction for understanding the material geographies of internal coloniality. This is not to deny the existence of conditions of urban impoverishment, nor that rural accumulation is enjoyed by some; instead, it is intended to propose that the point of dispossession is most often in the countryside in 'developing' countries with large agrarian populations.[1] However, in the process of turning towards these countries, capitalist diversity scholarship has not reconsidered its overwhelming focus on technological innovation and manufacturing industries (see Reslinger, 2013; Witt and Redding, 2013; Zhang and Whitley, 2013) or shifted proportionate analysis to significant rural sectors.[2] This equates to telling metropolitan stories under the sign of 'national' growth.

Two very distinct and atomized political economy literatures that are of concern to us here can be identified, one of which is engaged with national capitalist development and includes capitalist diversity scholarship (cf. Witt and Redding, 2013; Reslinger, 2013; Boschi and Gaitán, 2013) and the second of which is concerned with rural livelihoods and ecology (see Thawnghmung (2008) for a summary). Both have a strong normative focus which largely contradicts that of the other, with the first tending to argue uncritically in favour of national development and the second being more greatly concerned with the negative effects of capitalist development on ecology and livelihoods. I have argued that scholarship centred on national-scale development conceals and distorts the geographies of coloniality, and Thawnghmung (2008) has called for a much more focused rural political economy approach along the lines of classic works on rural livelihoods (cf. Scott, 1976; Popkin, 1979). However, Gellert (2008) warns against falling into the 'local trap' of political ecology, which often takes localized phenomena in isolation and instead suggests developing a dialectics of scale between the local, national and global. While it is certainly true that a rural political economy approach is imperative but not enough in itself, the scalar dialectics suggested by Gellert would still involve treating essentially metropolitan investment, accumulation and consumption as 'national' or 'global' phenomena. Instead, there is a case to be made for understanding (and politicizing) the relationality (and coloniality) between the metropolis and the province, both within and across national borders.

Rural regions form the frontier between capitalist and extracapitalist ways of being and, as such, become the site of the first point of socialization into the particular 'race-gender-class relations of domination' (Lahiri-Dutt, 2013, p. 990) that capitalist existence entails. In Indonesia, large-scale land acquisition for the purposes of developing nature-based industries disadvantages the rural poor by reducing their access to land, which may be their source of basic subsistence as well as their source of security in the event of economic difficulties. This involves the complicity of the state and domestic and foreign finance and results in the dispossession of local communities. As McCarthy et al. (2012, p. 544) explain, 'state policy supports large-scale acquisitions linked with international investment associated with commodity booms... while insufficiently addressing the structural constraints that limit smallholder production'.

Turning the lens onto rural nature-based industries such as extractives and logging reveals the disparate metropolitan–rural effects in terms of wealth and poverty creation. But this is not exclusively an Indonesian or Southeast Asian story. Thorp et al. (2012, p. 169) examine the conditions of 'inequality, conflict and environmental damage' appended to extractive industry activity in rural Africa and Latin America, noting an inverse relationship in many places between resource wealth and the well-being of rural inhabitants. Moreover, the commonalities and differences between the experience of rural dwellers across Asia, Latin America and Africa provide a compelling case for a comparative political economy of nature-based and extractive industries with a focus on their varied metropolitan–rural effects.

Yet, although the differential impact of extractive industries can be seen as partly contingent upon the form and effectiveness of institutions, the relation here is also reflexive, with the social contestations surrounding rural industries impacting in turn upon institutional formation. In other words, the relationship between conflicts in extractive regions, social movements based on labour or environmental activism and politico-economic relations in wider society are all deeply interrelated and implicated in processes of institutional change (Bebbington, 2012). This reminds us that resource governance is not simply a rural story but also feeds wider institutional processes at what we consider to be the national scale. With concern for logging in Indonesia, Gellert also foregrounds the problem of impoverishment within the extractive region (2008, p. 44) alongside wealth creation for a 'small coterie of industrialists and leaders of the Indonesian state', linked here to the export boom in the 1990s in plywood for the Japanese market (ibid., p. 47). At the same time, the technologies needed for industrial-scale logging demand metropolitan investment, whether domestic or foreign. Overall, Gellert's scalar dialectics bring the province into the analysis, but within CC scholarship there are few studies that look beyond the metropolitan picture.

In perhaps one of the closest approximations of a relational rural–metropolitan political economy, carried out through the expanding 'variegated capitalism' research agenda, Zhang and Peck (2014, p. 13) find a series of islanded economies within the great landmass of China, which 'remains an archipelago of capitalist urban formations within a sea of rural underdevelopment'. Their study serves to show why comparing China and, for instance, Singapore in a table of data is meaningless, Singapore being essentially a city with extraterritorial hinterlands for production (see Phelps and Wu, 2009), while China has the size and diversity of many nations. Moreover, it shows that labelling China as having a nationwide 'state', 'guanxi' or even a 'neoliberal' model of capitalism also tells us very little about how China's political economy functions. Instead, they present a complex picture of capitalism on a 'continental scale' (Zhang and Peck, 2014, p. 9), fed by capital from 'offshore' links, diasporic connections and other international sources of finance (ibid., p. 15). However, although the authors at least disrupt teleological expectations by performing a scalar shift down to five metropolitan zones of highly variegated organization, they still essentially reproduce the VoC approach's Western-centric institutionalist framework. Zhang and Peck do show that deprived rural regions essentially feed a 'floating' workforce population of around 261 million people, which makes up a cheap and mobile labour force sustaining metropolitan accumulation in the industrialized coastal regions to the east (ibid., p. 13). Yet, no insight is given into *how* the relations of exploitation between their urban cases and other (rural) regions are instigated and maintained. For example, the idea that Guangdong's 'dormitory labour regime' is sustained by conditions of poverty in rural regions is only implicit in the analysis, and overall they stop short of making explicit the internal geographies of coloniality.

Suggestion three: Disrupt the ontological status of the nation state

Zhang and Peck leave the impression that China is essentially a borderless continent, leaving aside the idea that the *hukou* system of two-tiered citizenship functions as a de facto internal border between rural dwellers and metropolitan residents. Yet, within such a borderless continent, many disparate and unequal 'nations' are being produced by the logics of capitalism, assisted by social forces, physical geographies and variegated political design. Not only does this demonstrate the absolute coevalness of China's poverty and wealth, but it also shows how capitalist forces, even without formal borders, produce distinct spatial pockets of diversity. In other words, China's sheer scale and the shifting patterns within its borders show us how differentiated space is produced under capitalism.

Rather than simply considering capitalist diversity as something produced by different national conditions (as the CC literatures tend to), we should consider how the 'nation' and other spatial scales are reflexively reproduced by the many facets of capitalism itself (see Lefebvre, 1991 [1974] on the production of social space). This becomes important in the Indonesian context: when we refer to 'Indonesian capitalism', we are including spaces and communities which are in no meaningful way either 'Indonesian' or 'capitalist', and the equivalent can be said for much of the postcolonial world. Various economic structures and processes have their role to play in bordering and claiming the nation as a distinct cognitive space, and corporations in particular play their own role in this process. Hence, the rest of this section considers the role of one corporation in the production of Indonesia.

Indonesia's furthest eastern province of West Papua (formerly Irian Jaya) is home to around 250 different Melanesian ethnic groups (Chauvel, 2003, p. 121). It was placed on a path towards independence at the end of the formal colonial era, because the Dutch colonists viewed Papua as too ethnically and culturally distinct from the other Indonesian islands to be subsumed under a postcolonial state administered from Jakarta, around 2500 kilometres away. However, independence plans were shelved in 1969 after a small sample of Papuans voted under coercion to remain part of Indonesia (Banivanua-Mar, 2008, p. 584). The discovery of mineral-rich mountains and the interest of the US mining firm Freeport McMoRan have persistently been implicated in the decision of Sukarno to hold on to Papua at all costs (see, for example, Cultural Survival, 2001). Freeport had actually begun operations in Papua two years before the vote, and these days the same company continues to be the largest tax contributor to the Indonesian state through funds from the Grasberg gold and copper mine, the largest of its kind in the world (see Jakarta Globe, 2013).

To reiterate with respect to Papua a point made repeatedly in this chapter, 'the significant mineral and timber-based wealth extracted from the region rarely ends up in the hands of indigenous land owners, and their land in turn is constitutionally framed as being owned by no one' (Banivanua-Mar, 2008, p. 585). The Grasberg mine – 'a great asset for the country' in the words of Freeport's chief executive (Jakarta Globe, 2013) – is a site of contestation between local rural campaign groups and metropolitan political forces both within and outside of Indonesia. And the state plays a role in rural contestations, too. Indonesia's much-anticipated neoliberal era in the wake of International Monetary Fund (IMF) reforms after the Asian crisis (Hadiz and Robison, 2013) has proved to be far from unidirectional, and more than a decade later the state is reasserting its power by rolling back privatization in the extractives sector.

Through the reform of taxation, the state is making a concerted effort to repatriate the profits of foreign firms, including Freeport. A graduated tax is planned to eventually become a complete export ban of raw mineral ores by 2017. These tax reforms are geared towards locating ore smelting operations on 'Indonesian' soil by placing pressure on mining firms operating in Indonesia to construct ore smelters and refineries.

In the meantime, copper concentrates are due to be taxed progressively up to 60 per cent by 2016 (Tax News, 2014). This is all being heavily contested by mining companies, and the final outcome cannot be predicted. Interestingly, however, the rationale for recent moves towards increased state control of the extractives industry is couched in terms of reversing the impoverishment of the local indigenous population in Papua. Yet, judging by the direction of past revenue, any benefits of tax reform are more likely to contribute to the fiscal viability of the Indonesian state and ultimately to be directed to metropolitan elites in distant Jakarta. Overall, then, Freeport's operations in Papua form an example of the extractives industry contributing towards the production of the nation in a remote and impoverished rural area, and this represents a reason for the state to hold on to territory with a separatist indigenous population.

Conclusion

In summary, a decolonial lens shows that the study of capitalist diversity suffers under the influence of teleological thinking, which serves to seal certain livelihoods, as well as poverty itself, in a coexisting 'past'. This has become much more problematic along with the recent broadening of CC analysis beyond its Triad core to encompass nations with large impoverished populations. This turn has also drawn in the concept of the developmental state through a shared concern for degrees of strategic coordination and the relation of this to economic growth. However, in order to better understand why recognizably developmental state structures have not resulted in the same broad prosperity as in Northeast Asia, this chapter has proposed decolonizing the concept of the developmental state. This involves the deconstruction of politically motivated Western scholarship and a reconsideration of the Japanese view of Japan's own historical development. Most importantly though, it requires a rethink of how the state has interacted with society, of the role that labour played in development and of the role of the countryside and the transformation of rural industries in these processes. This should lead to a greater understanding of how similar developmental state structures have not led to equivalent outcomes, such as in the case of Indonesia.

Under the impetus of national development, rural industries often bring impoverishment and dispossession to rural communities, making the rural province the first point of socialization into capitalist relations of domination, and adding to a pool of floating labour for exploitation in metropolitan zones of accumulation. Hence, a consideration of metropolitan–rural relations of coloniality is vital for the broadening field of CC research, not only to illuminate the differentiated local and metropolitan effects of rural industries but also to examine how the relations of contestation around these industries impact upon the formation of institutions.

Relatedly, a consideration of how capitalist forces produce spatial forms including the nation (rather than how the nation produces forms of capitalism) is suggested in order to disrupt the ontological status of the nation within studies of capitalist diversity. As observed in the case of Papua, capitalist development is inextricably linked to territorialization, especially in postcolonial states with disputed areas of territory and where rural industries play a role in the production of the nation as well as in the production of rural poverty. The new directions for globalizing capitalist diversity scholarship outlined here are intended to challenge references to national capitalism where this term covers populations who subscribe to neither capitalism nor the nation. Instead, it calls for attention to be paid to metropolitan accumulation and rural impoverishment as the material geographies of coloniality, which are hidden under the sign of national capitalism.

Notes

1. Rural populations in China (48 per cent), India (68 per cent) and Indonesia (48.5 per cent) remain large (World Bank, 2013).
2. Of Indonesian GDP, 'agriculture, livestock, forestry and fishery' industries make up 14.4 per cent and 'mining and quarrying' constitute 11.23 per cent, and although manufacturing comprises 23 per cent, this includes often rurally situated oil and gas, wood and wood products (Bank of Indonesia, 2013).

Bibliography

Banivanua-Mar, T. (2008) ' "A Thousand Miles of Cannibal Lands": Imagining Away Genocide in the Re-Colonization of West Papua', *Journal of Genocide Research*, 10:4, 583–602.

Bank of Indonesia (2013) *Quarterly Domestic Product by Industrial Origin at Current Prices*, available at: http://www.bi.go.id/sdds/series/NA/index_NA.asp (last accessed 18 February 2014).

Bebbington, A. (ed.) (2012) *Social Conflict, Economic Development and Extractive Industry: Evidence from South America* (Abingdon: Routledge).

Becker, U. (2013) 'Measuring Change of Capitalist Varieties: Reflections on Method, Illustrations from the BRICs', *New Political Economy*, 18:4, 503–32.

Blaney, D. and N. Inayatullah (2010) *Savage Economics: Wealth, Poverty and the Temporal Walls of Capitalism* (Abingdon: Routledge).

Boschi, R and F. Gaitán (2013) 'Politics and Development: Lessons from Latin America', in C.H. Santana and R. Boschi (eds.), *Development and Semi-periphery: Post-Neoliberal Trajectories in South America and Central Eastern Europe* (London: Anthem Press), 45–64.

Breslin, S. (2011) 'The "China Model" and the Global Crisis: From Friedrich List to a Chinese Mode of Governance?' *International Affairs*, 87:6, 1323–43.

Chakrabarty, D. (2000) *Provincializing Europe: Postcolonial Thought and Historical Difference* (Princeton: Princeton University Press).

Chang, H.-J. (2003) *Kicking Away the Ladder: Development Strategy in Historical Perspective* (London: Anthem Press).

Chauvel, R. (2003) 'Papua and Indonesia: Where Contending Nationalisms Meet', in D. Kingsbury and H. Aveling (eds.), *Autonomy and Disintegration in Indonesia* (Abingdon: Routledge), 115–27.

Cultural Survival (2001) *The Amungme, Kamoro & Freeport: How Indigenous Papuans Have Resisted the World's Largest Gold and Copper Mine*. Retrieved on 26 February 2014, from http://www.culturalsurvival.org/ourpublications/csq/article/the-amungme-kamoro-freeport-how-indigenous-papuans-have-resisted-worlds-

Ebenau, M. (2014) 'Comparative Capitalisms and Latin American Neo-developmentalism: A Critical Political Economy View', *Capital & Class*, 38:1, 102–14.

Edigheji, O. (ed.) (2010) *Constructing a Democratic Developmental State in South Africa: Potentials and Challenges* (Cape Town: HSRC Press).

Fine, B. (2010) 'Can South Africa Be a Developmental State?' in O. Edigheji (ed.), *Constructing a Democratic Developmental State in South Africa: Potentials and Challenges* (Cape Town: HSRC Press), 169–82.

Ford, M. (2000) 'Continuity and Change in Indonesian Labour Relations in the Habibie Interregnum', *Southeast Asian Journal of Social Science*, 28:2, 59–88.

Gellert, P.K. (2008) 'What's New with the Old? Scalar Dialectics and the Reorganization of Indonesia's Timber Industry', in J. Nevins and N.L. Peluso (eds.), *Taking Southeast Asia to Market: Commodities, Nature, and People in the Neoliberal Age* (Ithaca: Cornell University Press), 43–55.

Hadiz, V. and R. Robison (2013) 'The Political Economy of Oligarchy and the Reorganization of Power in Indonesia', *Indonesia*, 96, 35–57.

Hall, P.A. and D. Soskice (eds.) (2001) *Varieties of Capitalism: The Institutional Foundations of Comparative Advantage* (Oxford: Oxford University Press).

Jakarta Globe (2013) *US Mining Giant Freeport Faces Fight with Indonesia*, available at: http://www.thejakartaglobe.com/news/us-mining-giant-faces-fight-with-indonesia/ (last accessed 20 February 2014).

Jessop, B. (2014) 'Capitalist Diversity and Variety: Variegation, the World Market, Compossibility and Ecological Dominance', *Capital & Class*, 38:1, 45–58.

Johnson, C. (1982) *MITI and the Japanese Miracle* (Stanford: Stanford University Press).

Kang, D. (2002) *Crony Capitalism: Corruption and Development in South Korea and the Philippines* (Cambridge: Cambridge University Press).

Kim, W. (2009) 'Rethinking Colonialism and the Origins of the Developmental State in East Asia', *Journal of Contemporary Asia*, 39:3, 382–99.

Lahiri-Dutt, K. (2013) 'Gender (Plays) in Tanjung Bara Mining Camp in Eastern Kalimantan, Indonesia', *Gender, Place & Culture: A Journal of Feminist Geography*, 20:8, 979–98.

Lefebvre, H. (1991 [1974]) *The Production of Space* (Oxford: Blackwell).
McCarthy, J.F., J.A.C. Vel and S. Afiff (2012) 'Trajectories of Land Acquisition and Enclosure: Development Schemes, Virtual Land Grabs, and Green Acquisitions in Indonesia's Outer Islands', *Journal of Peasant Studies*, 39:2, 521–49.
Mignolo, W.D. (2000) *Local Histories/Global Designs: Coloniality, Subaltern Knowledges, and Border Thinking* (Princeton: Princeton University Press).
Petras, J. and H. Veltmeyer (2007) 'The "Development State" in Latin America: Whose Development, Whose State?' *Journal of Peasant Studies*, 34:3–4, 371–407.
Phelps, N.A. and F. Wu (2009) 'Capital's Search for Order: Foreign Direct Investment in Singapore's Overseas Parks in Southeast and East Asia', *Political Geography*, 28:1, 44–54.
Popkin, S. (1979) *The Rational Peasant* (Berkeley: University of California Press).
Quijano, A. (1997) 'Colonialidad del Poder, Cultura y Conocimiento en América Latina', *Anuario Mariateguiano*, 9, 113–21.
Reslinger, C. (2013) 'Is There an Asian Model of Technological Emergence?' *Socio-economic Review*, 11:2, 371–408.
Sargeson, S. (2013) 'Violence as Development: Land Expropriation and China's Urbanization', *Journal of Peasant Studies*, 40:6, 1063–85.
Schneider, B.R. (2009) 'Hierarchical Market Economies and Varieties of Capitalism in Latin America', *Journal of Latin American Studies*, 41:3, 553–75.
Scott, J. (1976) *The Moral Economy of the Peasant: Rebellion and Subsistence in Southeast Asia* (New Haven: Yale University Press).
Silvey, R. and R. Elmhirst (2003) 'Engendering Social Capital: Women Workers and Rural-Urban Networks in Indonesia's Crisis', *World Development*, 31:5, 865–79.
Storz, C., B. Amable, S. Casper and S. Lechevalier (2013) 'Bringing Asia into the Comparative Capitalism Perspective', *Socio-Economic Review*, 11:2, 217–32.
Taylor, N. (2014) 'Theorising Capitalist Diversity: The Uneven and Combined Development of Labour Forms', *Capital & Class*, 38:1, 129–41.
Tax News (2014) *US Copper Miners Contest New Indonesian Export Tax*, available at: http://www.tax-news.com/news/US_Copper_Miners_Contest_New_Indonesian_Export_Tax_63480.html. (last accessed 28 January 2014).
Thawnghmung, A.M. (2008) 'The Missing Countryside: The Price of Ignoring Rural Political Economy in Southeast Asia', in E. Martinez Kuhonta, D. Slater and T. Vu (eds.), *Southeast Asia in Political Science: Theory, Region and Qualitative Analysis* (Stanford: Stanford University Press), 252–73.
Thompson, H. (2012) 'The Limits of Blaming Neo-liberalism: Fannie Mae and Freddie Mac, the American State and the Financial Crisis', *New Political Economy*, 17:4, 399–419.
Thorp, R., S. Battistelli, Y. Guichaoua, J.C. Orihuela and M. Paredes (eds.) (2012) *The Developmental Challenges of Mining and Oil: Lessons from Africa and Latin America*. (Basingstoke: Palgrave Macmillan).
Vu, T. (2007) 'State Formation and the Origins of Developmental States in South Korea and Indonesia', *Studies in Comparative International Development*, 41:4, 27–56.
Wade, R. (1990) *Governing the Market: Economic Theory and the Role of Government in East Asian Industrialization* (Princeton: Princeton University Press).
Weiss, L. (2012) 'The Myth of the Neoliberal State', in C. Kyung-Sup, B. Fine and L. Weiss (eds.), *Developmental Politics in Transition: The Neoliberal Era and Beyond* (Basingstoke: Palgrave Macmillan), 27–42.

Witt, M.A. and G. Redding (2013) 'Asian Business Systems: Institutional Comparison, Clusters and Implications for Varieties of Capitalism and Business Systems Theory', *Socio-Economic Review*, 11:2, 265–300.
Wöhl, S. (2014) 'The State and Gender Relations in International Political Economy: A State-Theoretical Approach to Varieties of Capitalism in Crisis', *Capital & Class*, 38:1, 87–99.
World Bank (2013) *Rural Population*, available at: http://data.worldbank.org/indicator/SP.RUR.TOTL. (last accessed 18 February 2014).
World Bank (2014) *Indonesia Overview*, available at: http://www.worldbank.org/en/country/indonesia/overview. (last accessed 18 February 2014).
Zhang, J. and J. Peck (2014) 'Variegated Capitalism, Chinese Style: Regional Models, Multi-Scalar Constructions', *Regional Studies*, Latest Articles section.
Zhang, X. and R. Whitley (2013) 'Changing Macro-structural Varieties of East Asian Capitalism', *Socio-Economic Review*, 11:2, 301–36.

Conclusion: Towards a Critical, Global Comparative Political Economy

Christian May, Matthias Ebenau and Ian Bruff

The chapters in this volume are the results and elements of a lively debate among a diverse group of political economists about the state and purpose of Comparative Capitalisms (CC) research. The arguments they make, including their agreements and divergences, reflect a certain moment in the development of this academic field and of the political conjunctures that in one way or another impact upon it. Of course, as editors we would like to see this volume become a point of reference in this discussion. But – perhaps counterintuitively – we also hope for it to become quickly outdated, for in this case its principal utility would lie in helping to shift the fundamental coordinates of CC theory and empirical research by strengthening the various 'new directions' alluded to throughout the different chapters. After all, contemporary CC, like capitalism, is a dynamic field and things change fast.

Paving the road ahead

As stated in the chapters in the Part I of this volume, the CC debate is presently in a growing state of flux: the future of established approaches has been decisively put into question; neoinstitutionalist researchers have sought to adjust and broaden their theoretical and methodological toolkits in response to the challenges arising from the critique of the established approaches; at the same time, critical political economists, taking inspiration especially from neo-Marxist theories but also increasingly from feminist and postcolonial/decolonial perspectives, argue for the need for an even more fundamental reorientation of CC research. Thus, the field currently faces a wide range of disputes over numerous theoretical issues and research problems that are relevant to it. This collection also reflects this state of the debate: some of the chapters aim to redefine institutionalist approaches and thus respond to the aforementioned critiques they consider most relevant; other chapters are more radical in seeking to establish new paths for CC research.

What unites the different chapters is that they transcend the previously near-hegemonic position of Hall and Soskice's Varieties of Capitalism (VoC) approach. This means that the gravitational pull exerted by VoC's founding principles – an emphatic focus on the national level and on the influence of institutional factors relating to business behaviour and economic efficiency – is weakening (see Coates and Bruff et al. in this volume). Where 'second generation' attempts at renewing the VoC approach had given rise to mere 'incremental' theoretical innovations without hurting the theoretical core of the approach, the chapters that have formed part of this collection respond – each in their own way – to the observations made by David Coates in his chapter. That is, such incremental refinement of VoC and similar approaches will not help us to understand the present reality of capitalist crisis and contestation and even the possible return of capitalist models to their established trajectories.

Taking the bumpy roads thus indicated is necessarily more difficult than cruising down a well-paved intellectual highway such as that laid out by the established research agenda associated with the VoC approach. Nevertheless, it seems inevitable if the CC field is to continue helping us make sense of contemporary capitalism in all of its diversity *and* commonalities, the latter including its contradictory, highly unequal and crisis-prone nature. Metaphorically speaking, the protagonists of the 'new directions' proposed in this collection seek to pave alternative roads ahead by providing remedies to the flaws of conventional CC approaches.

New directions – but where to?

In what follows, we shall return to the most important challenges for contemporary CC research that were identified in the opening chapters. In so doing, we will provide some suggestions as to what a dialogue between post-VoC institutionalist and critical perspectives can contribute to meeting these challenges and to the broader objective of a critical, global renewal of scholarship on capitalist diversity. In this sense, we will point towards contributions to this collection as well as those that formed part of the wider project from which it has emerged (see also Ebenau et al. in this volume; for the wider project, see Bruff and Ebenau, 2014; Bruff et al., 2013; Ebenau et al., 2013).

Back to basics?

When first introducing the notion of 'new directions' (see Bruff et al.), we highlighted how they formed part of an ongoing self-transformation of the CC research agenda. Where, then, does the future of research on capitalist diversity lie? Broadly speaking, contributors to this book have given at least two partly contrasting answers: while some argued for the possibility of eventually generating a new, creative synthesis between post-VoC institutionalist and more critical approaches (see May and Nölke, McDonough, and Drahokoupil and Myant), others suggested (explicitly or implicitly) that a more decisive rupture with the neoinstitutionalist paradigm would be needed in order to respond effectively to its shortcomings (see Jessop, Lux & Wöhl, Wehr, and Tilley). The old question of 'choosing between paradigms' (Coates, 2005) therefore appears to be as relevant as ever. Nevertheless, what seems to be a commonality among virtually all of these authors, and thus a potential basis for continuing and deepening the dialogue, is the conviction that institutional analysis should no longer be considered the natural preserve of established neoinstitutionalist approaches (see also Bruff and Hartmann, 2014; Coates, 2014a; Kannankulam and Georgi, 2014).

An associated, recurrent theme throughout the volume is the proclaimed need to reconsider and reinvigorate older, 'classical' approaches to the politico-economic study of institutions (in this volume, see particularly May and Nölke, McDonough, and Gaitán and Boschi; see also Bieling, 2014; Hardy, 2014). Indeed, this return to the classics constitutes a welcome convergence between the new directions outlined in this book and more mainstream post-VoC perspectives (see, for example, Bohle and Greskovits, 2012; Höpner, 2004; Streeck, 2010). Perhaps the rationalist and strongly efficiency-centred reframing of the purpose of institutional analysis, which came with the VoC approach, will, in some years' time, be viewed as just a temporary diversion from a more encompassing enterprise of analysing the 'laws of motion' of capitalist political economies through the study of various institutions. In any case, this development implies that CC scholars will have to reconsider a great many of the 'big debates', which are taking place against the background of 21st-century capitalism (the most recent example being the runaway commercial success of Thomas Piketty's *Capital in the Twenty-First Century*). Marx, List, Polanyi, Schumpeter, Cardoso, Fraser – who of these, if any, has proposed the most incisive answers to the questions posed by capitalism is as much up for discussion as is the potential for generating new syntheses among their lines of thought. Here, as elsewhere, we call for taking the blinkers off. The contemporary situation is a welcome occasion to move out of the realms of theoretical restriction and self-marginalization.

Capitalist dynamics, crises and institutional change

Calling for a more 'dynamic' CC and showing ways of coming to terms with the complexity and diversity of contemporary processes of institutional and politico-economic change has been one of the key themes of the institutionalist post-VoC debate. In a nutshell, the main response has been to proclaim the need to return to non-rationalist types of institutionalist research. These are premised upon more complex and open-ended conceptions of change, but in and of themselves they have fallen short of providing convincing explanations of the interrelations between institutions and the (capitalist) societies the institutions are part of (see especially Lux, Wöhl, May, Nölke and McDonough).

In contrast, critical perspectives on capitalist diversity go beyond these approaches by positing that capitalism in itself is a dynamic reality whose contradictory tendencies and logics constantly push for changes in the multiple ways in which it is institutionalized. Crises, in such an understanding, are not understood as external shocks but as constitutive features of capitalist economies. Simply put, critical analysts expect that capitalism will necessarily go awry at times and in places. What is in need of an explanation, then, is *where, when* and *how* capitalist crises occur but also why and how they can sometimes be displaced in time and/or space (see Jessop and Suau Arinci et al.). Moreover, crises often constitute important turning points in the development of the institutional framing of capitalism and as such deserve to be studied more closely. Whether and how such critical visions of the crisis proneness of capitalism can be fruitfully combined with the more specifically institution-centred perspectives on change developed in the frame of the post-VoC debate is an important question for future theoretical developments in the CC field.

National diversity and relations of dependency in the world market

The critique of the tendency in conventional CC research towards comparing national 'containers' is by now well rehearsed, as can be seen elsewhere in the volume. Nevertheless, it is worth restating that little has happened so far to establish conceptually robust frameworks which incorporate the (transnational) interrelations of different varieties or models, both between each other and also with the world market, into the study of capitalist diversity (see Ebenau and May and Nölke).

Critical political economy approaches, with their long heritage of studying the capitalist world system and specific relations of dependency/domination within it, may breathe fresh air into this part of the debate. These approaches generally conceive of capitalist dynamics as necessarily transcendent of national borders and therefore see the institutional configurations they produce as 'variegated' across different scales, rather than separated into discrete varieties of capitalism as taken for granted in VoC and also many post-VoC approaches (see Jessop and Suau Arinci et al. in this volume; see also Gough, 2014).

Of course, the national level remains crucially important for the institutionalization of capitalist economies and hence for questions of capitalist diversity. Moreover, at present the notion of a fully integrated world market is probably a mere theoretical possibility. This gives CC scholarship considerable justification in continuing to enquire into the institutional differentiation of national capitalisms. Nevertheless, even where a national level of abstraction is chosen, critical, global analyses of capitalist diversity would consistently point to the need to examine specific 'national' instances in relation to other 'national' capitalisms and also to the wider system (Coates, 2014b; Hardy, 2014; Weiss, 2014). Different kinds and degrees of insertion into external structures crucially shape the ways in which capitalist dynamics are institutionalized on the national and local levels – for better or worse. However, it is equally important to recognize that dependency and peripherialization in the world market do not constitute one-way roads, lest we run the risk of lapsing back into 1990s-style hyperglobalist arguments (see Gaitán and Boschi). How to stake out and conceptually solidify the common ground between scholarship on capitalist diversity in a (national) 'varieties' or 'models' sense, and relational perspectives on capitalism as a globally integrated system, is thus a question of great relevance for developing further a critical, global CC agenda (see also Tilley).

Heralding diversity

One early criticism of the VoC approach concerned its apparent division of the world of capitalism into (just) two ideal-typical varieties. This, it was argued, could never do justice to the really existing diversity of capitalism around the globe (see also Ebenau). Undoubtedly, the critics were generally correct when making this argument, but (as argued by Drahokoupil and Myant) they tended to bend the stick too far the other way. This is the case because the originators of the VoC perspective had never associated it with an attempt to generate a meaningful world map of capitalism but rather with a more limited purpose: that of explaining why and how non-liberal economies can be efficient and stable in the contemporary era. One of the resulting shortcomings of post-VoC debates is their somewhat directionless search for ever new ways of cataloguing institutional diversity and different types of capitalism. The contributions in this volume attempt to transcend this debate. They neither try to fit non-OECD models of capitalism into one or the other of the existing typologies nor do they amend the latter in order accommodate these models. Instead, they demonstrate that globalizing CC research entails a *necessarily* multifaceted analysis of capitalism, thereby pointing to the need to change the parameters of the CC research programme as a whole (see Wehr, Suau Arinci et al. and Tilley; Taylor, 2014). For instance, the role of the state as an active shaper of capitalist orders, as emphasized by Gaitán and Boschi, is important not only in the Latin American context but, in different ways, in all forms of capitalism. At the same time, and more fundamentally speaking, acknowledging the epistemological and ideological foundations, as well as the geographical origins, of the theories and analytical tools that are in use throughout the CC field helps to de-essentialize many truisms and so-called stylized facts about capitalist varieties. This is a necessary step, because it enables us to become aware of how and why the various forms in which capitalism(s), understood as systematic orders of accumulation, are embedded in social/societal structures that shape not only the trajectories of these orders but also the frameworks within which we approach and study them.

The politics of CC research

The absence of the political within VoC work, and across CC research in general, has been pointed out by many. One important manifestation of this is the downplaying and/or pathologization of conflicts, tensions and political struggles in capitalism (Bailey and Shibata, 2014). Post-VoC debates have been marked by calls to re-emphasize the significance of the political (the state, power, conflict and so on). At the same time, however, other tendencies pushing the CC field towards an increasing depoliticization of the research agenda have continued. This includes, for instance, the aforementioned flurry of refined or new typologies, which serve no other purpose than to map an ever greater range of capitalist varieties. In addition, large parts of the post-VoC debates on the notion of institutional complementarity or on types and modes of institutional change have exhibited strong tendencies to abstract from the real-world issues to which they refer. This indicates that there is a significant difference between a mere analytical, technical incorporation of politics into the conceptual frameworks and an approach that is conscious of the political relevance and implications of making such a move (see Hürtgen, 2014; Gallas, 2014).

Hence, there remains a real danger that CC scholarship, even in its post-VoC guises, will continue to become increasingly technical, abstract and detached from the political nature of its object of study, namely the differentiated economic, social and political effects which capitalism generates. Thus, ironically, in our contemporary times, which are characterized by a resurgence of public and media interest in this thing called capitalism, many CC approaches appear to have less and less to say about capitalist realities. They thus perform less impressively on this point than even the classical VoC approach, which for all of its depoliticizing elements emerged – like most CC scholarship at the time – from a search for and defence of alternatives to neoliberalism in general and the US 'model' in particular (see Bruff et al.).

A shared feature of many of the chapters that comprise this volume is their foregrounding of the political implications of studying capitalist diversity. These include, among other things, the unequal distribution of capacities across different parts of the world to derive durable economic and social gains from capitalist accumulation (Suau Arinci et al.); the unequal distribution of abilities to displace and defer capitalist crises and/or to deal with their consequences (Jessop); the inextricable interlinking between the production of wealth and the production of poverty (Tilley); the connection between different forms of capitalism and gender inequalities (Lux and Wöhl); and the (potential) role of the state in producing more desirable economic and social models (Gaitán and Boschi). Therefore, the new directions in CC scholarship represented in this volume conceive of the analysis of capitalist diversity not merely as an academic interest but also as an essential precondition for understanding real social and political problems.

The above-mentioned chapters thus raise the alarm that driving out politics from CC research and debates is a problem that goes to the heart of investigations into capitalist diversity, rather than merely affecting the analytical approaches that we may apply for one specific purpose or another. In other words, it is one thing to criticize the neglect of group, class and other struggles from a purely academic point of view, that is, as an omitted variable, factor or problem. It is an entirely different issue to attempt to re-centre CC, at least partially, on the political stakes associated with capitalist diversity, namely its concrete implications for humans living in different parts of the world. In this regard, the contemporary debates on varieties or models of capitalism hold promises, which have been hardly recognized, let alone realized, thus far. This is despite the fact that these promises, which are inherent to the notion that most CC research is inherently progressive in nature and intent (cf. Bruff et al.), are of high potential relevance for social and political actors striving to give this mode of production a more humane character and/or eventually to transcend it towards a fundamentally different, post-capitalist, order. One of the basic questions for future CC scholarship is whether such a re-centring will eventually reinforce the division between institutionalists and proponents of more critical approaches or whether it can grow into a common objective for a CC agenda that is simultaneously conscious and critical of capitalism in its diverse manifestations across the globe.

Concluding remarks

Whatever one makes of each of these individual themes and the associated questions, we hope that this book and the various contributions it comprises have served to show that (i) research into capitalist diversity is an endeavour to which the new directions presented here have much to contribute and (ii) such research is therefore an undertaking which stands to gain from the insights generated by these alternative approaches. The CC field ought to avoid travelling along the VoC highway in the future, since this would ultimately lead us into a dead end. Rather, the challenge will be to pave the road(s) ahead towards a redefinition of the CC research agenda towards what we call a critical, global Comparative Political Economy: the transdisciplinary study of contemporary capitalism, which is capable of grasping its diversity and its commonalities, which can make sense of its structural contradictions, inequalities and crisis-proneness and which has a genuinely global horizon in terms of its theoretical foundations and its empirical scope.

Bibliography

Bailey, D. and S. Shibata (2014) 'Varieties of Contestation: The Comparative and Critical Political Economy of "Excessive" Demand', *Capital & Class*, 38:1, 239–51.
Bieling, H.-J. (2014) 'Comparative Analysis of Capitalism from a Regulationist Perspective Extended by Neo-Gramscian IPE', *Capital & Class*, 38:1, 31–43.
Bohle, D. and B. Greskovits (2012) *Capitalist Diversity on Europe's Periphery* (Ithaca: Cornell University Press).
Bruff, I. (2011) 'What about the Elephant in the Room? Varieties of Capitalism, Varieties in Capitalism', *New Political Economy*, 16:4, 481–500.

Bruff, I. and M. Ebenau (2014) 'Critical Political Economy and the Critique of Comparative Capitalisms Scholarship on Capitalist Diversity', *Capital & Class*, 38:1, 3–15.

Bruff, I., M. Ebenau, C. May and A. Nölke (eds.) (2013) *Vergleichende Kapitalismusforschung: Stand, Perspektiven, Kritik* (Münster: Westfälisches Dampfboot).

Bruff, I. and E. Hartmann (2014) 'Neo-Pluralist Political Science, Economic Sociology and the Conceptual Foundations of the Comparative Capitalisms Literatures', *Capital & Class*, 38:1, 73–85.

Coates, D. (2005) 'Choosing Between Paradigms – A Personal View', in D. Coates (ed), *Varieties of Capitalism, Varieties of Approaches* (Basingstoke and New York: Palgrave Macmillan), 265–71.

Coates, D. (2014a) 'Studying Comparative Capitalisms by Going Left and by Going Deeper', *Capital & Class*, 38:1, 18–30.

Coates, D. (2014b) 'The UK: Less a Liberal Market Economy, More a Post-Imperial One', *Capital & Class*, 38:1, 171–82.

Ebenau, M., R. Kößler, C. May and I. Wehr (eds.) (2013) *Die Welt des Kapitals*, Double Special issue of *PERIPHERIE: Zeitschrift für Politik und Ökonomie in der Dritten Welt*, 130–1, 143–348.

Gallas, A. (2014) 'The Silent Treatment of Class Domination: "Critical" Comparative Capitalisms Scholarship and the British State', *Capital & Class*, 38:1, 225–37.

Gough, J. (2014) 'The Difference Between Local and National Capitalism, and Why Local Capitalisms Differ from One Another: A Marxist Approach', *Capital & Class*, 38:1, 197–210.

Hardy, J. (2014) 'Transformation and Crisis in Central and Eastern Europe: A Combined and Uneven Development Perspective', *Capital & Class*, 38:1, 143–55.

Höpner, M. (2004) 'Der organisierte Kapitalismus in Deutschland und sein Niedergang', in R. Czada and R. Zintl (eds.), *Politik und Markt*, PVS-Sonderheft 34 (Wiesbaden: VS), 300–24.

Hürtgen, S. (2014) 'Labour as a Transnational Actor, and Labour's National Diversity as a Systematic Frame of Contemporary Competitive Transnationality', *Capital & Class*, 38:1, 211–23.

Kannankulam, J. and F. Georgi (2014) 'Varieties of Capitalism or Varieties of Relationships of Forces? Outlines of a Historical Materialist Policy Analysis', *Capital & Class*, 38:1, 59–71.

Streeck, W. (2010) 'E Pluribus Unum? Varieties and Commonalities of Capitalism', *MPIfG Working Papers*, 10/12 (Köln: Max-Planck-Institut für Gesellschaftsforschung).

Taylor, N. (2014) 'Theorising Capitalist Diversity: The Uneven and Combined Development of Labour Forms', *Capital & Class*, 38:1, 129–41.

Weiss, O. (2014) 'Economic Surplus and Capitalist Diversity', *Capital & Class*, 38:1, 157–70.

Index

Note: **Bold** page number denotes topic discussion.

Africa, 46–7, 142, 208, 211, 216
  South Africa, 47
  agro-sector and rural economy, 196–202, 214–17, 219–20
  metropolitan-rural exploitation, 207–8, 209–11, 214–16, *see also* post/decolonial theory, coloniality
Amable, Bruno, 34, 35, 52, 95, **135–6**
Argentina, *see* Latin America

Becker, Uwe, **7–8**, **35–6**, 51, 89, **137–9**, 158–9, 184, 210
Bizberg, Ilán, 50, 52, 185, 191
Brazil, *see* Latin America
BRIC(S), 51, 136–7, 175, 177

Cardoso, Fernando Henrique, 191–2, 226
Central and Eastern Europe (CEE), 46–7, 49, 55, 161–3, **163–9**
  Baltic Republics, 162, 164, 165, 166
  Commonwealth of Independent States (CIS), 163, **166–9**
  Slovenia, 49, 162–3, **163–5**
  Visegrád Four (Czech Republic, Hungary, Poland, Slovakia), 55–6, 136, 162–3, **163–5**
Chile, *see* Latin America
China, *see* East Asia
colonialism, *see* post/decolonial theory
comparative capitalisms (CC) debates
  critical and global CC, **38–40**, **55–7**, 79–80, **225–31**
  history, 46–48, *see also* Varieties of Capitalism, history; post-VoC CC theory

new directions, **1–3**, 24, 28–9, **34–7**, **37–8**, 79–80, 83, 156, 208, 220, **225–31**
state of the art, 28–9, 155–6, **224–5**
crises in capitalism, 3, 6, 34, 54, 67–8, 74–5, 77, 79, 101–2, 118–20, 122–4, 178, 180, 191, 202, 227
  Argentine crisis, 196–7, 200
  Asian crisis, 101, 213, 218
  Eurozone crisis, 38, 71, 77, 107, 108–10, 111–13, *see also* Western Europe
  gender and crisis, 102–7, 113–14, *see also* feminist political economy
  global economic crisis, 19–20, 22–3, 37–8, 66, 102, 159–63, 172, 209ff
  mid-1970s global economic crisis, 128
  see also Marxism
critical institutionalism, 4, 24, **84–97**
  concept of institutions, 85–6
  discourses, 91–2
  institutional analysis and comparison, 87–9, 96–7
  institutional change, 89–91
  power and domination, 94–5
  research agenda, 95–7
Crouch, Colin, 13, 19, 34, **88–9**

decolonial theory, *see* post/decolonial theory
dependency theory, 6, 45, 55–7, 134, 136, 140–1, 174–5, 184, 189–90, **191–3**, 194–5, 202, 227–8
development studies, 46–7, 140, 143, 173–4, 207

East Asia, 46–7, 135–6, 175, 208–10, 211–14
China, 2, 33, 47, 77, 139, 209, **216–17**
Japan, 12, 46, 136, 207, **211–14**, 219
South Korea, 136, 211–14
Taiwan, 211–14
see also China
economism, *see* mainstream CC's fallacies
extractivism, extractive industries, 73, 179–80, 200, 213–16, 218–19

feminist political economy, 4–5, **39–40**, 101–2, 104–6, 142, 143, 224
see also gender and varieties of capitalism
fixes (institutional, spatio-temporal and semantic), 54, **67–8**, 74, 78–9
France, *see* Western Europe
functionalism, *see* mainstream CC's fallacies

gender and varieties of capitalism, 5, 39, 47, **102–6, 114**, 140–2, 145, 214–15
see also France; Spain
Germany, *see* Western Europe
global inequalities, 47, 173
globalization of CC research, 2–3, 45, **46–8, 57–8**, 72–5, 134, **135–7**, 207
global critical institutionalism, 92–3, 96
global critical-materialist perspectives, 55–7, 192–6
global post-VoC perspectives, 51–5, 157–69, 190–1
global VoC perspectives, 48–51, 156, 190–1
Gordon, David, **120–2**
Great Moderation, **18–20**, 22–3

Hall, Peter, 1, 11, **14–16**, 23
Harvey, David, 74–5, 79
hyper-globalism and convergence discourse, 20, 30–1, 46–7, 66, 70, 172, 209

imperialism, *see* Marxism and neo-Marxism
India, *see* South and Southeast Asia
Indonesia, *see* South and Southeast Asia
informal labour, 92, 105, 141–2, 201, 214
in Latin American countries, 181–2
institutionalism
constructivist and discursive institutionalism, 2, 24, 51, **91–2**
historical institutionalism, 2, **16**, 24, 51, 52, 89–91
institutional change, 33, 53, 89–91, 130–1, 191, 227, *see also* crises in capitalism
institutional complementarity, 12–13, 16, 20, 22, 49–50, 51, **88–9**, 123, 127, 159, 169, 173, 229
institutionalism, old and new, **86–7**, 96, 226–7
path dependence, 24, 31, 92, 126–7
rational choice institutionalism, 15, **16**, 20–1, 24, 28, 33, 50–1, 52–3, **85–6**, 226–7
Ireland, *see* Western Europe

Japan, *see* East Asia
Johnson, Chalmers, 208, **211–12**

Latin America, 2, 45–7, 49–50, 51–2, 56–7, 101, 136–7, 173, **175–83**, 189–90, 208–9, 210–11, 216, 229
Andean countries (Bolivia, Colombia, Ecuador, Peru, Venezuela), 176, 179, 180, 181, 182, 183
Argentina, 6, 52, 176, 177, 178, 179, 180, 182, 183, 185, **196–202**
Brazil, 33, 50, 52, 143, 176, 177, 178, 179, 180, 181, 182, 183, 185, 200
Central America (including Panama), 177, 180, 182, 183

Chile, 52, 176, 177, 178, 179, 180, 181, 183, 185, 200
Mexico, 52, 105, 176, 177, 180, 182, 183, 185, 200

mainstream CC's fallacies
  economism and functionalism, 34, 50, 53–4, 93–4, 191
  Eurocentrism and Orientalism, 139–43, 208–11
  methodological nationalism, 33–4, 50, 54–5, 69–71, 93–4, 134, 140, 191, 217–19, 227–8
  paradigmatic closure, 1, 37, 226
  see also Varieties of Capitalism (VoC) theory; post-VoC CC theory
Marini, Ruy Mauro, 191, 193
super-exploitation, 193
Marxism and neo-Marxism, 2–3, 15, 16, 17, 18, 19, 20, 24, **38–9**, 65–9, 102, 142, 144, 224
  imperialism theory, 45, 48, 55, 57, 72, 120, 143
  neo-Gramscianism, 114, 144–5
  stage-theoretic tradition, **119–22**, **130–1**, see also Social Structure of Accumulation (SSA) approach
Marx, Karl, 4, 24, 65, 69–72, 79–80, 85–7, 96, 209, 226
  critique of political economy, 4, 65–6, 67, **69–72**, 79, 87–8
  see also Marxism; neo-Marxism
  methodological nationalism, see mainstream CC's fallacies
Mexico, see Latin America
Mignolo, Walter, 207–9

neodevelopmentalism and developmental states, 49–50, 52, 73, **173–5**, 179–80, 190–1, 196–8, 200, 207, **211–14**, 219–20
see also East Asia and Latin America
neoliberalism, 18–19, 30, 66, 69, 104–7, 114, 124, 128–30, 163, 172, 175, 182–3, 196, 209, 212, 218, 230

Offe, Claus, 144

patrimonial capitalism, 5, 51, 137–42, 158–9, 210
  debate and critique, **139–42**, 210
  see also political capitalism
Piketty, Thomas, 140, 226
political capitalism, 68, 73–4
post/decolonial theory, 6, 39–40, 135, 143–7, 207–8, 208–11, 219–20, 224
  colonialism, 134–5, 142–3, 210, 213–14, see also Africa; Southeast Asia
  coloniality of power, 207–9
  entangled modernity, 5, **143–7**
  see also mainstream CC's fallacies
post-VoC CC theory, 1–2, 7, 22–3, 34–7, 51–5, 83, 122, **225–30**
  debate and critique, 36–7
  exposition of key tenets, 1, 34–6, 155–6
  global post-VoC perspectives, see globalization of CC research
  poverty, 109, 112, 183, 207, 209–11, 213–17, 219–20, 230

regulation approaches, 17, 52, **67–9**, 84–5, 87, 89–90, 95, 120, 130–1, 135–6, 144–5, 191, 193–4
see also Marxism and neo-Marxism
Russia, 5, 138–9, 161–2, **167–8**

Schmidt, Vivien, 14, 34, 110
Schneider, Ben Ross, **49–50**, **136–7**, 141, 183, 190, 209–10
Shonfield, Andrew, 17, 73
social inequality, 49, 53, 94, 173
social movements, 200–1, 216, 229–30
Social Structure of Accumulation (SSA) approach, 5, 120–2, **122–5**
  comparison with VoC theory, 122–5, 127
  exposition of key tenets, 122–5
Soskice, David, 1, 11–13, **14–16**, 23, 49, 58
South and Southeast Asia, 46, 211–16
  India, 47, 139–40
  Indonesia, 105, **211–19**
Spain, see Western Europe

state and state theory in CC, 106–7, 173–5, 193–4, 211–14, 229
Streeck, Wolfgang, 13, 17, 18–19, 23, 34, **35–6**

Thelen, Kathleen, 13, 15, 16, 21, 34, 85, 90
trade unions and organized labour, 31, 52–3, 78, 113, 126, **181–3**, 200–1, 212–13, 229–30
transition studies, 2, 5–6, 46–8, 50, 136, 155–9
transnational corporations (TNCs), 49–50, 55–6, 136, 141, 163–6
typologies of capitalism, 5, 11–13, 17–18, 20–1, 29, 33, 35, 46–7, 48–50, 51–2, 57, **95–6**, 119, 141, 155–6, **163–9**, 172, 185, 209–10, 229–30

United Kingdom, *see* Western Europe
United States, 19–20, 23, 46, 75–6, 77, 111, 121, 140, 144, 177, 208–9, 230

variegated capitalism, 4, **75–9**, 134, 143–7, 227–8
 compossibility and incompossibility, 77–8
 ecological dominance, 78

Varieties of Capitalism (VoC) theory, 1
 debate and critique, 13–14, 22–3, 31–2, 102, 118–19, 155–6, 208–11
 dependent market economies (DMEs), **55–7**, 136
 exposition of key tenets, 11, 30–1
 'gendered' VoC perspectives, *see also* gender and varieties of capitalism
 global VoC perspectives, *see* globalization of CC research
 hierarchical market economies (HMEs), **49–50**, 136–7, 190, 209
 history, **15–22**, 30–4
 liberal and coordinated market economies, 12, 48–9, 73, 135, 208, 228–9
 second generation VoC approaches, 32–4

Weber, Max, 73–4, 138, 139, 141
welfare states, 30–1, 102, 103–4, 107–13, 126, 144, 147, 181–3
Western Europe
 France, 5, **110–13**, 114
 Germany, 12, 19, 23, 33–4, 35–6, 75–6, 95–6, 109
 Ireland, **125–30**
 Spain, **107–10**, 114
 United Kingdom, 12, 71, 113, 142

Printed and bound by CPI Group (UK) Ltd, Croydon, CR0 4YY